Network Programming

M. Priyadharshini

Published by

BONFRING®
Intellectual Integrity

Network Programming

9 789383 459902 >

ISBN 978-93-83459-90-2

Bonfring
309, 2nd Floor, 5th Street Extension, Gandhipuram,
Coimbatore-641 012.
Tamilnadu, India.
E-mail: info@bonfring.org
Website: www.bonfring.org
Phone: 0422-3928700

Preface

It is a pleasure to write a book on ***Network Programming.*** This book is an attempt to present clear and simple ideas about different aspects of Network Programming in a more interesting manner. All the chapters in this book are designed to cover the Basic Network Concepts and Network programming involves writing programs that communicate with other programs across a computer network. The book is focused on the students to inculcate the knowledge of programming skill and best practices to incorporate in the real world applications. This book contains the model question papers with answer keys. This book covers the introduction of Network Programming, Unix, Java and Socket Programming along with the various examples and case studies.

Year: 2014 **M. Priyadharshini**

Author's Profile

M. Priyadharshini graduated M.Phil., in the year 2013 from Sree Saraswathi Thyagaraja College, Pollachi, affiliated to Bharathiar University, Coimbatore, in the discipline of Computer Applications. She has obtained her MCA Degree in 2010 from M. Kumarasamy College of Engineering Karur, affiliated to Anna University, Chennai. She was the topper in the college during her studies in the college. In recognition of her merit, she was awarded Gold Medal for Best Student in the discipline of Computer Applications for the year 2010. She is an Assistant Professor for more than four years and continuously handling the Networking subject for MCA. She has published more than 2 research articles and has presented more than 10 research papers in national / international conferences. She has delivered Guest Lectures, organized a number of training programmes, and has a good communication with the Industry People to enhance the student towards their better career.

M. Priyadharshini,
SNS College of Engineering
SNS Kalvi Nagar, Kurumbapalayam(PO)
Coimbatore - 641107
mpriyadharshinimca@gmail.com

UNIT-I

Introduction

All operating Systems provide services for programs they run. Typical services include executing a new program, opening a file, reading a file, allocating a region of memory, getting the correct time of day, and so on.

Describing the UNIX System in a strictly linear fashion, without any forward references to terms that haven't been described yet, is nearly impossible. It describes the programming interface to the Unix systemthe system call interface and many of the functions provided in the standard C library. It is intended for anyone writing programs that run under Unix.

UNIX Architecture

In a strict sense, an operating system can be defined as the software that controls the hardware resources of the computer and provides an environment under which programs can run. Generally, call this software the kernel, since it is relatively small and resides at the core of the environment.

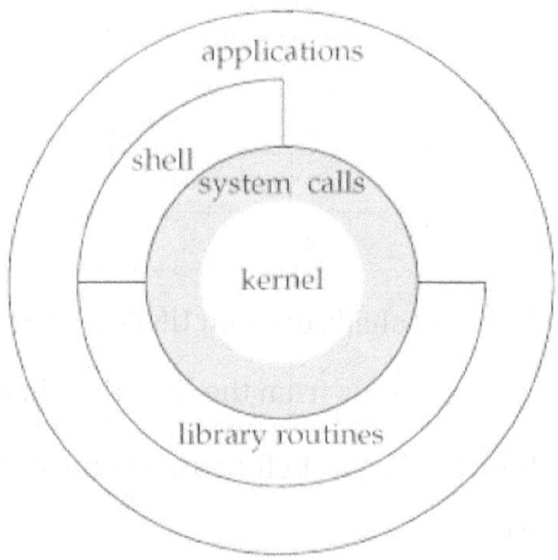

Architecture of the UNIX Operating System

The interface to the kernel is a layer of software called the system calls. Libraries of common functions are built on top of the system call interface, but applications are free to use both. The shell is a special application that provides an interface for running other applications.

An operating system is the kernel and all the other software that makes a computer useful and gives the computer its personality. This other software includes system utilities, applications, shells, libraries of common functions, and so on. For example, Linux is the kernel used by the GNU operating system.

Logging In

Login Name

When log in to a UNIX system, enter our login name, followed by our password. The system then looks up our login name in its password file, usually the file /etc/passwd. If look at our entry in the password file see that it's composed of seven colon-separated fields: the login name, encrypted password, numeric user ID (205), numeric group ID (105), a comment field, home directory (/home/sar), and shell program (/bin/ksh).

sar:x:205:105:Stephen Rago:/home/sar:/bin/ksh

Shells

A shell is a command-line interpreter that reads user input and executes commands. The user input to a shell is normally from the terminal (an interactive shell) or sometimes from a file (called a shell script). The common shells in use are summarized below.

Name	Path	FreeBSD 5.2.1	Linux 2.4.22	Mac OS X 10.3	Solaris 9
Bourne shell	/bin/sh	•	link to bash	link to bash	•
Bourne-again shell	/bin/bash	optional	•	•	•
C shell	/bin/csh	link to tcsh	link to tcsh	link to tcsh	•
Korn shell	/bin/ksh				•
TENEX C shell	/bin/tcsh	•	•	•	•

Common shells used on UNIX systems

The system knows which shell to execute for us from the final field in our entry in the password file.

The Bourne shell, developed by Steve Bourne at Bell Labs, has been in use since Version 7 and is provided with almost every UNIX system in existence.

The C shell, developed by Bill Joy at Berkeley, is provided with all the BSD releases. Additionally, the C shell was provided by AT&T with System V/386 Release 3.2 and is also in System V Release 4 (SVR4).

The Korn shell is considered a successor to the Bourne shell and was first provided with SVR4. The Korn shell, developed by David Korn at Bell Labs, runs on most UNIX systems, but before SVR4 was usually an extra-cost add-on, so it is not as widespread as the other two shells. It is upward compatible with the Bourne shell and includes those features that made the C shell popular: job control, command line editing, and so on.

The Bourne-again shell is the GNU shell provided with all Linux systems. It was designed to be POSIX-conformant, while still remaining compatible with the Bourne shell. It supports features from both the C shell and the Korn shell.

The TENEX C shell is an enhanced version of the C shell. It borrows several features, such as command completion, from the TENEX operating system (developed in 1972 at Bolt Beranek and Newman). The TENEX C shell adds many features to the C shell and is often used as a replacement for the C shell.

Files and Directories

File System

The UNIX file system is a hierarchical arrangement of directories and files. Everything starts in the directory called root whose name is the single character /.

A directory is a file that contains directory entries. Logically, can think of each directory entry as containing a filename along with a structure of information describing the attributes of the file. The attributes of a file are such things as type of file regular file, directory the size of the file, the owner of the file, permissions for the file whether other users may access this file and when the file was last modified. The stat and fstat functions return a structure of information containing all the attributes of a file.

Filename

The names in a directory are called filenames. The only two characters that cannot appear in a filename are the slash character (/) and the null character. The slash separates the filenames that form a pathname (described next) and the null character terminates a pathname.

Two filenames are automatically created whenever a new directory is created: . (called dot) and .. (called dot-dot). Dot refers to the current directory, and dot-dot refers to the parent directory. In the root directory, dot-dot is the same as dot.

The Research UNIX System and some older UNIX System V file systems restricted a filename to 14 characters. BSD versions extended this limit to 255 characters. Today, almost all commercial UNIX file systems support at least 255-character filenames.

Pathname

A sequence of one or more filenames, separated by slashes and optionally starting with a slash, forms a pathname. A pathname that begins with a slash is called an absolute pathname; otherwise, it's called a relative pathname. Relative pathnames refer to files relative to the current directory. The name for the root of the file system (/) is a special-case absolute pathname that has no filename component.

The notation ls(1) is the normal way to reference a particular entry in the UNIX system manuals.

Note that the directory listing is not in alphabetical order. The ls command sorts the names before printing them.

There are many details to consider in this 20-line program.

- First, include a header of our own: apue.h. include this header in almost every program in this text. This header includes some standard system headers and defines numerous constants and function prototypes that use throughout the examples in the text.
- The declaration of the main function uses the style supported by the ISO C standard.
- We take an argument from the command line, argv[1], as the name of the directory to list.
- Because the actual format of directory entries varies from one UNIX system to another, use the functions opendir, readdir, and closedir to manipulate the directory.
- The opendir function returns a pointer to a DIR structure, and pass this pointer to the readdir function. don't care what's in the DIR structure. then call readdir in a loop, to read each directory entry. The readdir function returns a pointer to a dirent structure or, when it's finished with the directory, a null pointer. All examine in the dirent structure is the name of each directory entry (d_name). Using this name, could then call the stat function to determine all the attributes of the file.
- We call two functions of our own to handle the errors: err_sys and err_quit. can see from the preceding output that the err_sys function prints an informative message describing what type of error was encountered ("Permission denied" or "Not a directory").
- When the program is done, it calls the function exit with an argument of 0. The function exit terminates a program. By convention, an argument of 0 means OK, and an argument between 1 and 255 means that an error occurred.

```
#include "apue.h"
#include <dirent.h>
int
main(int argc, char *argv[])
{
DIR *dp;
struct dirent *dirp;
if (argc != 2)
err_quit("usage: ls directory_name");
if ((dp = opendir(argv[1])) == NULL)
err_sys("can't open %s", argv[1]);
while ((dirp = readdir(dp)) != NULL)
printf("%s\n", dirp->d_name);
closedir(dp);
```

```
exit(0);
}
```

List all the files in a directory

Above program that just prints the name of every file in a directory, and nothing else. If the source file is named myls.c, compile it into the default a.out executable file by

```
cc myls.c
Some sample output is
$ ./a.out /dev
.
..
console
tty
mem
kmem
null
mouse
stdin
stdout
stderr
zero
many more lines that aren't shown
cdrom
$ ./a.out /var/spool/cron
can't open /var/spool/cron: Permission denied
$ ./a.out /dev/tty
can't open /dev/tty: Not a directory
```

Working Directory

Every process has a working directory, sometimes called the current working directory. This is the directory from which all relative pathnames are interpreted. A process can change its working directory with the chdir function.

For example, the relative pathname doc/memo/joe refers to the file or directory joe, in the directory memo, in the directory doc, which must be a directory within the working directory. From looking just at this pathname, know that both doc and memo have to be directories, but can't tell whether joe is a file or a directory. The pathname /usr/lib/lint is an absolute pathname that refers to the file or directory lint in the directory lib, in the directory usr, which is in the root directory.

Home Directory

When log in, the working directory is set to our home directory. Our home directory is obtained from our entry in the password file.

Input and Output

File Descriptors

File descriptors are normally small non-negative integers that the kernel uses to identify the files being accessed by a particular process. Whenever it opens an existing file or creates a new file, the kernel returns a file descriptor that use when want to read or write the file.

Standard Input, Standard Output, and Standard Error

By convention, all shells open three descriptors whenever a new program is run: standard input, standard output, and standard error. If nothing special is done, as in the simple command ls

then all three are connected to the terminal. Most shells provide a way to redirect any or all of these three descriptors to any file. For example,

ls > file.list

Executes the ls command with its standard output redirected to the file named file.list.

Unbuffered I/O

Unbuffered I/O is provided by the functions open, read, write, lseek, and close. These functions all work with file descriptors.

Standard I/O

The standard I/O functions provide a buffered interface to the unbuffered I/O functions. Using standard I/O prevents us from having to worry about choosing optimal buffer sizes, such as the BUFFSIZE. Another advantage of using the standard I/O functions is that they simplify dealing with lines of input (a common occurrence in UNIX applications). The fgets function, for example, reads an entire line. The read function, on the other hand, reads a specified number of bytes. The standard I/O library provides functions that let us control the style of buffering used by the library. The most common standard I/O function is printf. In programs that call printf, we'll always include <stdio.h> normally by including apue.h as this header contains the function prototypes for all the standard I/O functions.

Programs and Processes

Program

A program is an executable file residing on disk in a directory. A program is read into memory and is executed by the kernel as a result of one of the six exec functions.

Processes and Process ID

An executing instance of a program is called a process, a term used on almost every page of this text. Some operating systems use the term task to refer to a program that is being executed.

The UNIX System guarantees that every process has a unique numeric identifier called the process ID. The process ID is always a non-negative integer.

Print the process ID

```
#include "apue.h"
int
main(void)
{
printf("hello world from process ID %d\n", getpid());
exit(0);
}
```

If compile this program into the file a.out and execute it, have

```
$ ./a.out
hello world from process ID 851
$ ./a.out
hello world from process ID 854
```

When this program runs, it calls the function getpid to obtain its process ID.

Process Control

There are three primary functions for process control: fork, exec, and waitpid. (The exec function has six variants, but often refer to them collectively as simply the exec function.)

Example

The process control features of the UNIX System are demonstrated using a simple program that reads commands from standard input and executes the commands. This is a bare-bones implementation of a shell-like program. There are several features to consider in this 30-line program.

- We use the standard I/O function fgets to read one line at a time from the standard input. When type the end-of-file character (which is often Control-D) as the first character of a line, fgets returns a null pointer, the loop stops, and the process terminates.
- Because each line returned by fgets is terminated with a new line character, followed by a null byte, use the standard C function strlen to calculate the length of the string, and then replace the new line with a null byte. do this because the execlp function wants a null terminated argument, not a new line-terminated argument.
- We call fork to create a new process, which is a copy of the caller. say that the caller is the parent and that the newly created process is the child. Then fork returns the non-negative process ID of the new child process to the parent, and returns 0 to the child. Because fork creates a new process, say that it is called once by the parent but returns twice in the parent and in the child.
- In the child, call execlp to execute the command that was read from the standard input. This replaces the child process with the new program file. The combination of a fork, followed by an exec, is what some operating systems call spawning a new process. In the UNIX System, the two parts are separated into individual functions.
- Because the child calls execlp to execute the new program file, the parent wants to wait for the child to terminate. This is done by calling waitpid, specifying which process want to wait for: the pid argument, which is the process ID of the child. The waitpid function also returns the termination status of the childthe status variablebut in this simple program, don't do anything with this value. could examine it to determine exactly how the child terminated.
- The most fundamental limitation of this program is that can't pass arguments to the command that execute. can't, for example, specify the name of a directory to list. can execute ls only on the working directory. To allow arguments would require that parse the input line, separating the arguments by some convention, probably spaces or tabs, and then pass each argument as a separate argument to the execlp function. Nevertheless, this program is still a useful demonstration of the process control functions of the UNIX System.

Read commands from standard input and execute them

```
#include "apue.h"
#include <sys/wait.h>
int
main(void)
{
char buf[MAXLINE]; /* from apue.h */
pid_t pid;
```

```
int status;
printf("%% "); /* print prompt (printf requires %% to print %) */
while (fgets(buf, MAXLINE, stdin) != NULL) {
if (buf[strlen(buf) - 1] == "\n")
buf[strlen(buf) - 1] = 0; /* replace newline with null */
if ((pid = fork()) < 0) {
err_sys("fork error");
} else if (pid == 0) { /* child */
execlp(buf, buf, (char *)0);
err_ret("couldn't execute: %s", buf);
exit(127);
}
/* parent */
if ((pid = waitpid(pid, &status, 0)) < 0)
err_sys("waitpid error");
printf("%% ");
}
exit(0);
}
```

If run this program, get the following results. Note that our program has a different promp the percent signto distinguish it from the shell's prompt.

```
$ ./a.out
% date
Sun Aug 1 03:04:47 EDT 2004 programmers work late
% who
sar :0 Jul 26 22:54
sar pts/0 Jul 26 22:54 (:0)
sar pts/1 Jul 26 22:54 (:0)
sar pts/2 Jul 26 22:54 (:0)
% pwd
/home/sar/bk/apue/2e
% ls
Makefile
a.out
```

shell1.c

% ^D type the end-of-file character

$ the regular shell prompt

Threads and Thread IDs

Usually, a process has only one thread of control one set of machine instructions executing at a time. Some problems are easier to solve when more than one thread of control can operate on different parts of the problem. Additionally, multiple threads of control can exploit the parallelism possible on multiprocessor systems. All the threads within a process share the same address space, file descriptors, stacks, and process related attributes. Because they can access the same memory, the threads need to synchronize access to shared data among themselves to avoid inconsistencies. As with processes, threads are identified by IDs. Thread IDs, however, are local to a process. A thread ID from one process has no meaning in another process. use thread IDs to refer to specific threads as manipulate the threads within a process.

Error Handling

When an error occurs in one of the UNIX System functions, a negative value is often returned, and the integer errno is usually set to a value that gives additional information. For example, the open function returns either a non-negative file descriptor if all is OK or 1 if an error occurs. An error from open has about 15 possible errno values, such as file doesn't exist, permission problem, and so on. Some functions use a convention other than returning a negative value. For example, most functions that return a pointer to an object return a null pointer to indicate an error.

The file <errno.h> defines the symbol errno and constants for each value that errno can assume. Each of these constants begins with the character E. Also, the first page of Section 2 of the UNIX system manuals, named intro(2), usually lists all these error constants. For example, if errno is equal to the constant EACCES, this indicates a permission problem, such as insufficient permission to open the requested file.

On Linux, the error constants are listed in the errno(3) manual page. POSIX and ISO C define errno as a symbol expanding into a modifiable lvalue of type integer. This can be either an integer that contains the error number or a function that returns a pointer to the error number. The historical definition is extern int errno; But in an environment that supports threads, the process address space is shared among multiple threads, and each thread needs its own local copy of errno to prevent one thread from interfering with another. Linux, for example, supports multithreaded access to errno by defining it as extern int *__errno_location(void);

#define errno (*__errno_location())

There are two rules to be aware of with respect to errno. First, its value is never cleared by a routine if an error does not occur. Therefore, should examine its value only when the return value from a function indicates that an error occurred. Second, the value of errno is never set to 0 by any of the functions, and none of the constants defined in <errno.h> has a value of 0.

Two functions are defined by the C standard to help with printing error messages.

Demonstrate strerror and perror

```
#include "apue.h"
#include <errno.h>
int
main(int argc, char *argv[])
{
fprintf(stderr, "EACCES: %s\n", strerror(EACCES));
errno = ENOENT;
perror(argv[0]);
exit(0);
}
```

If this program is compiled into the file a.out, have

```
$ ./a.out
EACCES: Permission denied
./a.out: No such file or directory
```

Error Recovery

The errors defined in <errno.h> can be divided into two categories: fatal and nonfatal. A fatal error has no recovery action. The best can do is print an error message on the user's screen or write an error message into a log file, and then exit. Nonfatal errors, on the other hand, can sometimes be dealt with more robustly. Most nonfatal errors are temporary in nature, such as with a resource shortage, and might not occur when there is less activity on the system.

Resource-related nonfatal errors include EAGAIN, ENFILE, ENOBUFS, ENOLCK, ENOSPC, ENOSR, EWOULDBLOCK, and sometimes ENOMEM. EBUSY can be treated as a nonfatal error when it indicates that a shared resource is in use.

User Identification

User ID

The user ID from our entry in the password file is a numeric value that identifies us to the system. This user ID is assigned by the system administrator when our login name is assigned, and cannot change it. The user ID is normally assigned to be unique for every user. We'll see how the kernel uses the user ID to check whether have the appropriate permissions to perform certain operations.

We call the user whose user ID is 0 either root or the super user. The entry in the password file normally has a login name of root, and refer to the special privileges of this user as super user privileges. If a process has super user privileges, most file permission checks are bypassed. Some operating system functions are restricted to the super user. The super user has free rein over the system. Client versions of Mac OS X ship with the super user account disabled; server versions ship with the account already enabled.

Group ID

Our entry in the password file also specifies our numeric group ID. This too is assigned by the system administrator when our login name is assigned. Typically, the password file contains multiple entries that specify the same group ID. Groups are normally used to collect users together into projects or departments. This allows the sharing of resources, such as files, among members of the same group.

There is also a group file that maps group names into numeric group IDs. The group file is usually /etc/group. The use of numeric user IDs and numeric group IDs for permissions is historical. With every file on disk, the file system stores both the user ID and the group ID of a file's owner. Storing both of these values requires only four bytes, assuming that each is stored as a two-byte integer. If the full ASCII login name and group name were used instead, additional disk space would be required. In addition, comparing strings during permission checks is more expensive than comparing integers.

Users, however, work better with names than with numbers, so the password file maintains the mapping between login names and user IDs, and the group file provides the mapping between group names and group IDs. The ls -l command, for example, prints the login name of the owner of a file, using the password file to map the numeric user ID into the corresponding login name.

Early UNIX systems used 16-bit integers to represent user and group IDs. Contemporary UNIX systems use 32-bit integers.

Example

The program prints the user ID and the group ID.

user ID and group ID

```
#include "apue.h"
int
main(void)
{
printf("uid = %d, gid = %d\n", getuid(), getgid());
```

```
exit(0);
}
```

We call the functions getuid and getgid to return the user ID and the group ID. Running the program yields

```
$ ./a.out
uid = 205, gid = 105
```

Supplementary Group IDs

In addition to the group ID specified in the password file for a login name, most versions of the UNIX System allow a user to belong to additional groups. This started with 4.2BSD, which allowed a user to belong to up to 16 additional groups. These supplementary group IDs are obtained at login time by reading the file /etc/group and finding the first 16 entries that list the user as a member.

Signals

Signals are a technique used to notify a process that some condition has occurred. For example, if a process divides by zero, the signal whose name is SIGFPE (floating-point exception) is sent to the process. The process has three choices for dealing with the signal.

- Ignore the signal. This option isn't recommended for signals that denote a hardware exception, such as dividing by zero or referencing memory outside the address space of the process, as the results are undefined.
- Let the default action occur. For a divide-by-zero condition, the default is to terminate the process.
- Provide a function that is called when the signal occurs (this is called "catching" the signal). By providing a function of our own, we'll know when the signal occurs and can handle it as wish.

Many conditions generate signals. Two terminal keys, called the interrupt key often the DELETE key or Control-Cand the quit keyoften Control-backslashare used to interrupt the currently running process. Another way to generate a signal is by calling the kill function. can call this function from a process to send a signal to another process. There are limitations: have to be the owner of the other process (or the superuser) to be able to send it a signal.

Read commands from standard input and execute them

```
#include "apue.h"
#include <sys/wait.h>
+ static void sig_int(int); /* our signal-catching function */
+
int
main(void)
```

```
{
char buf[MAXLINE]; /* from apue.h */
pid_t pid;
int status;
+ if (signal(SIGINT, sig_int) == SIG_ERR)
+ err_sys("signal error");
+
printf("%% "); /* print prompt (printf requires %% to print %) */
while (fgets(buf, MAXLINE, stdin) != NULL) {
if (buf[strlen(buf) - 1] == "\n")
buf[strlen(buf) - 1] = 0; /* replace newline with null */
if ((pid = fork()) < 0) {
err_sys("fork error");
} else if (pid == 0) { /* child */
execlp(buf, buf, (char *)0);
err_ret("couldn't execute: %s", buf);
exit(127);
}
/* parent */
if ((pid = waitpid(pid, &status, 0)) < 0)
err_sys("waitpid error");
printf("%% ");
}
exit(0);
}
+
+ void
+ sig_int(int signo)
+ {
+ printf("interrupt\n%% ");
+ }
```

Time Values

UNIX systems have maintained two different time values:

- Calendar time. This value counts the number of seconds since the Epoch: 00:00:00 January 1, 1970, Coordinated Universal Time (UTC). (Older manuals refer to UTC as Greenwich Mean Time.) These time values are used to record the time when a file was last modified, for example.
- The primitive system data type time_t holds these time values.
- Process time. This is also called CPU time and measures the central processor resources used by a process. Process time is measured in clock ticks, which have historically been 50, 60, or 100 ticks per second.
- The primitive system data type clock_t holds these time values.

When measure the execution time of a process, the UNIX System maintains three values for a process:

- Clock time
- User CPU time
- System CPU time

System Calls and Library Functions

All operating systems provide service points through which programs request services from the kernel. All implementations of the UNIX System provide a well-defined, limited number of entry points directly into the kernel called system calls.

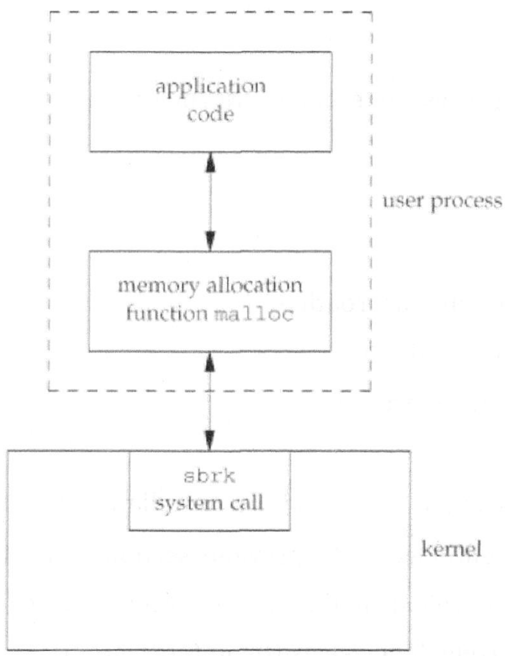

Separation of malloc function and sbrk system callChapter

Process Environment

Introduction

Before looking at the process control primitives in the next chapter, need to examine the environment of a single process. The main function is called when the program is executed, how command-line arguments are passed to the new program, what the typical memory layout looks like, how to allocate additional memory, how the process can use environment variables, and various ways for the process to terminate. The longjmp and setjmp functions and their interaction with the stack.

Main Function

A C program starts execution with a function called main. The prototype for the main function is int main(int argc, char *argv[]); where argc is the number of command-line arguments, and argv is an array of pointers to the arguments.

When a C program is executed by the kernel by one of the exec functions, a special start-up routine is called before the main function is called. The executable program file specifies this routine as the starting address for the program; this is set up by the link editor when it is invoked by the C compiler. This start-up routine takes values from the kernel the command-line arguments and the environment and sets things up so that the main function is called as shown earlier.

Process Termination

There are eight ways for a process to terminate. Normal termination occurs in five ways:

- Return from main
- Calling exit
- Calling _exit or _Exit
- Return of the last thread from its start routine
- Calling pthread_exit from the last thread

Abnormal termination occurs in three ways:

- Calling abort
- Receipt of a signal Response of the last thread to a cancellation request
- The start-up routine that mentioned in the previous section is also written so that if the main function returns, the exit function is called. If the start-up routine were coded in C (it is often coded in assembler) the call to main could look like exit(main(argc, argv));

Exit Functions

Three functions terminate a program normally: _exit and _Exit, which return to the kernel immediately, and exit, which performs certain cleanup processing and then returns to the kernel.

```
#include <stdlib.h>
void exit(int status);
void _Exit(int status);
#include <unistd.h>
void _exit(int status);
```

The reason for the different headers is that exit and _Exit are specified by ISO C, whereas _exit is specified by POSIX.1.

All three exit functions expect a single integer argument, which call the exit status. Most UNIX System shells provide a way to examine the exit status of a process. If (a) any of these functions is called without an exit status, (b) main does a return without a return value, or (c) the main function is not declared to return an integer, the exit status of the process is undefined. However, if the return type of main is an integer and main "falls off the end" (an implicit return), the exit status of the process is 0.

This behavior is new with the 1999 version of the ISO C standard. Historically, the exit status was undefined if the end of the main function was reached without an explicit return statement or call to the exit function.

Returning an integer value from the main function is equivalent to calling exit with the same value.

Thus

```
exit(0);
```

is the same as

```
return(0);
```

from the main function.

If compile the same program on different systems, are likely to get different exit codes, depending on the contents of the stack and register contents at the time that the main function returns:

```
$ cc hello.c
$ ./a.out
hello, world
$ echo $? print the exit status
13
```

Now if enable the 1999 ISO C compiler extensions, see that the exit code changes:

```
$ cc -std=c99 hello.c enable gcc's 1999 ISO C extensions
hello.c:4: warning: return type defaults to 'int'
$ ./a.out
```

```
hello, world
$ echo $? role="italicAlt"print the exit status
0
```

Note the compiler warning when enable the 1999 ISO C extensions. This warning is printed because the type of the main function is not explicitly declared to be an integer. If were to add this declaration, the message would go away. However, if were to enable all recommended warnings from the compiler (with the -Wall flag), then would see a warning message something like "control reaches end of nonvoid function."

The declaration of main as returning an integer and the use of exit instead of return produces needless warnings from some compilers and the lint(1) program. The problem is that these compilers don't know that an exit from main is the same as a return. One way around these

warnings, which become annoying after a while, is to use return instead of exit from main. But doing this prevents us from using the UNIX System's grep utility to locate all calls to exit from a program. Another solution is to declare main as returning void, instead of int, and continue calling exit. This gets rid of the compiler warning but doesn't look right (especially in a programming text), and can generate other compiler warnings, since the return type of main is supposed to be a signed integer. In this text, show main as returning an integer, since that is the definition specified by both ISO C and POSIX.1. Different compilers vary in the verbosity of their warnings. Note that the GNU C compiler usually doesn't emit these extraneous compiler warnings unless additional warning options are used.

atexit Function

With ISO C, a process can register up to 32 functions that are automatically called by exit. These are called exit handlers and are registered by calling the atexit function.

```
#include <stdlib.h>
int atexit(void (*func)(void));
Returns: 0 if OK, nonzero on error
```

This declaration says that pass the address of a function as the argument to atexit. When this function is called, it is not passed any arguments and is not expected to return a value. The exit function calls these functions in reverse order of their registration. Each function is called as many times as it was registered.

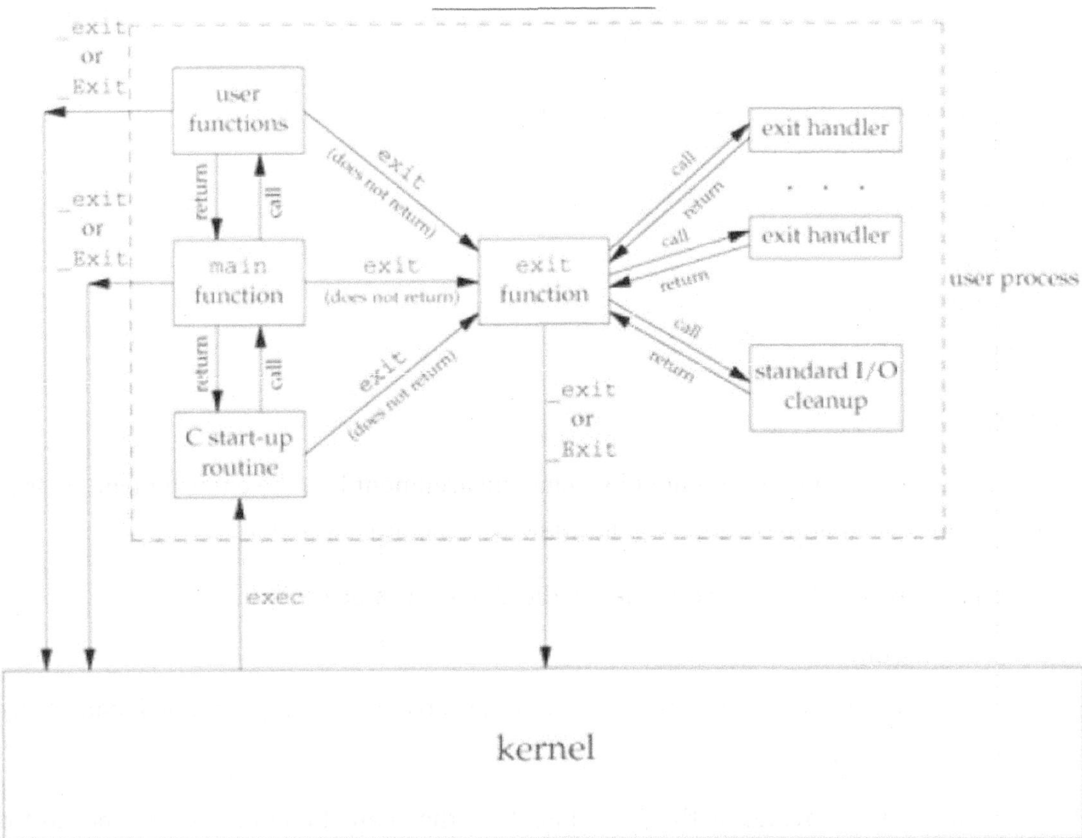

How a C program is started and how it terminates

Command-Line Arguments

When a program is executed, the process that does the exec can pass command-line arguments to the new program. This is part of the normal operation of the UNIX system shells.

Example

The program in echoes all its command-line arguments to standard output. Note that the normal echo(1) program doesn't echo the zeroth argument.

Echo all command-line arguments to standard output

```
#include "apue.h"
int
main(int argc, char *argv[])
{
int i;
for (i = 0; i < argc; i++) /* echo all command-line args */
printf("argv[%d]: %s\n", i, argv[i]);
```

```
exit(0);
}
```

If compile this program and name the executable echoarg, have

```
$ ./echoarg arg1 TEST foo
argv[0]: ./echoarg
argv[1]: arg1
argv[2]: TEST
argv[3]: foo
```

Environment List

Each program is also passed an environment list. Like the argument list, the environment list is an array of character pointers, with each pointer containing the address of a null-terminated C string.

The address of the array of pointers is contained in the global variable environ:

```
extern char **environ;
```

By convention, the environment consists of name=value strings. Most predefined names are entirely uppercase, but this is only a convention.

Most UNIX systems have provided a third argument to the main function that is the address of the environment list:

```
int main(int argc, char *argv[], char *envp[]);
```

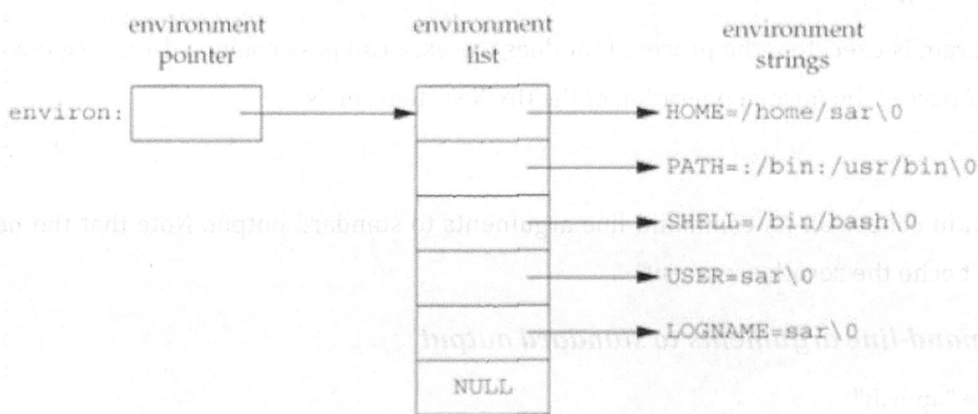

Environment consisting of five C character strings

Because ISO C specifies that the main function be written with two arguments, and because this third argument provides no benefit over the global variable environ, POSIX.1 specifies that environ should be used instead of the (possible) third argument. Access to specific environment variables is normally through the getenv and putenv functions, instead of through the environ variable. But to go through the entire environment, the environ pointer must be used.

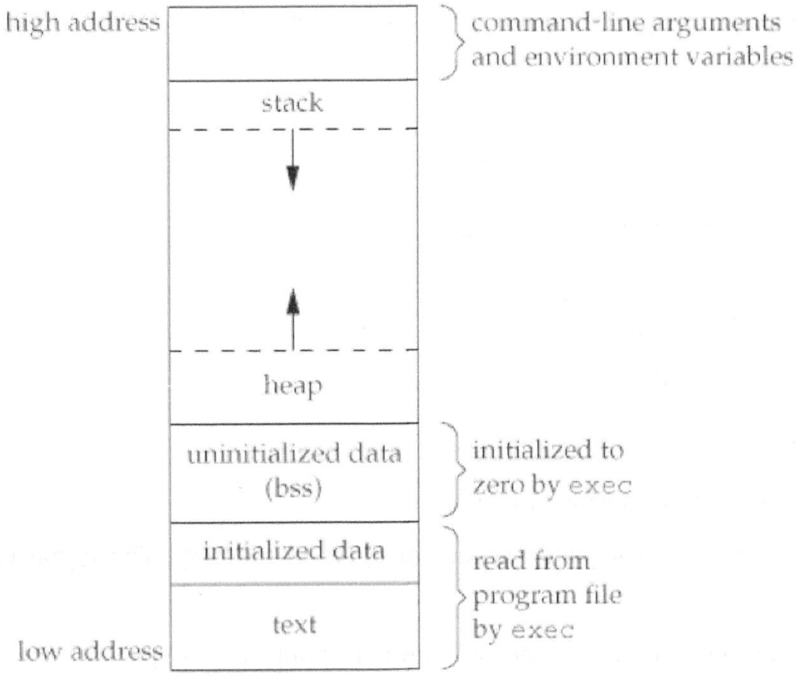

Typical memory arrangement

Shared Libraries

Most UNIX systems today support shared libraries. Arnold [1986] describes an early implementation under System V, and Gingell et al. [1987] describe a different implementation under SunOS. Shared libraries remove the common library routines from the executable file, instead maintaining a single copy of the library routine somewhere in memory that all processes reference. This reduces the size of each executable file but may add some runtime overhead, either when the program is first executed or the first time each shared library function is called. Another advantage of shared librries is that library functions can be replaced with new versions without having to relink edit every program that uses the library.

Different systems provide different ways for a program to say that it wants to use or not use the shared libraries. Options for the cc(1) and ld(1) commands are typical. As an example of the size differences, the following executable file the classic hello.c program was first created without shared libraries:

```
$ cc -static hello1.c prevent gcc from using shared libraries
$ ls -l a.out
-rwxrwxr-x 1 sar 475570 Feb 18 23:17 a.out
$ size a.out
text data bss dec hex filename
375657 3780 3220 382657 5d6c1 a.out
```

If compile this program to use shared libraries, the text and data sizes of the executable file are greatly decreased:

```
$ cc hello1.c gcc defaults to use shared libraries
$ ls -l a.out
-rwxrwxr-x 1 sar 11410 Feb 18 23:19 a.out
$ size a.out
text data bss dec hex filename
872 256 4 1132 46c a.out
```

Memory Allocation

ISO C specifies three functions for memory allocation:

- malloc, which allocates a specified number of bytes of memory. The initial value of the memory is indeterminate.
- calloc, which allocates space for a specified number of objects of a specified size. The space is initialized to all 0 bits.
- realloc, which increases or decreases the size of a previously allocated area. When the size increases, it may involve moving the previously allocated area somewhere else, to provide the additional room at the end. Also, when the size increases, the initial value of the space between the old contents and the end of the new area is indeterminate.

```
#include <stdlib.h>
void *malloc(size_t size);
void *calloc(size_t nobj, size_t size);
void *realloc(void *ptr, size_t newsize);
All three return: non-null pointer if OK, NULL on error
void free(void *ptr);
```

The pointer returned by the three allocation functions is guaranteed to be suitably aligned so that it can be used for any data object. For example, if the most restrictive alignment requirement on a particular system requires that doubles must start at memory locations that are multiples of 8, then all pointers returned by these three functions would be so aligned. Because the three alloc functions return a generic void * pointer, if #include <stdlib.h> (to obtain the function prototypes), do not explicitly have to cast the pointer returned by these functions when assign it to a pointer of a different type.

The function free causes the space pointed to by ptr to be deallocated. This freed space is usually put into a pool of available memory and can be allocated in a later call to one of the three alloc functions. The realloc function lets us increase or decrease the size of a previously allocated area. (The most common usage is to increase an area.) For example, if allocate room for 512 elements in an array that fill in at runtime but find that need room for more than 512 elements, can call realloc. If there is room beyond the end of the existing region for the requested space, then realloc doesn't have to move anything; it simply allocates the additional area at the end and returns the same pointer that passed it. But if there isn't room at the end of the existing region, realloc allocates another area that is large enough, copies the existing 512-element array to the new area, frees the old area, and returns the pointer to the new area. Because the area may move, shouldn't have any pointers into this area.

Note that the final argument to realloc is the new size of the region, not the difference between the old and new sizes. As a special case, if ptr is a null pointer, realloc behaves like malloc and allocates a region of the specified newsize.

Older versions of these routines allowed us to realloc a block that had freed since the last call to malloc, realloc, or calloc. This trick dates back to Version 7 and exploited the search strategy of malloc to perform storage compaction. Solaris still supports this feature, but many other platforms do not. This feature is deprecated and should not be used.

The allocation routines are usually implemented with the sbrk(2) system call. This system call expands (or contracts) the heap of the process.

Although sbrk can expand or contract the memory of a process, most versions of malloc and free never decrease their memory size. The space that free is available for a later allocation, but the freed space is not usually returned to the kernel; that space is kept in the malloc pool. It is important to realize that most implementations allocate a little more space than is requested and use the additional space for record keeping the size of the allocated block, a pointer to the next allocated block, and the like. This means that writing past the end of an allocated area could overwrite this record-keeping information in a later block. These types of errors are often catastrophic, but difficult to find, because the error may not show up until much later. Also, it is possible to overwrite this record keeping by writing before the start of the allocated area.

Writing past the end or before the beginning of a dynamically-allocated buffer can corrupt more than internal record-keeping information. The memory before and after a dynamically-allocated buffer can potentially be used for other dynamically-allocated objects. These objects can be unrelated to the code corrupting them, making it even more difficult to find the source of the corruption.

Other possible errors that can be fatal are freeing a block that was already freed and calling free with a pointer that was not obtained from one of the three alloc functions. If a process calls malloc, but forgets to call free, its memory usage continually increases; this is called leakage. By not calling free to return unused space, the size of a process's address space slowly increases until no free space is left. During this time, performance can degrade from excess paging overhead.

Because memory allocation errors are difficult to track down, some systems provide versions of these functions that do additional error checking every time one of the three alloc functions or free is called. These versions of the functions are often specified by including a special library for the link editor. There are also publicly available sources that you can compile with special flags to enable additional runtime checking.

FreeBSD, Mac OS X, and Linux support additional debugging through the setting of environment variables. In addition, options can be passed to the FreeBSD library through the symbolic link /etc/malloc.conf.

Alternate Memory Allocators

Many replacements for malloc and free are available. Some systems already include libraries providing alternate memory allocator implementations. Other systems provide only the standard allocator, leaving it up to software developers to download alternatives, if desired.

libmalloc

SVR4-based systems, such as Solaris, include the libmalloc library, which provides a set of interfaces matching the ISO C memory allocation functions. The libmalloc library includes mallopt, a function that allows a process to set certain variables that control the operation of the storage allocator. A function called mallinfo is also available to provide statistics on the memory allocator.

Vmalloc

A memory allocator that allows processes to allocate memory using different techniques for different regions of memory. In addition to the functions specific to vmalloc, the library also provides emulations of the ISO C memory allocation functions.

Quick-fit

The standard malloc algorithm used either a best-fit or a first-fit memory allocation strategy. Quick-fit is faster than either, but tends to use more memory. The algorithm, which is based on splitting up memory into buffers of various sizes and maintaining unused buffers on different free lists, depending on the size of the buffers. Free implementations of malloc and free based on quick-fit are readily available from several FTP sites.

Alloca Function

One additional function is also worth mentioning. The function alloca has the same calling sequence as malloc; however, instead of allocating memory from the heap, the memory is allocated from the stack frame of the current function. The advantage is that don't have to free the space; it goes away automatically when the function returns. The alloca function increases the size of the stack frame. The disadvantage is that some systems can't support alloca, if it's impossible to increase the size of the stack frame after the function has been called. Nevertheless, many software packages use it, and implementations exist for a wide variety of systems. All four platforms discussed in this text provide the alloca function.

Environment Variables

As mentioned earlier, the environment strings are usually of the form name=value The UNIX kernel never looks at these strings; their interpretation is up to the various applications. The shells, for example, use numerous environment variables. Some, such as HOME and USER, are set automatically at login, and others are for us to set. normally set environment variables in a shell start-up file to control the shell's actions. If set the environment variable MAILPATH, for example, it tells the Bourne shell, GNU Bourne-again shell, and Korn shell where to look for mail. ISO C defines a function that can use to fetch values from the environment, but this standard says that the contents of the environment are implementation defined.

```
#include <stdlib.h>
char *getenv(const char *name);
```

Returns: pointer to value associated with name, NULL if not found

Variable	POSIX.1	FreeBSD 5.2.1	Linux 2.4.22	Mac OS X 10.3	Solaris 9	Description
COLUMNS	•	•	•	•	•	terminal width
DATEMSK	XSI		•		•	getdate(3) template file pathname
HOME	•	•	•	•	•	home directory
LANG	•	•	•	•	•	name of locale
LC_ALL	•	•	•	•	•	name of locale
LC_COLLATE	•	•	•	•	•	name of locale for collation
LC_CTYPE	•	•	•	•	•	name of locale for character classification
LC_MESSAGES	•	•	•	•	•	name of locale for messages
LC_MONETARY	•	•	•	•	•	name of locale for monetary editing
LC_NUMERIC	•	•	•	•	•	name of locale for numeric editing
LC_TIME	•	•	•	•	•	name of locale for date/time formatting
LINES	•	•	•	•	•	terminal height
LOGNAME	•	•	•	•	•	login name
MSGVERB	XSI	•			•	fmtmsg(3) message components to process
NLSPATH	XSI	•	•	•	•	sequence of templates for message catalogs
PATH	•	•	•	•	•	list of path prefixes to search for executable file
PWD	•	•	•	•	•	absolute pathname of current working directory
SHELL	•	•	•	•	•	name of user's preferred shell
TERM	•	•	•	•	•	terminal type
TMPDIR	•	•	•	•	•	pathname of directory for creating temporary files
TZ	•	•	•	•	•	time zone information

Environment variables defined in the Single UNIX Specification

Setjmp and longjmp Functions

In C, goto a label that's in another function. Instead, must use the setjmp and longjmp functions to perform this type of branching. These two functions are useful for handling error conditions that occur in a deeply nested function call. It consists of a main loop that reads lines from standard input and calls the function do_line to process each line. This function then calls get_token to fetch the next token from the input line. The first token of a line is assumed to be a command of some form, and a switch statement selects each command. For the single command shown, the function cmd_add is called.

```
#include <setjmp.h>
int setjmp(jmp_buf env);
Returns: 0 if called directly, nonzero if returning from a call to longjmp
void longjmp(jmp_buf env, int val);
```

To call setjmp from the location that want to return to, which in this example is in the main function. In this case, setjmp returns 0 because called it directly. In the call to setjmp, the argument env is of the special type jmp_buf. This data type is some form of array that is capable of holding all the information required to restore the status of the stack to the state when call longjmp. Normally, the env variable is a global variable, since we'll need to reference it from another function.

getrlimit and setrlimit Functions

Every process has a set of resource limits, some of which can be queried and changed by the getrlimit and setrlimit functions

```
#include <sys/resource.h>
int getrlimit(int resource, struct rlimit *rlptr);
int setrlimit(int resource, const struct rlimit
*rlptr);
Both return: 0 if OK, nonzero on error
```

Three rules govern the changing of the resource limits.

- A process can change its soft limit to a value less than or equal to its hard limit. A process can lower its hard limit to a value greater than or equal to its soft limit. This lowering of the hard limit is irreversible for normal users.
- Only a superuser process can raise a hard limit.

Process Control

Introduction

The process control provided by the UNIX System. This includes the creation of new processes, program execution, and process termination. also look at the various IDs that are the property of the processreal, effective, and saved; user and group IDsand how they're affected by the process control primitives. Interpreter files and the system function are also covered. conclude the chapter by looking at the process accounting provided by most UNIX systems.

Process Identifiers

Every process has a unique process ID, a non-negative integer. Because the process ID is the only well-known identifier of a process that is always unique, it is often used as a piece of other identifiers, to guarantee uniqueness. For example, applications sometimes include the process ID as part of a filename in an attempt to generate unique filenames. Although unique, process IDs are reused. As processes terminate, their IDs become candidates for reuse. Most UNIX systems implement algorithms to delay reuse, however, so that newly created processes are assigned IDs different from those used by processes that terminated recently. This prevents a new process from being mistaken for the previous process to have used the same ID.

There are some special processes, but the details differ from implementation to implementation. Process ID 0 is usually the scheduler process and is often known as the swapper. No program on disk corresponds to this process, which is part of the kernel and is known as a system process. Process ID 1 is usually the init process and is invoked by the kernel at the end of the bootstrap procedure. The program file for this process was /etc/init in older versions of the UNIX System and is /sbin/init in newer versions. This process is responsible for bringing up a UNIX system after the kernel has been bootstrapped. init usually reads the system-dependent initialization filesthe /etc/rc* files or /etc/inittab and the files in /etc/init.dand brings the system to a certain state, such as multiuser. The init process never dies. It is a normal user process, not a system process within the kernel, like the swapper, although it does run with superuser privileges. Later in this chapter, we'll see how init becomes the parent process of any orphaned child process.

Each UNIX System implementation has its own set of kernel processes that provide operating system services. For example, on some virtual memory implementations of the UNIX System, process ID 2 is the pagedaemon. This process is responsible for supporting the paging of the virtual memory system. In addition to the process ID, there are other identifiers for every process. The following functions return these identifiers.

```
#include <unistd.h>
pid_t getpid(void);
Returns: process ID of calling process
```

pid_t getppid(void);

Returns: parent process ID of calling process

uid_t getuid(void);

Returns: real user ID of calling process

uid_t geteuid(void);

Returns: effective user ID of calling process

gid_t getgid(void);

Returns: real group ID of calling process

gid_t getegid(void);

Returns: effective group ID of calling process

Note that none of these functions has an error return.

fork Function

An existing process can create a new one by calling the fork function.

#include <unistd.h>

pid_t fork(void);

Returns: 0 in child, process ID of child in parent, 1 on error

The new process created by fork is called the child process. This function is called once but returns twice. The only difference in the returns is that the return value in the child is 0, whereas the return value in the parent is the process ID of the new child. The reason the child's process ID is returned to the parent is that a process can have more than one child, and there is no function that allows a process to obtain the process IDs of its children. The reason fork returns 0 to the child is that a process can have only a single parent, and the child can always call getppid to obtain the process ID of its parent. (Process ID 0 is reserved for use by the kernel, so it's not possible for 0 to be the process ID of a child.) Both the child and the parent continue executing with the instruction that follows the call to fork. The child is a copy of the parent. For example, the child gets a copy of the parent's data space, heap, and stack. Note that this is a copy for the child; the parent and the child do not share these portions of memory.

Current implementations don't perform a complete copy of the parent's data, stack, and heap, since a fork is often followed by an exec. Instead, a technique called copy-on-write (COW) is used. These regions are shared by the parent and the child and have their protection changed by the kernel to read-only. If either process tries to modify these regions, the kernel then makes a copy of that piece of memory only, typically a "page" in a virtual memory system.

Variations of the fork function are provided by some platforms. All four platforms discussed in this book support the vfork(2) variant discussed in the next section. Linux 2.4.22 also provides new process creation through the clone(2) system call. This is a generalized form of fork that allows the caller to control what is shared between parent and child. FreeBSD 5.2.1 provides the rfork(2) system call, which is similar to the Linux clone system call. The rfork call is derived from the Plan 9 operating system

Example

The program demonstrates the fork function, showing how changes to variables in a child process do not affect the value of the variables in the parent process.

```
#include "apue.h"
int glob = 6; /* external variable in initialized data */
char buf[] = "a write to stdout\n";
int
main(void)
{
int var; /* automatic variable on the stack */
pid_t pid;
var = 88;
if (write(STDOUT_FILENO, buf, sizeof(buf)-1) != sizeof(buf)-1)
err_sys("write error");
printf("before fork\n"); /* we don't flush stdout */
if ((pid = fork()) < 0) {
err_sys("fork error");
} else if (pid == 0) { /* child */
glob++; /* modify variables */
var++;
} else {
sleep(2); /* parent */
}
printf("pid = %d, glob = %d, var = %d\n", getpid(), glob, var);
exit(0);
}
```

If execute this program, get

```
$ ./a.out
```

```
a write to stdout
before fork
pid = 430, glob = 7, var = 89 child's variables were changed
pid = 429, glob = 6, var = 88 parent's copy was not changed
$ ./a.out > temp.out
$ cat temp.out
a write to stdout
before fork
pid = 432, glob = 7, var = 89
before fork
pid = 431, glob = 6, var = 88
```

In general, never know whether the child starts executing before the parent or vice versa. T is depends on the scheduling algorithm used by the kernel. If it's required that the child and parent synchronize, some form of inter process communication is required.

When write to standard output, subtract 1 from the size of buf to avoid writing the terminating null byte. Although strlen will calculate the length of a string not including the terminating null byte, sizeof calculates the size of the buffer, which does include the terminating null byte. Another difference is that using strlen requires a function call, whereas sizeof calculates the buffer length at compile time, as the buffer is initialized with a known string, and its size is fixed.

Example of fork function

```
#include "apue.h"
int glob = 6; /* external variable in initialized data */
char buf[] = "a write to stdout\n";
int
main(void)
{
int var; /* automatic variable on the stack */
pid_t pid;
var = 88;
if (write(STDOUT_FILENO, buf, sizeof(buf)-1) != sizeof(buf)-1)
err_sys("write error");
printf("before fork\n"); /* don't flush stdout */
if ((pid = fork()) < 0) {
err_sys("fork error");
```

```
} else if (pid == 0) { /* child */
glob++; /* modify variables */
var++;
} else {
sleep(2); /* parent */
}
printf("pid = %d, glob = %d, var = %d\n", getpid(), glob, var);
exit(0);
}
```

File Sharing

When redirect the standard output of the parent from the program in Figure 8.1, the child's standard output is also redirected. Indeed, one characteristic of fork is that all file descriptors that are open in the parent are duplicated in the child. say "duplicated" because it's as if the dup function had been called for each descriptor. The parent and the child share a file table entry for every open descriptor Consider a process that has three different files opened for standard input, standard output, and standard error.

It is important that the parent and the child share the same file offset. Consider a process that forks a child, then waits for the child to complete. Assume that both processes write to standard output as part of their normal processing. If the parent has its standard output redirected (by a shell, perhaps) it is essential that the parent's file offset be updated by the child when the child writes to standard output. In this case, the child can write to standard output while the parent is waiting for it; on completion of the child, the parent can continue writing to standard output, knowing that its output will be appended to whatever the child wrote. If the parent and the child did not share the same file offset, this type of interaction would be more difficult to accomplish and would require explicit actions by the parent.

If both parent and child write to the same descriptor, without any form of synchronization, such as having the parent wait for the child, their output will be intermixed (assuming it's a descriptor that was open before the fork).

There are two normal cases for handling the descriptors after a fork. The parent waits for the child to complete. In this case, the parent does not need to do anything with its descriptors. When the child terminates, any of the shared descriptors that the child read from or wrote to will have their file offsets updated accordingly. Both the parent and the child go their own ways. Here, after the fork, the parent closes the descriptors that it doesn't need, and the child does the same thing. This way, neither interferes with the other's open descriptors. This scenario is often the case with network servers.

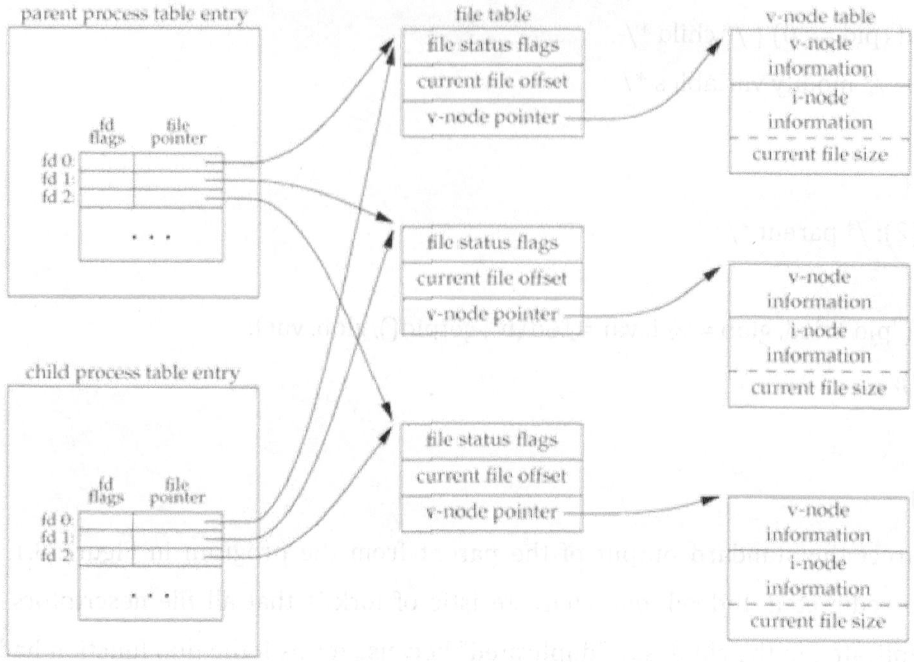

Sharing of open files between parent and child after fork

Besides the open files, there are numerous other properties of the parent that are inherited by the child: Real user ID, real group ID, effective user ID, effective group ID Supplementary group IDs Process group ID Session ID Controlling terminal The set-user-ID and set-group-ID flags Current working directory Root directory File mode creation mask Signal mask and dispositions The close-on-exec flag for any open file descriptors Environment Attached shared memory segments Memory mappings Resource limits The differences between the parent and child are The return value from fork The process IDs are different.

The two processes have different parent process IDs: the parent process ID of the child is the parent; the parent process ID of the parent doesn't change. The child's tms_utime, tms_stime, tms_cutime, and tms_cstime values are set to 0 File locks set by the parent are not inherited by the child Pending alarms are cleared for the child The set of pending signals for the child is set to the empty set.

There are two normal cases for handling the descriptors after a fork.

- The parent waits for the child to complete. In this case, the parent does not need to do anything with its descriptors. When the child terminates, any of the shared descriptors that the child read from or wrote to will have their file offsets updated accordingly.
- Both the parent and the child go their own ways. Here, after the fork, the parent closes the descriptors that it doesn't need, and the child does the same thing. This way, neither interferes with the other's open descriptors. This scenario is often the case with network servers.

Besides the open files, there are numerous other properties of the parent that are inherited by the child:

- Real user ID, real group ID, effective user ID, effective group ID

- Supplementary group IDs
- Process group ID
- Session ID
- Controlling terminal
- The set-user-ID and set-group-ID flags
- Current working directory
- Root directory
- File mode creation mask
- Signal mask and dispositions
- The close-on-exec flag for any open file descriptors
- Environment
- Attached shared memory segments
- Memory mappings
- Resource limits
- The differences between the parent and child are
- The return value from fork
- The process IDs are different
- The two processes have different parent process IDs: the parent process ID of the child is the
- parent; the parent process ID of the parent doesn't change
- The child's tms_utime, tms_stime, tms_cutime, and tms_cstime values are set to 0
- File locks set by the parent are not inherited by the child
- Pending alarms are cleared for the child
- The set of pending signals for the child is set to the empty set

The two main reasons for fork to fail are (a) if too many processes are already in the system, which usually means that something else is wrong, or (b) if the total number of processes for this real user ID exceeds the system's limit. The CHILD_MAX specifies the maximum number of simultaneous processes per real user ID.

There are two uses for fork:

- When a process wants to duplicate itself so that the parent and child can each execute different sections of code at the same time. This is common for network servers the parent waits for a service request from a client. When the request arrives, the parent calls fork and lets the child handle the request. The parent goes back to waiting for the next service request to arrive.
- When a process wants to execute a different program. This is common for shells. In this case, the child does an exec right after it returns from the fork.

Some operating systems combine the operations from step 2a fork followed by an exec into a single operation called a spawn.

The UNIX System separates the two, as there are numerous cases where it is useful to fork without doing an exec. Also, separating the two allows the child to change the per process attributes between the fork and the exec, such as I/O redirection, user ID, signal disposition, and so on.

The Single UNIX Specification does include spawn interfaces in the advanced real-time option group. These interfaces are not intended to be replacements for fork and exec, however. They are intended to support systems that have difficulty implementing fork efficiently, especially systems without hardware support for memory management.

vfork Function

The function vfork has the same calling sequence and same return values as fork. But the semantics of the two functions differ. The vfork function originated with 2.9BSD. Some consider the function a blemish, but all the platforms covered in this book support it. In fact, the BSD developers removed it from the 4.4BSD release, but all the open source BSD distributions that derive from 4.4BSD added support for it back into their own releases. The vfork function is marked as an obsolete interface in Version 3 of the Single UNIX Specification.

The vfork function is intended to create a new process when the purpose of the new process is to exec a new program (step 2 at the end of the previous section). The vfork function creates the new process, just like fork, without copying the address space of the parent into the child, as the child won't reference that address space; the child simply calls exec (or exit) right after the vfork. Instead, while the child is running and until it calls either exec or exit, the child runs in the address space of the parent. This optimization provides an efficiency gain on some paged virtual-memory implementations of the UNIX System. (As mentioned in the previous section, implementations use copy-on-write to improve the efficiency of a fork followed by an exec, but no copying is still faster than some copying.)

Another difference between the two functions is that vfork guarantees that the child runs first, until the child calls exec or exit. When the child calls either of these functions, the parent resumes. (This can lead to deadlock if the child depends on further actions of the parent before calling either of these two functions.)

Example

```
#include "apue.h"
int glob = 6; /* external variable in initialized data */
int
main(void)
{
```

```
int var; /* automatic variable on the stack */
pid_t pid;
var = 88;
printf("before vfork\n"); /* we don't flush stdio */
if ((pid = vfork()) < 0) {
err_sys("vfork error");
} else if (pid == 0) { /* child */
glob++; /* modify parent's variables */
var++;
_exit(0); /* child terminates */
}
/*
* Parent continues here.
*/
printf("pid = %d, glob = %d, var = %d\n", getpid(), glob, var);
exit(0);
}
```

Running this program gives us

```
$ ./a.out
before vfork
pid = 29039, glob = 7, var = 89
```

Here, the incrementing of the variables done by the child changes the values in the parent. Because the child runs in the address space of the parent, this doesn't surprise us. This behavior, however, differs from fork. The _exit does not perform any flushing of standard I/O buffers. If call exit instead, the results are indeterminate.

Depending on the implementation of the standard I/O library, might see no difference in the output, or might find that the output from the parent's printf has disappeared. If the child calls exit, the implementation flushes the standard I/O streams. If this is the only action taken by the library, then will see no difference with the output generated if the child called _exit. If the implementation also closes the standard I/O streams, however, the memory representing the FILE object for the standard output will be cleared out. Because the child is borrowing the parent's address space, when the parent resumes and calls printf, no output will appear and printf will return -1. Note that the parent's STDOUT_FILENO is still valid, as the child gets a copy of the parent's file descriptor array.

Most modern implementations of exit will not bother to close the streams. Because the process is about to exit, the kernel will close all the file descriptors open in the process. Closing them in the library simply adds overhead without any benefit.

exit Functions

A process can terminate normally in five ways:

- Executing a return from the main function. This is equivalent to calling exit.
- Calling the exit function. This function is defined by ISO C and includes the calling of all exit handlers that have been registered by calling atexit and closing all standard I/O streams. Because ISO C does not deal with file descriptors, multiple processes (parents and children), and job control, the definition of this function is incomplete for a UNIX system.
- Calling the _exit or _Exit function. ISO C defines _Exit to provide a way for a process to terminate without running exit handlers or signal handlers. Whether or not standard I/O streams are flushed depends on the implementation. On UNIX systems, _Exit and _exit are synonymous and do not flush standard I/O streams. The _exit function is called by exit and handles the UNIX system-specific details; _exit is specified by POSIX.1. In most UNIX system implementations, exit(3) is a function in the standard C library, whereas _exit(2) is a system call.
- Executing a return from the start routine of the last thread in the process. The return value of the thread is not used as the return value of the process, however. When the last thread returns from its start routine, the process exits with a termination status of 0.
- Calling the pthread_exit function from the last thread in the process. As with the previous case, the exit status of the process in this situation is always 0, regardless of the argument passed to pthread_exit.

The three forms of abnormal termination are as follows:

- Calling abort. This is a special case of the next item, as it generates the SIGABRT signal.
- When the process receives certain signals. The signal can be generated by the process itselffor example, by calling the abort function by some other process, or by the kernel. Examples of signals generated by the kernel include the process referencing a memory location not within its address space or trying to divide by 0.
- The last thread responds to a cancellation request. By default, cancellation occurs in a deferred manner: one thread requests that another be canceled, and sometime later, the target thread terminates.

wait and waitpid Functions

When a process terminates, either normally or abnormally, the kernel notifies the parent by sending the SIGCHLD signal to the parent. Because the termination of a child is an asynchronous eventit can happen at any time while the parent is runningthis signal is the asynchronous notification from the kernel to the parent. The parent can choose to ignore this signal, or it can provide a function that is called when the signal occurs: a signal handler. The default action for this signal is to be ignored.

For now, need to be aware that a process that calls wait or waitpid can

- Block, if all of its children are still running
- Return immediately with the termination status of a child, if a child has terminated and is waiting for its termination status to be fetched
- Return immediately with an error, if it doesn't have any child processes

If the process is calling wait because it received the SIGCHLD signal, expect wait to return immediately. But if call it at any random point in time, it can block.

```
#include <sys/wait.h>
pid_t wait(int *statloc);
pid_t waitpid(pid_t pid, int *statloc, int options);
```

Both return: process ID if OK, 0 (see later), or 1 on error

The differences between these two functions are as follows.

- The wait function can block the caller until a child process terminates, whereas waitpid has an option that prevents it from blocking.
- The waitpid function doesn't wait for the child that terminates first; it has a number of options that control which process it waits for.

If a child has already terminated and is a zombie, wait returns immediately with that child's status. Otherwise, it blocks the caller until a child terminates. If the caller blocks and has multiple children, wait returns when one terminates. can always tell which child terminated, because the process ID is returned by the function.

Solaris supports one additional, but nonstandard, option constant. WNOWAIT has the system keep the process whose termination status is returned by waitpid in a wait state, so that it may be waited for again.

- The waitpid function provides three features that aren't provided by the wait function.
- The waitpid function lets us wait for one particular process, whereas the wait function returns the status of any terminated child. We'll return to this feature when discuss the popen function.
    1. The waitpid function provides a nonblocking version of wait. There are times when want to fetch a child's status, but don't want to block.
    2. The waitpid function provides support for job control with the WUNtrACED and WCONTINUED options.

Example

If want to write a process so that it forks a child but don't want to wait for the child to complete and don't want the child to become a zombie until terminate, the trick is to call fork twice. To call sleep in the second child to ensure that the first child terminates before printing the parent process ID. After a fork, either the parent or the child can continue executing; never know which will resume execution first. If didn't put the second child to sleep, and if it resumed execution after the fork before its parent, the parent process ID that it printed would be that of its parent, not process ID 1.

Avoid zombie processes by calling fork twice

```
#include "apue.h"
#include <sys/wait.h>
int
main(void)
{
pid_t pid;
if ((pid = fork()) < 0) {
err_sys("fork error");
} else if (pid == 0) { /* first child */
if ((pid = fork()) < 0)
err_sys("fork error");
else if (pid > 0)
exit(0); /* parent from second fork == first child */
/*
* We're the second child; our parent becomes init as soon
* as our real parent calls exit() in the statement above.
* Here's where we'd continue executing, knowing that when
* we're done, init will reap our status.
*/
sleep(2);
printf("second child, parent pid = %d\n", getppid());
exit(0);
}
if (waitpid(pid, NULL, 0) != pid) /* wait for first child */
err_sys("waitpid error");
/*
```

```
* We're the parent (the original process); continue executing,
* knowing that we're not the parent of the second child.
*/
exit(0);
}
```

Executing the program that gives

```
$ ./a.out
$ second child, parent pid = 1
```

waitid Function

The XSI extension of the Single UNIX Specification includes an additional function to retrieve the exit status of a process. The waitid function is similar to waitpid, but provides extra flexibility.

```
#include <sys/wait.h>
int waitid(idtype_t idtype, id_t id, siginfo_t
*infop, int options);
```

Returns: 0 if OK, 1 on error

Like waitpid, waitid allows a process to specify which children to wait for. Instead of encoding this information in a single argument combined with the process ID or process group ID, two separate arguments are used. The id parameter is interpreted based on the value of idtype.

wait3 and wait4 Functions

Most UNIX system implementations provide two additional functions: wait3 and wait4. Historically, these two variants descend from the BSD branch of the UNIX System. The only feature provided by these two functions that isn't provided by the wait, waitid, and waitpid functions is an additional argument that allows the kernel to return a summary of the resources used by the terminated process and all its child processes.

```
#include <sys/types.h>
#include <sys/wait.h>
#include <sys/time.h>
#include <sys/resource.h>
pid_t wait3(int *statloc, int options, struct
rusage *rusage);
pid_t wait4(pid_t pid, int *statloc, int options,
struct rusage *rusage);
```

Both return: process ID if OK, 0, or 1 on error

The resource information includes such statistics as the amount of user CPU time, the amount of system CPU time, number of page faults, number of signals received, and the like. Refer to the geTRusage(2) manual page for additional details.

Race Conditions

A race condition occurs when multiple processes are trying to do something with shared data and the final outcome depends on the order in which the processes run. The fork function is a lively breeding ground for race conditions, if any of the logic after the fork either explicitly or implicitly depends on whether the parent or child runs first after the fork. In general, cannot predict which process runs first. Even if knew which process would run first, what happens after that process starts running depends on the system load and the kernel's scheduling algorithm.

If the second child runs before the first child, then its parent process will be the first child. But if the first child runs first and has enough time to exit, then the parent process of the second child is init. Even calling sleep, as did, guarantees nothing. If the system was heavily loaded, the second child could resume after sleep returns, before the first child has a chance to run. Problems of this form can be difficult to debug because they tend to work "most of the time." A process that wants to wait for a child to terminate must call one of the wait functions. If a process wants to wait for its parent to terminate.

```
while (getppid() != 1)
    sleep(1);
```

The problem with this type of loop, called polling, is that it wastes CPU time, as the caller is awakened every second to test the condition. To avoid race conditions and to avoid polling, some form of signaling is required between multiple processes.

For a parent and child relationship, often have the following scenario. After the fork, both the parent and the child have something to do. For example, the parent could update a record in a log file with the child's process ID, and the child might have to create a file for the parent. In this example, require that each process tell the other when it has finished its initial set of operations, and that each wait for the other to complete, before heading off on its own.

exec Functions

The fork function is to create a new process (the child) that then causes another program to be executed by calling one of the exec functions. When a process calls one of the exec functions, that process is completely replaced by the new program, and the new program starts executing at its main function. The process ID does not change across an exec, because a new process is not created; exec merely replaces the current processits text, data, heap, and stack segmentswith a brand new program from disk.

There are six different exec functions, but we'll often simply refer to "the exec function," which means that could use any of the six functions. These six functions round out the UNIX System process control primitives. With fork, can create new processes; and with the exec functions, can initiate new programs. The exit function and the wait functions handle termination and waiting for termination. These are the only process control primitives need. We'll use these primitives in later sections to build additional functions, such as popen and system.

```
#include <unistd.h>
int execl(const char *pathname, const char *arg0,
... /* (char *)0 */ );
int execv(const char *pathname, char *const argv []);
int execle(const char *pathname, const char *arg0, ...
/* (char *)0, char *const envp[] */ );
int execve(const char *pathname, char *const
argv[], char *const envp []);
int execlp(const char *filename, const char *arg0,
... /* (char *)0 */ );
int execvp(const char *filename, char *const argv []);
All six return: 1 on error, no return on success
```

The first difference in these functions is that the first four take a pathname argument, whereas the last two take a filename argument. When a filename argument is specified

- If filename contains a slash, it is taken as a pathname.
- Otherwise, the executable file is searched for in the directories specified by the PATH environment variable.

The PATH variable contains a list of directories, called path prefixes, that are separated by colons. For example, the name=value environment string PATH=/bin:/usr/bin:/usr/local/bin/:. specifies four directories to search. The last path prefix specifies the current directory. (A zero-length prefix also means the current directory.

If either execlp or execvp finds an executable file using one of the path prefixes, but the file isn't a machine executable that was generated by the link editor, the function assumes that the file is a shell script and tries to invoke /bin/sh with the filename as input to the shell. The next difference concerns the passing of the argument list (l stands for list and v stands for vector). The functions execl, execlp, and execle require each of the command-line arguments to the new program to be specified as separate arguments. mark the end of the arguments with a null pointer. For the other three functions (execv, execvp, and execve), have to build an array of pointers to the arguments, and the address of this array is the argument to these three functions.Before using ISO C prototypes, the normal way to show the command-line arguments for the three functions execl, execle, and execlp was char *arg0, char *arg1, ..., char *argn, (char *)0

This specifically shows that the final command-line argument is followed by a null pointer. If this null pointer is specified by the constant 0, must explicitly cast it to a pointer; if don't, it's interpreted as an integer argument. If the size of an integer is different from the size of a char *, the actual arguments to the exec function will be wrong.

The final difference is the passing of the environment list to the new program. The two functions whose names end in an e (execle and execve) allow us to pass a pointer to an array of pointers to the environment strings. The other four functions, however, use the environ variable in the calling process to copy the existing environment for the new program.

Normally, a process allows its environment to be propagated to its children, but in some cases, a process wants to specify a certain environment for a child. One example of the latter is the login program when a new login shell is initiated. the process ID does not change after an exec, but the new program inherits additional properties from the calling process:

- Process ID and parent process ID
- Real user ID and real group ID
- Supplementary group IDs
- Process group ID
- Session ID
- Controlling terminal
- Time left until alarm clock
- Current working directory
- Root directory
- File mode creation mask
- File locks
- Process signal mask
- Pending signals
- Resource limits
- Values for tms_utime, tms_stime, tms_cutime, and tms_cstime

The handling of open files depends on the value of the close-on-exec flag for each descriptor.

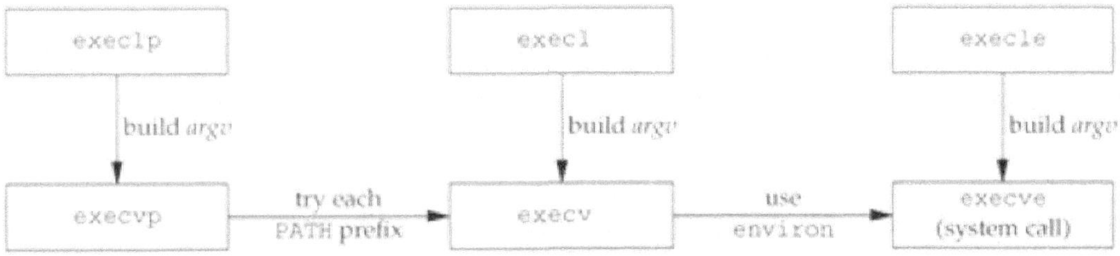

Relationship of the six exec functions

Changing User IDs and Group IDs

In the UNIX System, privileges, such as being able to change the system's notion of the current date, and access control, such as being able to read or write a particular file, are based on user and group IDs. When our programs need additional privileges or need to gain access to resources that they currently aren't allowed to access, they need to change their user or group ID to an ID that has the appropriate privilege or access. Similarly, when our programs need to lower their privileges or prevent access to certain resources, they do so by changing either their user ID or group ID to an ID without the privilege or ability access to the resource.

In general, try to use the least-privilege model when design our applications. Following this model, our programs should use the least privilege necessary to accomplish any given task. This reduces the likelihood that security can be compromised by a malicious user trying to trick our programs into using their privileges in unintended ways.

We can set the real user ID and effective user ID with the setuid function. Similarly, can set the real group ID and the effective group ID with the setgid function.

```
#include <unistd.h>
int setuid(uid_t uid);
int setgid(gid_t gid);
Both return: 0 if OK, 1 on error
```

There are rules for who can change the IDs. Let's consider only the user ID for now. (Everything describe for the user ID also applies to the group ID.)

- If the process has superuser privileges, the setuid function sets the real user ID, effective user ID, and saved set-user-ID to uid.
- If the process does not have superuser privileges, but uid equals either the real user ID or the saved set-user-ID, setuid sets only the effective user ID to uid. The real user ID and the saved set-user-ID are not changed.
- If neither of these two conditions is true, errno is set to EPERM, and 1 is returned.

Here, are assuming that _POSIX_SAVED_IDS is true. If this feature isn't provided, then delete all preceding references to the saved set-user-ID. The saved IDs are a mandatory feature in the 2001 version of POSIX.1.

They used to be optional in older versions of POSIX. To see whether an implementation supports this feature, an application can test for the constant _POSIX_SAVED_IDS at compile time or call sysconf with the _SC_SAVED_IDS argument at runtime. can make a few statements about the three user IDs that the kernel maintains.

- Only a superuser process can change the real user ID. Normally, the real user ID is set by the login(1) program when log in and never changes. Because login is a superuser process, it sets all three user IDs when it calls setuid.
- The effective user ID is set by the exec functions only if the set-user-ID bit is set for the
- program file. If the set-user-ID bit is not set, the exec functions leave the effective user ID as its current value. can call setuid at any time to set the effective user ID to either the real user ID or the saved set-user-ID. Naturally, can't set the effective user ID to any random value.
- The saved set-user-ID is copied from the effective user ID by exec. If the file's set-user-ID bit is set, this copy is saved after exec stores the effective user ID from the file's user ID.

setreuid and setregid Functions

Historically, BSD supported the swapping of the real user ID and the effective user ID with the setreuid function.

```
#include <unistd.h>
int setreuid(uid_t ruid, uid_t euid);
int setregid(gid_t rgid, gid_t egid);
Both return: 0 if OK, 1 on error
```

The value of 1 for any of the arguments to indicate that the corresponding ID should remain unchanged. The rule is simple: an unprivileged user can always swap between the real user ID and the effective user ID. This allows a set-user-ID program to swap to the user's normal permissions and swap back again later for set-user-ID operations. When the saved set-user-ID feature was introduced with POSIX.1, the rule was enhanced to also allow an unprivileged user to set its effective user ID to its saved set-user-ID.

Both setreuid and setregid are XSI extensions in the Single UNIX Specification. As such, all UNIX System implementations are expected to provide support for them.

4.3BSD didn't have the saved set-user-ID feature described earlier. It used setreuid and setregid instead. This allowed an unprivileged user to swap back and forth between the two values. Be aware, however, that when programs that used this feature spawned a shell, they had to set the real user ID to the normal user ID before the exec. If they didn't do this, the real user ID could be privileged (from the swap done by setreuid) and the shell process could call setreuid to swap the two and assume the permissions of the more privileged user.

seteuid and setegid Functions

POSIX.1 includes the two functions seteuid and setegid. These functions are similar to setuid and setgid, but only the effective user ID or effective group ID is changed.

```
#include <unistd.h>
int seteuid(uid_t uid);
int setegid(gid_t gid);
Both return: 0 if OK, 1 on error
```

An unprivileged user can set its effective user ID to either its real user ID or its saved set-user-ID. For a privileged user, only the effective user ID is set to uid. (This differs from the setuid function, which changes all three user IDs.)

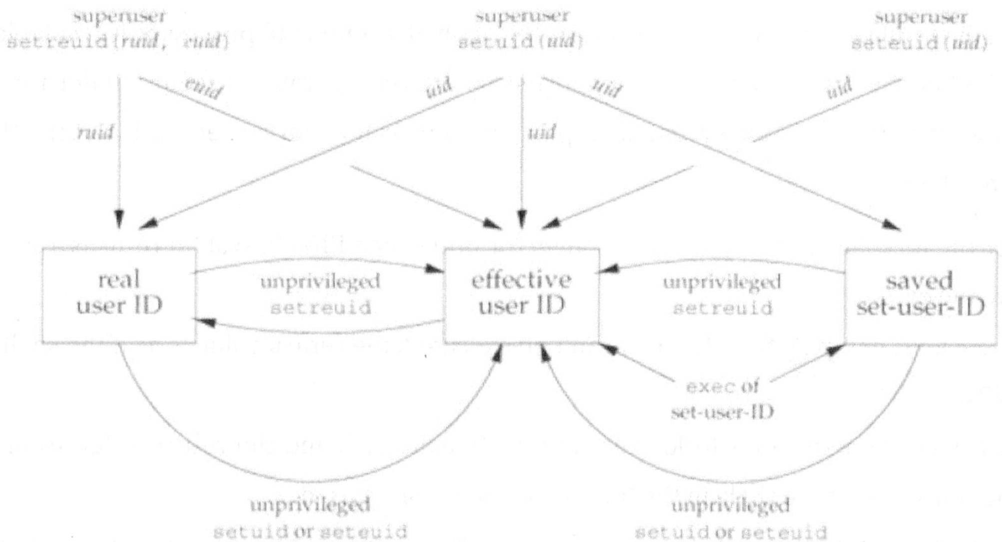

Summary of all the functions that set the various user IDs

Group IDs

Everything that we've said so far in this section also applies in a similar fashion to group IDs. The supplementary group IDs are not affected by setgid, setregid, or setegid.

Interpreter Files

All contemporary UNIX systems support interpreter files. These files are text files that begin with a line of the form #! pathname [optional-argument]

The space between the exclamation point and the pathname is optional. The most common of these interpreter files begin with the line #!/bin/sh

System Function

It is convenient to execute a command string from within a program. For example, assume that want to put a time-and-date stamp into a certain file. The call time to get the current calendar time, then call localtime to convert it to a broken-down time, and then call strftime to format the result, and write the results to the file.

```
system("date > file");
```

ISO C defines the system function, but its operation is strongly system dependent. POSIX.1 includes the system interface, expanding on the ISO C definition to describe its behavior in a POSIX environment.

```
#include <stdlib.h>
int system(const char *cmdstring);
Returns: (see below)
```

If cmdstring is a null pointer, system returns nonzero only if a command processor is available. This feature determines whether the system function is supported on a given operating system. Under the UNIX System, system is always available. Because system is implemented by calling fork, exec, and waitpid, there are three types of return values.

- If either the fork fails or waitpid returns an error other than EINTR, system returns 1 with errno set to indicate the error.
- If the exec fails, implying that the shell can't be executed, the return value is as if the shell had executed exit(127).
- Otherwise, all three functionsfork, exec, and waitpidsucceed, and the return value from system is the termination status of the shell, in the format specified for waitpid.

Some older implementations of system returned an error (EINTR) if waitpid was interrupted by a caught signal. Because there is no cleanup strategy that an application can use to recover from this type of error, POSIX later added the requirement that system not return an error in this case.

Process Accounting

Most UNIX systems provide an option to do process accounting. When enabled, the kernel writes an accounting record each time a process terminates. These accounting records are typically a small amount of binary data with the name of the command, the amount of CPU time used, the user ID and group ID, the starting time, and so on.

Process accounting is not specified by any of the standards. Thus, all the implementations have annoying differences. For example, the I/O counts maintained on Solaris 9 are in units of bytes, whereas FreeBSD 5.2.1 and Mac OS X 10.3 maintain units of blocks, although there is no distinction between different block sizes, making the counter effectively useless. Linux 2.4.22, on the other hand, doesn't try to maintain I/O statistics at all.

Each implementation also has its own set of administrative commands to process raw accounting data. For example, Solaris provides runacct(1m) and acctcom(1), whereas FreeBSD provides the sa(8) command to process and summarize the raw accounting data.

User Identification

Any process can find out its real and effective user ID and group ID.

```
#include <unistd.h>
char *getlogin(void);
Returns: pointer to string giving login name if OK, NULL on error
```

Process Times

In this three times that can measure: wall clock time, user CPU time, and system CPU time. Any process can call the times function to obtain these values for itself and any terminated children.

```
#include <sys/times.h>
clock_t times(struct tms *buf);
Returns: elapsed wall clock time in clock ticks if OK, 1 on error
```

Process Relationships

Introduction

First, every process has a parent process (the initial kernel-level process is usually its own parent). The parent is notified when the child terminates, and the parent can obtain the child's exit status.

Terminal Logins

Let's start by looking at the programs that are executed when log in to a UNIX system. In early UNIX systems, such as Version 7, users logged in using dumb terminals that were connected to the host with hard-wired connections. The terminals were either local (directly connected) or remote (connected through a modem). In either case, these logins came through a terminal device driver in the kernel. For example, the common devices on PDP-11s were DH-11s and DZ-11s. A host had a fixed number of these terminal devices, so there was a known upper limit on the number of simultaneous logins.

As bit-mapped graphical terminals became available, windowing systems were developed to provide users with new ways to interact with host computers. Applications were developed to create "terminal windows" to emulate character-based terminals, allowing users to interact with hosts in familiar ways (i.e., via the shell command line).

BSD Terminal Logins

This procedure has not changed much over the past 30 years. The system administrator creates a file, usually /etc/ttys, that has one line per terminal device. Each line specifies the name of the device and other parameters that are passed to the getty program. One parameter is the baud rate of the terminal, for example.

When the system is bootstrapped, the kernel creates process ID 1, the init process, and it is init that brings the system up multiuser. The init process reads the file /etc/ttys and, for every terminal device that allows a login, does a fork followed by an exec of the program getty.

If log in correctly, login will Change to our home directory (chdir) Change the ownership of our terminal device (chown) so own it Change the access permissions for our terminal device so have permission to read from and write to it Set our group IDs by calling setgid and initgroups Initialize the environment with all the information that login has: our home directory (HOME), shell (SHELL), user name (USER and LOGNAME), and a default path (PATH) Change to our user ID (setuid) and invoke our login shell, as in execl("/bin/sh", "-sh", (char *)0);

The minus sign as the first character of argv[0] is a flag to all the shells that they are being invoked as a login shell. The shells can look at this character and modify their startup accordingly.

When we enter our user name, getty's job is complete, and it then invokes the login program, similar to execle("/bin/login", "login", "-p", username, (char *)0, envp);

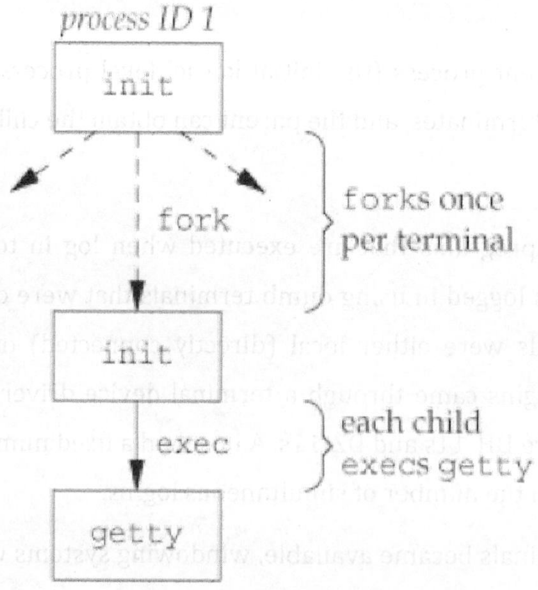

Processes invoked by init to allow terminal logins

Mac OS X Terminal Logins

On Mac OS X, the terminal login process follows the same steps as in the BSD login process, since Mac OS X is based in part on FreeBSD. With Mac OS X, however, are presented with a graphicalbased login screen from the start.

Linux Terminal Logins

The Linux login procedure is very similar to the BSD procedure. Indeed, the Linux login command is derived from the 4.3BSD login command. The main difference between the BSD login procedure and the Linux login procedure is in the way the terminal configuration is specified. On Linux, /etc/inittab contains the configuration information specifying the terminal devices for which init should start a getty process, similar to the way it is done on System V. Depending on the version of getty in use, the terminal characteristics are specified either on the command line (as with agetty) or in the file /etc/gettydefs (as with mgetty).

Solaris Terminal Logins

Solaris supports two forms of terminal logins: (a) getty style, as described previously for BSD, and (b) ttymon logins, a feature introduced with SVR4. Normally, getty is used for the console, and ttymon is used for other terminal logins.

Network Logins

The main (physical) difference between logging in to a system through a serial terminal and logging in to a system through a network is that the connection between the terminal and the computer isn't point-to-point. In this case, login is simply a service available, just like any other network service, such as FTP or SMTP.

With the terminal logins that described in the previous section, init knows which terminal devices are enabled for logins and spawns a getty process for each device. In the case of network logins, however, all the logins come through the kernel's network interface drivers (e.g., the Ethernet driver), and don't know ahead of time how many of these will occur. Instead of having a process waiting for each possible login, now have to wait for a network connection request to arrive.

BSD Network Logins

In BSD, a single process waits for most network connections: the inetd process, sometimes called the Internet superserver.

As part of the system start-up, init invokes a shell that executes the shell script /etc/rc. One of the daemons that is started by this shell script is inetd. Once the shell script terminates, the parent process of inetd becomes init; inetd waits for TCP/IP connection requests to arrive at the host. When a connection request arrives for it to handle, inetd does a fork and exec of the appropriate program.

Mac OS X Network Logins

Logging in to a Mac OS X system over a network is identical to a BSD system, because Mac OS X is based partially on FreeBSD.

Linux Network Logins

Network logins under Linux are the same as under BSD, except that an alternate inetd process is used, called the extended Internet services daemon, xinetd. The xinetd process provides a finer level of control over services it starts than does inetd.

Solaris Network Logins

The scenario for network logins under Solaris is almost identical to the steps under BSD and Linux. An inetd server is used similar to the BSD version. The Solaris version has the additional ability to run under the service access facility framework, although it is not configured to do so. Instead, the inetd server is started by init.

Process Groups

In addition to having a process ID, each process also belongs to a process group. A process group is a collection of one or more processes, usually associated with the same job that can receive signals from the same terminal. Each process group has a unique process group ID. Process group IDs are similar to process IDs: they are positive integers and can be stored in a pid_t data type. The function getpgrp returns the process group ID of the calling process.

```
#include <unistd.h>
pid_t getpgrp(void);
Returns: process group ID of calling process
```

In older BSD-derived systems, the getpgrp function took a pid argument and returned the process group for that process. The Single UNIX Specification defines the getpgid function as an XSI extension that mimics this behavior.

```
#include <unistd.h>
pid_t getpgid(pid_t pid);
Returns: process group ID if OK, 1 on error
```

If pid is 0, the process group ID of the calling process is returned. Thus,

```
getpgid(0);
```

is equivalent to

```
getpgrp();
```

Each process group can have a process group leader. The leader is identified by its process group ID being equal to its process ID.

A process joins an existing process group or creates a new process group by calling setpgid.

```
#include <unistd.h>
int setpgid(pid_t pid, pid_t pgid);
Returns: 0 if OK, 1 on error
```

This function sets the process group ID to pgid in the process whose process ID equals pid. If the two arguments are equal, the process specified by pid becomes a process group leader. If pid is 0, the process ID of the caller is used. Also, if pgid is 0, the process ID specified by pid is used as the process group ID.

A process can set the process group ID of only itself or any of its children. Furthermore, it can't change the process group ID of one of its children after that child has called one of the exec functions.

In most job-control shells, this function is called after a fork to have the parent set the process group ID of the child, and to have the child set its own process group ID. One of these calls is redundant, but by doing both, are guaranteed that the child is placed into its own process group before either process assumes that this has happened. If didn't do this, would have a race condition, since the child's process group membership would depend on which process executes first.

Sessions

A session is a collection of one or more process groups.

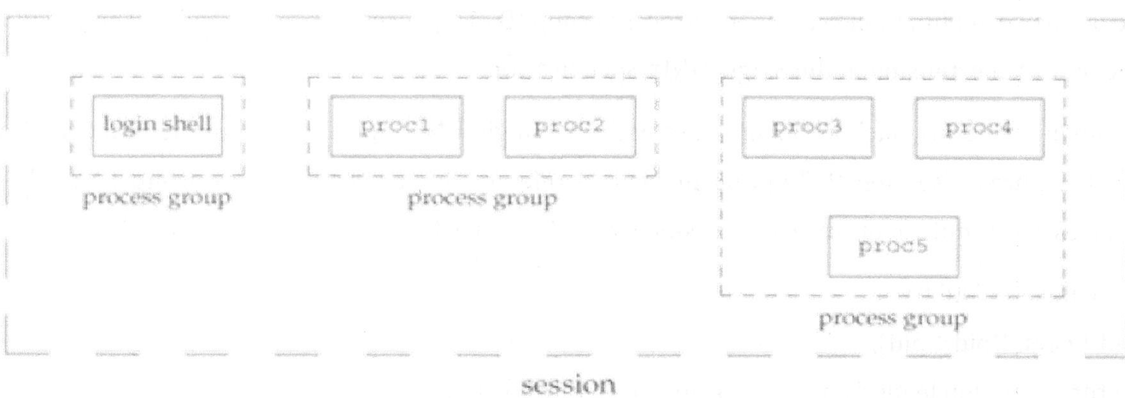

Arrangement of processes into process groups and sessions

The processes in a process group are usually placed there by a shell pipeline.

```
proc1 | proc2 &
proc3 | proc4 | proc5
```

A process establishes a new session by calling the setsid function.

```
#include <unistd.h>
pid_t setsid(void);
Returns: process group ID if OK, 1 on error
```

If the calling process is not a process group leader, this function creates a new session. Three things happen.

- The process becomes the session leader of this new session. (A session leader is the process that creates a session.) The process is the only process in this new session.
- The process becomes the process group leader of a new process group. The new process group ID is the process ID of the calling process.
- The process has no controlling terminal. (We'll discuss controlling terminals in the next section.) If the process had a controlling terminal before calling setsid, that association is broken.

This function returns an error if the caller is already a process group leader. To ensure this is not the case, the usual practice is to call fork and have the parent terminate and the child continue. are guaranteed that the child is not a process group leader, because the process group ID of the parent is inherited by the child, but the child gets a new process ID. Hence, it is impossible for the child's process ID to equal its inherited process group ID.

The Single UNIX Specification talks only about a "session leader." There is no "session ID" similar to a process ID or a process group ID. Obviously, a session leader is a single process that has a unique process ID, so could talk about a session ID that is the process ID of the session leader. This concept of a session ID was introduced in SVR4. Historically, BSD-based systems didn't support this notion, but have since been updated to include it. The getsid function returns the process group ID of a process's session leader. The getsid function is included as an XSI extension in the Single UNIX Specification.

Some implementations, such as Solaris, join with the Single UNIX Specification in the practice of avoiding the use of the phrase "session ID," opting instead to refer to this as the "process group ID of the session leader." The two are equivalent, since the session leader is always the leader of a process group.

```
#include <unistd.h>
pid_t getsid(pid_t pid);
Returns: session leader's process group ID if OK, 1 on error
```

If pid is 0, getsid returns the process group ID of the calling process's session leader. For security reasons, some implementations may restrict the calling process from obtaining the process group ID of the session leader if pid doesn't belong to the same session as the caller.

Controlling Terminal

Sessions and process groups have a few other characteristics.

- A session can have a single controlling terminal. This is usually the terminal device (in the case of a terminal login) or pseudo-terminal device (in the case of a network login) on which log in.
- The session leader that establishes the connection to the controlling terminal is called the controlling process.
- The process groups within a session can be divided into a single foreground process group and one or more background process groups.
- If a session has a controlling terminal, it has a single foreground process group, and all other process groups in the session are background process groups.
- Whenever type the terminal's interrupt key (often DELETE or Control-C), this causes the interrupt signal be sent to all processes in the foreground process group.
- Whenever type the terminal's quit key (often Control-backslash), this causes the quit signal to be sent to all processes in the foreground process group.
- If a modem (or network) disconnect is detected by the terminal interface, the hang-up signal is sent to the controlling process (the session leader).

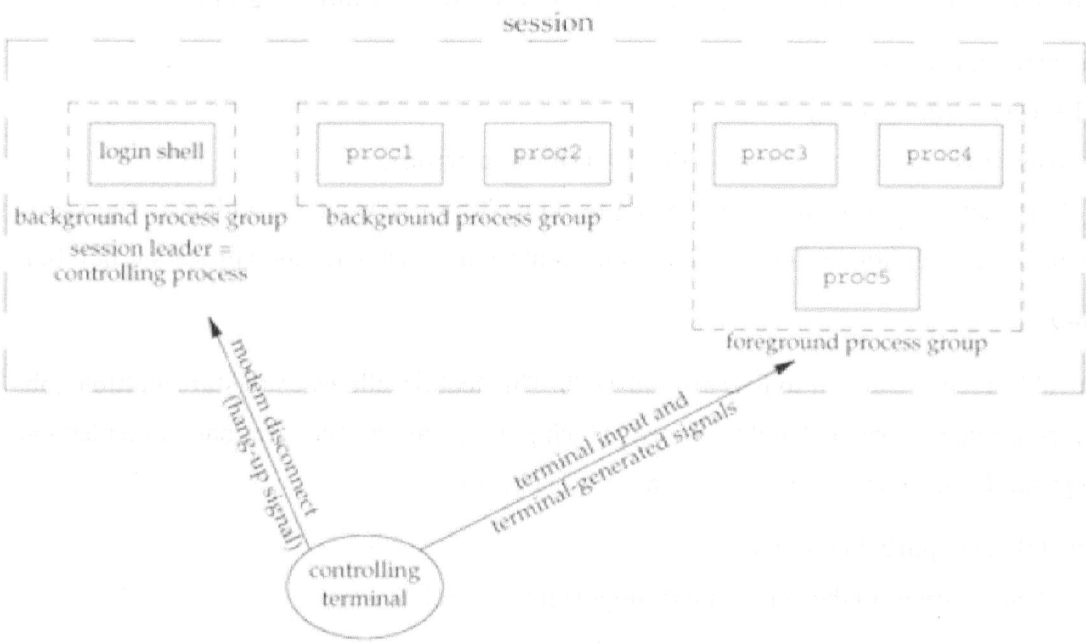

Process groups and sessions showing controlling terminal

tcgetpgrp, tcsetpgrp, and tcgetsid Functions

The kernel which process group is the foreground process group, so that the terminal device driver knows where to send the terminal input and the terminal-generated signals.

```
#include <unistd.h>
pid_t tcgetpgrp(int filedes);
Returns: process group ID of foreground process group if OK, 1 on error
int tcsetpgrp(int filedes, pid_t pgrpid);
Returns: 0 if OK, 1 on error
```

The function tcgetpgrp returns the process group ID of the foreground process group associated with the terminal open on filedes.

If the process has a controlling terminal, the process can call tcsetpgrp to set the foreground process group ID to pgrpid. The value of pgrpid must be the process group ID of a process group in the same session, and filedes must refer to the controlling terminal of the session.

Most applications don't call these two functions directly. They are normally called by job-control shells.

The Single UNIX Specification defines an XSI extension called tcgetsid to allow an application to obtain the process group ID for the session leader given a file descriptor for the controlling TTY.

```
#include <termios.h>
pid_t tcgetsid(int filedes);
Returns: session leader's process group ID if OK, 1 on error
```

Applications that need to manage controlling terminals can use tcgetsid to identify the session ID of the controlling terminal's session leader (which is equivalent to the session leader's process group ID).

Job Control

Job control is a feature added to BSD around 1980. This feature allows us to start multiple jobs (groups of processes) from a single terminal and to control which jobs can access the terminal and which jobs are to run in the background. Job control requires three forms of support:

- A shell that supports job control
- The terminal driver in the kernel must support job control
- The kernel must support certain job-control signals

SVR3 provided a different form of job control called shell layers. The BSD form of job control, however, was selected by POSIX.1 and is what describe here. In earlier versions of the standard, job control support was optional, but POSIX.1 now requires platforms to support it.

From our perspective, using job control from a shell, can start a job in either the foreground or the background. A job is simply a collection of processes, often a pipeline of processes. For example,

```
vi main.c
```

starts a job consisting of one process in the foreground. The commands

```
pr *.c | lpr &
make all &
```

start two jobs in the background. All the processes invoked by these background jobs are in the background.

As said, to use the features provided by job control, need to be using a shell that supports job control. With older systems, it was simple to say which shells supported job control and which didn't. The C shell supported job control, the Bourne shell didn't, and it was an option with the Korn shell, depending whether the host supported job control. But the C shell has been ported to systems (e.g., earlier versions of System V) that don't support job control, and the SVR4 Bourne shell, when invoked by the name jsh instead of sh, supports job control. The Korn shell continues to support job control if the host does. The Bourne-again shell also supports job control. We'll just talk generically about a shell that supports job control, versus one that doesn't, when the difference between the various shells doesn't matter.

When start a background job, the shell assigns it a job identifier and prints one or more of the process IDs. The following script shows how the Korn shell handles this:

```
$ make all > Make.out &
[1] 1475
$ pr *.c | lpr &
[2] 1490
$ just press RETURN
[2] + Done pr *.c | lpr &
[1] + Done make all > Make.out &
```

The make is job number 1 and the starting process ID is 1475. The next pipeline is job number 2 and the process ID of the first process is 1490. When the jobs are done and when press RETURN, the shell tells us that the jobs are complete. The reason have to press RETURN is to have the shell print its prompt. The shell doesn't print the changed status of background jobs at any random timeonly right before it prints its prompt, to let us enter a new command line. If the shell didn't do this, it could output while were entering an input line.

The interaction with the terminal driver arises because a special terminal character affects the foreground job: the suspend key (typically Control-Z). Entering this character causes the terminal driver to send the SIGTSTP signal to all processes in the foreground process group. The jobs in any background process groups aren't affected. The terminal driver looks for three special characters, which generate signals to the foreground process group.

- The interrupt character (typically DELETE or Control-C) generates SIGINT.
- The quit character (typically Control-backslash) generates SIGQUIT.
- The suspend character (typically Control-Z) generates SIGTSTP.

Another job control condition can arise that must be handled by the terminal driver. Since can have a foreground job and one or more background jobs, which of these receives the characters that enter at the terminal? Only the foreground job receives terminal input. It is not an error for a background job to try to read from the terminal, but the terminal driver detects this and sends a special signal to the background job: SIGTTIN. This signal normally stops the background job; by using the shell, are notified of this and can bring the job into the foreground so that it can read from the terminal.

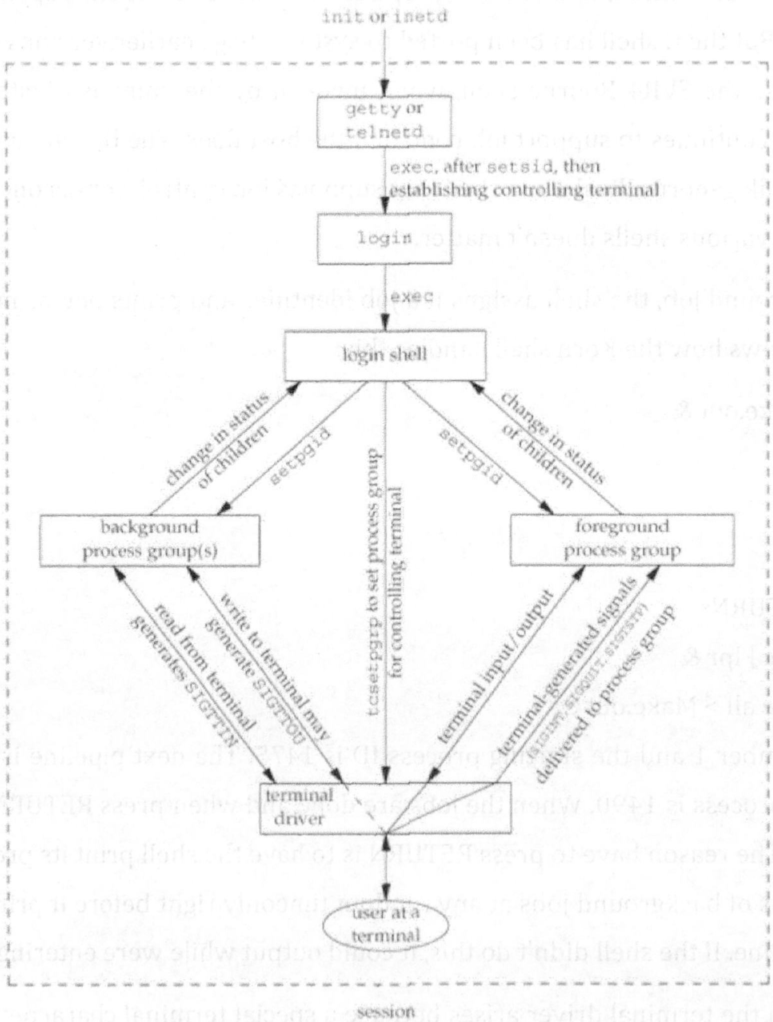

Summary of job control features with foreground and background jobs, and terminal driver

Shell Execution of Programs

Let's examine how the shells execute programs and how this relates to the concepts of process groups, controlling terminals, and sessions.

To do this, we'll use the ps command again. First, we'll use a shell that doesn't support job controlthe classic Bourne shell running on Solaris. If execute

ps -o pid,ppid,pgid,sid,comm

the output is

PID PPID PGID SID COMMAND

949 947 949 949 sh

1774 949 949 949 ps

The parent of the ps command is the shell, which would expect. Both the shell and the ps command are in the same session and foreground process group (949). say that 949 is the foreground process group because that is what you get when you execute a command with a shell that doesn't support job control. Some platforms support an option to have the ps(1) command print the process group ID associated with the session's controlling terminal. This value would be shown under the TPGID column. Unfortunately, the output of the ps command often differs among versions of the UNIX System. For example, Solaris 9 doesn't support this option. Under FreeBSD 5.2.1 and Mac OS X 10.3, the command

ps -o pid,ppid,pgid,sess,tpgid,command

and under Linux 2.4.22, the command

ps -o pid,ppid,pgrp,session,tpgid,comm

print exactly the information want.

Orphaned Process Groups

A process whose parent terminates is called an orphan and is inherited by the init process. now look at entire process groups that can be orphaned and how POSIX.1 handles this situation.

Example

Consider a process that forks a child and then terminates. Although this is nothing abnormal (it happens all the time), what happens if the child is stopped (using job control) when the parent terminates? How will the child ever be continued, and does the child know that it has been orphaned? The parent process has forked a child that stops, and the parent is about to exit.

This program has some new features. Here, are assuming a job-control shell. Recall from the previous section that the shell places the foreground process into its own process group (6099 in this example) and that the shell stays in its own process group (2837). The child inherits the process group of its parent (6099). After the fork,

- The parent sleeps for 5 seconds. This is our (imperfect) way of letting the child execute before the parent terminates.
- The child establishes a signal handler for the hang-up signal (SIGHUP). This is so can see whether SIGHUP is sent to the child.
- The child sends itself the stop signal (SIGTSTP) with the kill function. This stops the child, similar to our stopping a foreground job with our terminal's suspend character (Control-Z).
- When the parent terminates, the child is orphaned, so the child's parent process ID becomes 1, the init process ID.
- At this point, the child is now a member of an orphaned process group. The POSIX.1 definition of an orphaned process group is one in which the parent of every member is either itself a member of the group or is not a member of the group's session. Another way of wording this is that the process group is not orphaned as long as a process in the group has a parent in a different process group but in the same session. If the process group is not orphaned, there is a chance that one of those parents in a different process group but in the same session will restart a stopped process in the process group that is not orphaned. Here, the parent of every process in the group (e.g., process 1 is the parent of process 6100) belongs to another session.
- Since the process group is orphaned when the parent terminates, POSIX.1 requires that every process in the newly orphaned process group that is stopped (as our child is) be sent the hangup signal (SIGHUP) followed by the continue signal (SIGCONT).
- This causes the child to be continued, after processing the hang-up signal. The default action for the hang-up signal is to terminate the process, so have to provide a signal handler to catch the signal. therefore expect the printf in the sig_hup function to appear before the printf in the pr_ids function.

Creating an orphaned process group

```
#include "apue.h"
#include <errno.h>
static void
sig_hup(int signo)
{
printf("SIGHUP received, pid = %d\n"; getpid());
}
static void
```

```
pr_ids(char *name)
{
printf("%s: pid = %d, ppid = %d, pgrp = %d, tpgrp = %d\n",
name, getpid(), getppid(), getpgrp(), tcgetpgrp(STDIN_FILENO));
fflush(stdout);
}
int
main(void)
{
char c;
pid_t pid;
pr_ids("parent");
if ((pid = fork()) < 0) {
err_sys("fork error");
} else if (pid > 0) { /* parent */
sleep(5); /*sleep to let child stop itself */
exit(0); /* then parent exits */
} else { /* child */
pr_ids("child");
signal(SIGHUP, sig_hup); /* establish signal handler */
kill(getpid(), SIGTSTP); /* stop ourself */
pr_ids("child"); /* prints only if we're continued */
if (read(STDIN_FILENO, &c, 1) != 1)
printf("read error from controlling TTY, errno = %d\n",
errno);
exit(0);
}
}
```

Here is the output from the Program

```
$ ./a.out
parent: pid = 6099, ppid = 2837, pgrp = 6099, tpgrp = 6099
child: pid = 6100, ppid = 6099, pgrp = 6099, tpgrp = 6099
$ SIGHUP received, pid = 6100
child: pid = 6100, ppid = 1, pgrp = 6099, tpgrp = 2837
```

read error from controlling TTY, errno = 5

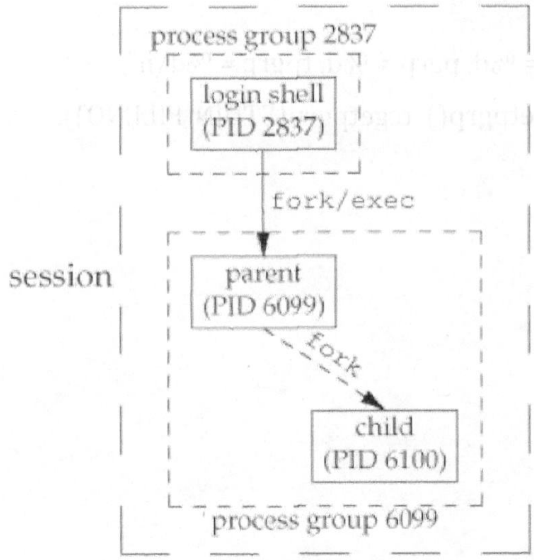

Example of a process group about to be orphaned

Note that our shell prompt appears with the output from the child, since two processesour login shell and the childare writing to the terminal. As expect, the parent process ID of the child has become 1. After calling pr_ids in the child, the program tries to read from standard input.

As saw earlier in this chapter, when a background process group tries to read from its controlling terminal, SIGTTIN is generated for the background process group. But here have an orphaned process group; if the kernel were to stop it with this signal, the processes in the process group would probably never be continued. POSIX.1 specifies that the read is to return an error with errno set to EIO (whose value is 5 on this system) in this situation.

Finally, note that our child was placed in a background process group when the parent terminated, since the parent was executed as a foreground job by the shell.

FreeBSD Implementation

The various attributes of a process, process group, session, and controlling terminal, it's worth looking at how all this can be implemented. We'll look briefly at the implementation used by FreeBSD.

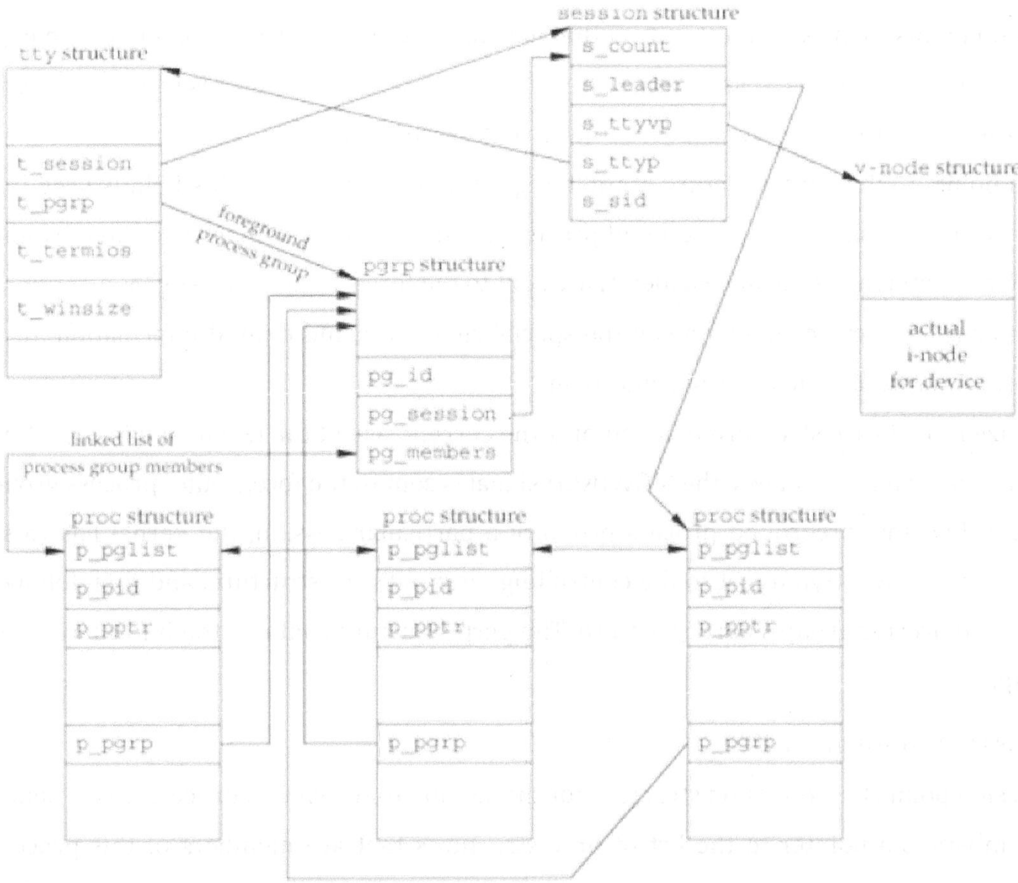

FreeBSD implementation of sessions and process groups

Let's look at all the fields that labeled, starting with the session structure. One of these structures is allocated for each session (e.g., each time setsid is called).

- s_count is the number of process groups in the session. When this counter is decremented to 0, the structure can be freed.
- s_leader is a pointer to the proc structure of the session leader.
- s_ttyvp is a pointer to the vnode structure of the controlling terminal.
- s_ttyp is a pointer to the tty structure of the controlling terminal.
- s_sid is the session ID. Recall that the concept of a session ID is not part of the Single UNIX Specification.

When setsid is called, a new session structure is allocated within the kernel. Now s_count is set to 1, s_leader is set to point to the proc structure of the calling process, s_sid is set to the process ID, and s_ttyvp and s_ttyp are set to null pointers, since the new session doesn't have a controlling terminal.

Let's move to the tty structure. The kernel contains one of these structures for each terminal device and each pseudo-terminal device.

- t_session points to the session structure that has this terminal as its controlling terminal. (Note that the tty structure points to the session structure and vice versa.) This pointer is used by the terminal to send a hang-up signal to the session leader if the terminal loses carrier.
- t_pgrp points to the pgrp structure of the foreground process group. This field is used by the terminal driver to send signals to the foreground process group. The three signals generated by entering special characters (interrupt, quit, and suspend) are sent to the foreground process group.
- t_termios is a structure containing all the special characters and related information for this terminal, such as baud rate, is echo on or off, and so on.
- t_winsize is a winsize structure that contains the current size of the terminal window. When the size of the terminal window changes, the SIGWINCH signal is sent to the foreground process group.

Note that to find the foreground process group of a particular session, the kernel has to start with the session structure, follow s_ttyp to get to the controlling terminal's tty structure, and then follow t_pgrp to get to the foreground process group's pgrp structure. The pgrp structure contains the information for a particular process group.

- pg_id is the process group ID.
- pg_session points to the session structure for the session to which this process group belongs.
- pg_members is a pointer to the list of proc structures that are members of this process group. The p_pglist structure in that proc structure is a doubly-linked list entry that points to both the next process and the previous process in the group, and so on, until a null pointer is encountered in the proc structure of the last process in the group.

The proc structure contains all the information for a single process.

- p_pid contains the process ID.
- p_pptr is a pointer to the proc structure of the parent process.
- p_pgrp points to the pgrp structure of the process group to which this process belongs.
- p_pglist is a structure containing pointers to the next and previous processes in the process group, as mentioned earlier.

The vnode structure is allocated when the controlling terminal device is opened. All references to /dev/tty in a process go through this vnode structure. show the actual i-node as being part of the v-node.

Signals

Introduction

Signals are software interrupts. Most nontrivial application programs need to deal with signals. Signals provide a way of handling asynchronous events: a user at a terminal typing the interrupt key to stop a program or the next program in a pipeline terminating prematurely.

Signals have been provided since the early versions of the UNIX System, but the signal model provided with systems such as Version 7 was not reliable. Signals could get lost, and it was difficult for a process to turn off selected signals when executing critical regions of code. Both 4.3BSD and SVR3 made changes to the signal model, adding what are called reliable signals. But the changes made by Berkeley and AT&T were incompatible. Fortunately, POSIX.1 standardized the reliable-signal routines, and that is what describe here.

Signal Concepts

First, every signal has a name. These names all begin with the three characters SIG. For example, SIGABRT is the abort signal that is generated when a process calls the abort function. SIGALRM is the alarm signal that is generated when the timer set by the alarm function goes off. Version 7 had 15 different signals; SVR4 and 4.4BSD both have 31 different signals. FreeBSD 5.2.1, Mac OS X 10.3, and Linux 2.4.22 support 31 different signals, whereas Solaris 9 supports 38 different signals. Both Linux and Solaris, however, support additional application-defined signals as real-time extensions

These names are all defined by positive integer constants (the signal number) in the header <signal.h>.

Implementations actually define the individual signals in an alternate header file, but this header file is included by <signal.h>. It is considered bad form for the kernel to include header files meant for user-level applications, so if the applications and the kernel both need the same definitions, the information is placed in a kernel header file that is then included by the user level header file. Thus, both FreeBSD 5.2.1 and Mac OS X 10.3 define the signals in <sys/signal.h>. Linux 2.4.22 defines the signals in <bits/signum.h>, and Solaris 9 defines them in <sys/iso/signal_iso.h>.

No signal has a signal number of 0. The kill function uses the signal number of 0 for a special case. POSIX.1 calls this value the null signal.

Numerous conditions can generate a signal.

- The terminal-generated signals occur when users press certain terminal keys. Pressing the DELETE key on the terminal (or Control-C on many systems) normally causes the interrupt signal (SIGINT) to be generated. This is how to stop a runaway program.
- Hardware exceptions generate signals: divide by 0, invalid memory reference, and the like. These conditions are usually detected by the hardware, and the kernel is notified. The kernel then generates the appropriate signal for the process that was running at the time the condition occurred. For example, SIGSEGV is generated for a process that executes an invalid memory reference.
- The kill(2) function allows a process to send any signal to another process or process group. Naturally, there are limitations: have to be the owner of the process that we're sending the signal to, or have to be the super user.

- The kill(1) command allows us to send signals to other processes. This program is just an interface to the kill function. This command is often used to terminate a runaway background process.
- Software conditions can generate signals when something happens about which the process should be notified. These aren't hardware-generated conditions (as is the divide-by-0 condition), but software conditions. Examples are SIGURG (generated when out-of-band data arrives over a network connection), SIGPIPE (generated when a process writes to a pipe after the reader of the pipe has terminated), and SIGALRM (generated when an alarm clock set by the process expires).

Signals are classic examples of asynchronous events. Signals occur at what appear to be random times to the process. The process can't simply test a variable (such as errno) to see whether a signal has occurred; instead, the process has to tell the kernel "if and when this signal occurs, do the following." can tell the kernel to do one of three things when a signal occurs. call this the disposition of the signal, or the action associated with a signal.

- Ignore the signal. This works for most signals, but two signals can never be ignored: SIGKILL and SIGSTOP. The reason these two signals can't be ignored is to provide the kernel and the superuser with a surefire way of either killing or stopping any process. Also, if ignore some of the signals that are generated by a hardware exception (such as illegal memory reference or divide by 0), the behavior of the process is undefined.
- Catch the signal. To do this, tell the kernel to call a function of ours whenever the signal occurs. In our function, can do whatever want to handle the condition. If we're writing a command interpreter, for example, when the user generates the interrupt signal at the keyboard, probably want to return to the main loop of the program, terminating whatever command were executing for the user. If the SIGCHLD signal is caught, it means that a child process has terminated, so the signal-catching function can call waitpid to fetch the child's process ID and termination status. As another example, if the process has created temporary files, may want to write a signal-catching function for the SIGTERM signal (the termination signal that is the default signal sent by the kill command) to clean up the temporary files. Note that the two signals SIGKILL and SIGSTOP can't be caught.
- Let the default action apply. Default action for most signals is to terminate the process.

When the default action is labeled "terminate+core," it means that a memory image of the process is left in the file named core of the current working directory of the process. (Because the file is named core, it shows how long this feature has been part of the UNIX System.) This file can be used with most UNIX System debuggers to examine the state of the process at the time it terminated.

The generation of the core file is an implementation feature of most versions of the UNIX System. Although this feature is not part of POSIX.1, it is mentioned as a potential implementation-specific action in the Single UNIX Specification's XSI extension.

The name of the core file varies among implementations. On FreeBSD 5.2.1, for example, the core file is named cmdname.core, where cmdname is the name of the command corresponding to the process that received the signal. On Mac OS X 10.3, the core file is named core.pid, where pid is the ID of the process that received the signal. (These systems allow the core filename to be configured via a sysctl parameter.)

Most implementations leave the core file in the current working directory of the corresponding process; Mac OS X places all core files in /cores instead.

SIGABRT This signal is generated by calling the abort function. The process terminates abnormally.

SIGALRM This signal is generated when a timer set with the alarm function expires. This signal is also generated when an interval timer set by the setitimer(2) function expires.

SIGBUS This indicates an implementation-defined hardware fault. Implementations usually generate this signal on certain types of memory faults.

SIGCANCEL This signal is used internally by the Solaris threads library. It is not meant for general use.

SIGCHLD Whenever a process terminates or stops, the SIGCHLD signal is sent to the parent. By default, this signal is ignored, so the parent must catch this signal if it wants to be notified whenever a child's status changes. The normal action in the signal-catching function is to call one of the wait functions to fetch the child's process ID and termination status. Earlier releases of System V had a similar signal named SIGCLD (without the H). The semantics of this signal were different from those of other signals, and as far back as SVR2, the manual page strongly discouraged its use in new programs. (Strangely enough, this warning disappeared in the SVR3 and SVR4 versions of the manual page.) Applications should use the standard SIGCHLD signal, but be aware that many systems define SIGCLD to be the same as SIGCHLD for backward compatibility. If you maintain software that uses SIGCLD, you need to check your system's manual page to see what semantics it follows.

SIGCONT This job-control signal is sent to a stopped process when it is continued. The default action is to continue a stopped process, but to ignore the signal if the process wasn't stopped. A full-screen editor, for example, might catch this signal and use the signal handler to make a note to redraw the terminal screen.

SIGEMT This indicates an implementation-defined hardware fault. The name EMT comes from the PDP-11 "emulator trap" instruction. Not all platforms support this signal. On Linux, for example, SIGEMT is supported only for selected architectures, such as SPARC, MIPS, and PA-RISC.

SIGFPE This signals an arithmetic exception, such as divide by 0, floating-point overflow, and so on.

SIGFREEZE This signal is defined only by Solaris. It is used to notify processes that need to take special action before freezing the system state, such as might happen when a system goes into hibernation or suspended mode.

SIGHUP This signal is sent to the controlling process (session leader) associated with a controlling terminal if a disconnect is detected by the terminal interface. The signal is sent to the process pointed to by the s_leader field in the session structure. This signal is generated for this condition only if the terminal's CLOCAL flag is not set. (The CLOCAL flag for a terminal is set if the attached terminal is local. The flag tells the terminal driver to ignore all modem status lines.

Note that the session leader that receives this signal may be in the background; This differs from the normal terminal-generated signals (interrupt, quit, and suspend), which are always delivered to the foreground process group. This signal is also generated if the session leader terminates. In this case, the signal is sent to each process in the foreground process group. This signal is commonly used to notify daemon processes to reread their configuration files. The reason SIGHUP is chosen for this is that a daemon should not have a controlling terminal and would normally never receive this signal.

SIGILL This signal indicates that the process has executed an illegal hardware instruction. 4.3BSD generated this signal from the abort function. SIGABRT is now used for this.

SIGINFO This BSD signal is generated by the terminal driver when type the status key (often Control-T). This signal is sent to all processes in the foreground process group. This signal normally causes status information on processes in the foreground process group to be displayed on the terminal. Linux doesn't provide support for SIGINFO except on the Alpha platform, where it is defined to be the same value as SIGPWR.

SIGINT This signal is generated by the terminal driver when type the interrupt key (often DELETE or Control-C). This signal is sent to all processes in the foreground process group. This signal is often used to terminate a runaway program, especially when it's generating a lot of unwanted output on the screen.

SIGIO This signal indicates an asynchronous I/O event.

The default action for SIGIO as either "terminate" or "ignore." Unfortunately, the default depends on the system. Under System V, SIGIO is identical to SIGPOLL, so its default action is to terminate the process. Under BSD, the default is to ignore the signal. Linux 2.4.22 and Solaris 9 define SIGIO to be the same value as SIGPOLL, so the default behavior is to terminate the process. On FreeBSD 5.2.1 and Mac OS X 10.3, the default is to ignore the signal.

SIGIOT This indicates an implementation-defined hardware fault. The name IOT comes from the PDP-11 mnemonic for the "input/output TRAP" instruction. Earlier versions of System V generated this signal from the abort function.

SIGABRT is now used for this. On FreeBSD 5.2.1, Linux 2.4.22, Mac OS X 10.3, and Solaris 9, SIGIOT is defined to be the same value as SIGABRT.

SIGKILL This signal is one of the two that can't be caught or ignored. It provides the system administrator with a sure way to kill any process.

SIGLWP This signal is used internally by the Solaris threads library, and is not available for general use.

SIGPIPE If write to a pipeline but the reader has terminated, SIGPIPE is generated. This signal is also generated when a process writes to a socket of type SOCK_STREAM that is no longer connected.

SIGPOLL This signal can be generated when a specific event occurs on a pollable device. describe this signal with the poll function. SIGPOLL originated with SVR3, and loosely corresponds to the BSD SIGIO and SIGURG signals. On Linux and Solaris, SIGPOLL is defined to have the same value as SIGIO.

SIGPROF This signal is generated when a profiling interval timer set by the setitimer(2) function expires.

SIGPWR This signal is system dependent. Its main use is on a system that has an uninterruptible power supply (UPS). If power fails, the UPS takes over and the software can usually be notified. Nothing needs to be done at this point, as the system continues running on battery power. But if the battery gets low (if the power is off for an extended period), the software is usually notified again; at this point, it behooves the system to shut everything down within about 1530 seconds. This is when SIGPWR should be sent. Most systems have the process that is notified of the low-battery condition send the SIGPWR signal to the init process, and init handles the shutdown. Linux 2.4.22 and Solaris 9 have entries in the inittab file for this purpose: powerfail and powerwait (or powerokwait). The default action for SIGPWR as either "terminate" or "ignore." Unfortunately, the default depends on the system. The default on Linux is to terminate the process. On Solaris, the signal is ignored by default.

SIGQUIT This signal is generated by the terminal driver when type the terminal quit key (often Control-backslash). This signal is sent to all processes in the foreground process group. This signal not only terminates the foreground process group (as does SIGINT), but also generates a core file.

SIGSEGV This signal indicates that the process has made an invalid memory reference. The name SEGV stands for "segmentation violation."

SIGSTKFLT This signal is defined only by Linux. This signal showed up in the earliest versions of Linux, intended to be used for stack faults taken by the math coprocessor. This signal is not generated by the kernel, but remains for backward compatibility.

SIGSTOP This job-control signal stops a process. It is like the interactive stop signal (SIGTSTP), but SIGSTOP cannot be caught or ignored.

SIGSYS This signals an invalid system call. Somehow, the process executed a machine instruction that the kernel thought was a system call, but the parameter with the instruction that indicates the type of system call was invalid. This might happen if you build a program that uses a new system call and you then try to run the same binary on an older version of the operating system where the system call doesn't exist.

SIGTERM This is the termination signal sent by the kill(1) command by default. SIGTHAW This signal is defined only by Solaris and is used to notify processes that need to take special action when the system resumes operation after being suspended.

SIGTRAP This indicates an implementation-defined hardware fault. The signal name comes from the PDP-11 TRAP instruction. Implementations often use this signal to transfer control to a debugger when a breakpoint instruction is executed.

SIGTSTP This interactive stop signal is generated by the terminal driver when type the terminal suspend key (often Control-Z). This signal is sent to all processes in the foreground process group. Unfortunately, the term stop has different meanings. When discussing job control and signals, talk about stopping and continuing jobs. The terminal driver, however, has historically used the term stop to refer to stopping and starting the terminal output using the Control-S and Control- Q characters. Therefore, the terminal driver calls the character that generates the interactive stop signal the suspend character, not the stop character.

SIGTTIN This signal is generated by the terminal driver when a process in a background process group tries to read from its controlling terminal. As special cases, if either (a) the reading process is ignoring or blocking this signal or (b) the process group of the reading process is orphaned, then the signal is not generated; instead, the read operation returns an error with errno set to EIO.

SIGTTOU This signal is generated by the terminal driver when a process in a background process group tries to write to its controlling terminal. Unlike the SIGTTIN signal just described, a process has a choice of allowing background writes to the controlling terminal. If background writes are not allowed, then like the SIGTTIN signal, there are two special cases: if either (a) the writing process is ignoring or blocking this signal or (b) the process group of the writing process is orphaned, then the signal is not generated; instead, the write operation returns an error with errno set to EIO. Regardless of whether background writes are allowed, certain terminal operations (other than writing) can also generate the SIGTTOU signal: tcsetattr, tcsendbreak, tcdrain, tcflush, tcflow, and tcsetpgrp.

SIGURG This signal notifies the process that an urgent condition has occurred. This signal is optionally generated when out-of-band data is received on a network connection.

SIGUSR1 This is a user-defined signal, for use in application programs.

SIGUSR2 This is another user-defined signal, similar to SIGUSR1, for use in application programs.

SIGVTALRM This signal is generated when a virtual interval timer set by the etitimer(2) function expires.

SIGWAITING This signal is used internally by the Solaris threads library, and is not vailable for general use.

SIGWINCH The kernel maintains the size of the window associated with each terminal and pseudo terminal. A process can get and set the window size with the ioctl function. If a process changes the window size from its previous value using the ioctl set-window-size command, the kernel generates the SIGWINCH signal for the foreground process group.

SIGXCPU The Single UNIX Specification supports the concept of resource limits as an XSI extension; If the process exceeds its soft CPU time limit, the SIGXCPU signal is generated. The default action for SIGXCPU as either "terminate with a core file" or "ignore." Unfortunately, the default depends on the operating system. Linux 2.4.22 and Solaris 9 support a default action of terminate with a core file, whereas FreeBSD 5.2.1 and Mac OS X 10.3 support a default action of ignore. The Single UNIX Specification requires that the default action be to terminate the process abnormally. Whether a core file is generated is left up to the implementation.

SIGXFSZ This signal is generated if the process exceeds its soft file size limit. Just as with SIGXCPU, the default action taken with SIGXFSZ depends on the operating system. On Linux 2.4.22 and Solaris 9, the default is to terminate the process and create a core file. On FreeBSD 5.2.1 and Mac OS X 10.3, the default is to be ignored. The Single UNIX Specification requires that the default action be to terminate the process abnormally. Whether a core file is generated is left up to the implementation.

SIGXRES This signal is defined only by Solaris. This signal is optionally used to notify processes that have exceeded a preconfigured resource value. The Solaris resource control mechanism is a general facility for controlling the use of shared resources among independent application sets.

signal Function

The simplest interface to the signal features of the UNIX System is the signal function.

```
#include <signal.h>
void (*signal(int signo, void (*func)(int)))(int);
```

Returns: previous disposition of signal (see following) if OK, SIG_ERR on error

The signal function is defined by ISO C, which doesn't involve multiple processes, process groups, terminal I/O, and the like. Therefore, its definition of signals is vague enough to be almost useless for UNIX systems.

Implementations derived from UNIX System V support the signal function, but it provides the old unreliable-signal semantics. This function provides backward compatibility for applications that require the older semantics. New applications should not use these unreliable signals.

4.4BSD also provides the signal function, but it is defined in terms of the sigaction function, so using it under 4.4BSD provides the newer reliablesignal semantics. FreeBSD 5.2.1 and Mac OS X 10.3 follow this strategy.

Solaris 9 has roots in both System V and BSD, but it chooses to follow the System V semantics for the signal function.

On Linux 2.4.22, the semantic of signal can follow either the BSD or System V semantics, depending on the version of the C library and how you compile your application.

Because the semantics of signal differ among implementations, it is better to use the sigaction function instead. When describe the sigaction function, provide an implementation of signal that uses it. All the examples in this text use the signal function.

The signo argument is just the name of the signal. The value of func is (a) the constant SIG_IGN, (b) the constant SIG_DFL, or (c) the address of a function to be called when the signal occurs. If specify SIG_IGN, are telling the system to ignore the signal. When specify SIG_DFL, are setting the action associated with the signal to its default value. When specify the address of a function to be called when the signal occurs, are arranging to "catch" the signal.

Process Creation

When a process calls fork, the child inherits the parent's signal dispositions. Here, since the child starts off with a copy of the parent's memory image, the address of a signal-catching function has meaning in the child.

Unreliable Signals

In earlier versions of the UNIX System (such as Version 7), signals were unreliable. By this mean that signals could get lost: a signal could occur and the process would never know about it. Also, a process had little control over a signal: a process could catch the signal or ignore it. Sometimes, would like to tell the kernel to block a signal: don't ignore it, just remember if it occurs, and tell us later when we're ready. Changes were made with 4.2BSD to provide what are called reliable signals. A different set of changes was then made in SVR3 to provide reliable signals under System V. POSIX.1 chose the BSD model to standardize.

Interrupted System Calls

A characteristic of earlier UNIX systems is that if a process caught a signal while the process was blocked in a "slow" system call, the system call was interrupted. The system call returned an error and errno was set to EINTR. This was done under the assumption that since a signal occurred and the process caught it, there is a good chance that something has happened that should wake up the blocked system call.

Here, have to differentiate between a system call and a function. It is a system call within the kernel that is interrupted when a signal is caught.

To support this feature, the system calls are divided into two categories: the "slow" system calls and all the others. The slow system calls are those that can block forever. Included in this category are

- Reads that can block the caller forever if data isn't present with certain file types (pipes, terminal devices, and network devices)
- Writes that can block the caller forever if the data can't be accepted immediately by these same file types
- Opens that block until some condition occurs on certain file types (such as an open of a terminal device that waits until an attached modem answers the phone)
- The pause function (which by definition puts the calling process to sleep until a signal is caught) and the wait function
- Certain ioctl operations
- Some of the inter process communication functions.

The notable exception to these slow system calls is anything related to disk I/O. Although a read or a write of a disk file can block the caller temporarily (while the disk driver queues the request and then the request is executed), unless a hardware error occurs, the I/O operation always returns and unblocks the caller quickly.

One condition that is handled by interrupted system calls, for example, is when a process initiates a read from a terminal device and the user at the terminal walks away from the terminal for an extended period. In this example, the process could be blocked for hours or days and would remain so unless the system was taken down.

POSIX.1 semantics for interrupted reads and writes changed with the 2001 version of the standard. Earlier versions gave implementations a choice for how to deal with reads and writes that have processed partial amounts of data. If read has received and transferred data to an application's buffer, but has not yet received all that the application requested and is then interrupted, the operating system could either fail the system call with errno set to EINTR or allow the system call to succeed, returning the partial amount of data received. Similarly, if write is interrupted after transferring some of the data in an application's buffer, the operation system could either fail the system call with errno set to EINTR or allow the system call to succeed, returning the partial amount of data written. Historically, implementations derived from System V fail the system call, whereas BSD-derived implementations return partial success. With the 2001 version of the POSIX.1 standard, the BSD-style semantics are required.

Reentrant Functions

When a signal that is being caught is handled by a process, the normal sequence of instructions being executed by the process is temporarily interrupted by the signal handler. The process then continues executing, but the instructions in the signal handler are now executed. If the signal handler returns (instead of calling exit or longjmp, for example), then the normal sequence of instructions that the process was executing when the signal was caught continues executing. (This is similar to what happens when a hardware interrupt occurs.) But in the signal handler, can't tell where the process was executing when the signal was caught. What if the process was in the middle of allocating additional memory on its heap using malloc, and call malloc from the signal handler? Or, what if the process was in the middle of a call to a function, such as getpwnam, that stores its result in a static location, and call the same function from the signal handler? In the malloc example, havoc can result for the process, since malloc usually maintains a linked list of all its allocated areas, and it may have been in the middle of changing this list. In the case of getpwnam, the information returned to the normal caller can get overwritten with the information returned to the signal handler.

The Single UNIX Specification specifies the functions that are guaranteed to be reentrant.

SIGCLD Semantics

Two signals that continually generate confusion are SIGCLD and SIGCHLD. First, SIGCLD (without the H) is the System V name, and this signal has different semantics from the BSD signal, named SIGCHLD. The POSIX.1 signal is also named SIGCHLD.

The semantics of the BSD SIGCHLD signal are normal, in that its semantics are similar to those of all other signals. When the signal occurs, the status of a child has changed, and need to call one of the wait functions to determine what has happened.

System V, however, has traditionally handled the SIGCLD signal differently from other signals. SVR4- based systems continue this questionable tradition (i.e., compatibility constraint) if set its disposition using either signal or sigset (the older, SVR3-compatible functions to set the disposition of a signal). This older handling of SIGCLD consists of the following.

If the process specifically sets its disposition to SIG_IGN, children of the calling process will not generate zombie processes. Note that this is different from its default action (SIG_DFL), is to be gnored. Instead, on termination, the status of these child processes is discarded. If it subsequently calls one of the wait functions, the calling process will block until all its children have terminated, and then wait returns 1 with errno set to ECHILD. (The default disposition of this signal is to be ignored, but this default will not cause the preceding semantics to occur. Instead, specifically have to set its disposition to SIG_IGN.)

POSIX.1 does not specify what happens when SIGCHLD is ignored, so this behavior is

allowed. The Single UNIX Specification includes an XSI extension specifying that this behavior be supported for SIGCHLD.

4.4BSD always generates zombies if SIGCHLD is ignored. If want to avoid zombies, have to wait for our children. FreeBSD 5.2.1 works like 4.4BSD. Mac OS X 10.3, however, doesn't create zombies when SIGCHLD is ignored.

With SVR4, if either signal or sigset is called to set the disposition of SIGCHLD to be ignored, zombies are never generated. Solaris 9 and Linux 2.4.22 follow SVR4 in this behavior.

With sigaction, can set the SA_NOCLDWAIT flag to avoid zombies. This action is supported on all four platforms: FreeBSD 5.2.1, Linux 2.4.22, Mac OS X 10.3, and Solaris 9.

If set the disposition of SIGCLD to be caught, the kernel immediately checks whether any child processes are ready to be waited for and, if so, calls the SIGCLD handler.

Reliable-Signal Terminology and Semantics

To define some of the terms used throughout our discussion of signals. First, a signal is generated for a process (or sent to a process) when the event that causes the signal occurs. The event could be a hardware exception (e.g., divide by 0), a software condition (e.g., an alarm timer expiring), a terminal-generated signal, or a call to the kill function. When the signal is generated, the kernel usually sets a flag of some form in the process table.

The signal is delivered to a process when the action for a signal is taken. During the time between the generation of a signal and its delivery, the signal is said to be pending.

A process has the option of blocking the delivery of a signal. If a signal that is blocked is generated for a process, and if the action for that signal is either the default action or to catch the signal, then the signal remains pending for the process until the process either (a) unblocks the signal or (b) changes the action to ignore the signal. The system determines what to do with a blocked signal when the signal is delivered, not when it's generated. This allows the process to change the action for the signal before it's delivered. The sigpending function can be called by a process to determine which signals are blocked and pending.

kill and raise Functions

The kill function sends a signal to a process or a group of processes. The raise function allows a process to send a signal to itself.

Raise was originally defined by ISO C. POSIX.1 includes it to align itself with the ISO C standard, but POSIX.1 extends the specification of raise to deal with threads. Since ISO C does not deal with multiple processes, it could not define a function, such as kill, that requires a process ID argument.

```
#include <signal.h>
int kill(pid_t pid, int signo);
int raise(int signo);
```

Both return: 0 if OK, 1 on error

The call

```
raise(signo);
```

is equivalent to the call

kill(getpid(), signo);

There are four different conditions for the pid argument to kill.

- pid > 0 The signal is sent to the process whose process ID is pid.
- pid == 0 The signal is sent to all processes whose process group ID equals the process group ID of the sender and for which the sender has permission to send the signal. Note that the term all processes excludes an implementation-defined set of system processes. For most UNIX systems, this set of system processes includes the kernel processes and init (pid 1).
- pid < 0 The signal is sent to all processes whose process group ID equals the absolute value of pid and for which the sender has permission to send the signal. Again, the set of all processes excludes certain system processes, as described earlier.
- pid == 1 The signal is sent to all processes on the system for which the sender has permission to send the signal. As before, the set of processes excludes certain system processes.

alarm and pause Functions

The alarm function allows us to set a timer that will expire at a specified time in the future. When the timer expires, the SIGALRM signal is generated. If ignore or don't catch this signal, its default action is to terminate the process.

```
#include <unistd.h>
unsigned int alarm(unsigned int seconds);
Returns: 0 or number of seconds until previously set alarm
```

The pause function suspends the calling process until a signal is caught.

```
#include <unistd.h>
int pause(void);
Returns: 1 with errno set to EINTR
```

The only time pause returns is if a signal handler is executed and that handler returns. In that case, pause returns 1 with errno set to EINTR.

This function looks like the sleep function, but this simple implementation has three problems.

- If the caller already has an alarm set, that alarm is erased by the first call to alarm. can correct this by looking at the return value from the first call to alarm. If the number of seconds until some previously set alarm is less than the argument, then should wait only until the previously set alarm expires. If the previously set alarm will go off after ours, then before returning should reset this alarm to occur at its designated time in the future.

- We have modified the disposition for SIGALRM. If we're writing a function for others to call, should save the disposition when we're called and restore it when we're done. can correct this by saving the return value from signal and resetting the disposition before return.
- There is a race condition between the first call to alarm and the call to pause. On a busy system, it's possible for the alarm to go off and the signal handler to be called before call pause. If that happens, the caller is suspended forever in the call to pause (assuming that some other signal isn't caught).

Signal Sets

A data type to represent multiple signalsa signal set. We'll use this with such functions as sigprocmask (in the next section) to tell the kernel not to allow any of the signals in the set to occur. As mentioned earlier, the number of different signals can exceed the number of bits in an integer, so in general, can't use an integer to represent the set with one bit per signal. POSIX.1 defines the data type sigset_t to contain a signal set and the following five functions to manipulate signal sets.

```
#include <signal.h>
int sigemptyset(sigset_t *set);
int sigfillset(sigset_t *set);
int sigaddset(sigset_t *set, int signo);
int sigdelset(sigset_t *set, int signo);
All four return: 0 if OK, 1 on error
int sigismember(const sigset_t *set, int signo);
Returns: 1 if true, 0 if false, 1 on error
```

The function sigemptyset initializes the signal set pointed to by set so that all signals are excluded. The function sigfillset initializes the signal set so that all signals are included. All applications have to call either sigemptyset or sigfillset once for each signal set, before using the signal set, because cannot assume that the C initialization for external and static variables (0) corresponds to the implementation of signal sets on a given system. Once have initialized a signal set, can add and delete specific signals in the set. The function sigaddset adds a single signal to an existing set, and sigdelset removes a single signal from a set. In all the functions that take a signal set as an argument, always pass the address of the signal set as the argument.

sigprocmask Function

The signal mask of a process is the set of signals currently blocked from delivery to that process. A process can examine its signal mask, change its signal mask, or perform both operations in one step by calling the following function.

```
#include <signal.h>
int sigprocmask(int how, const sigset_t *restrict set,
```

sigset_t *restrict oset);

Returns: 0 if OK, 1 on error

First, if oset is a non-null pointer, the current signal mask for the process is returned through oset.

Second, if set is a non-null pointer, the how argument indicates how the current signal mask is modified. SIG_BLOCK is an inclusive-OR operation, whereas SIG_SETMASK is an assignment. Note that SIGKILL and SIGSTOP can't be blocked.

how	Description
SIG_BLOCK	The new signal mask for the process is the union of its current signal mask and the signal set pointed to by *set*. That is, *set* contains the additional signals that we want to block.
SIG_UNBLOCK	The new signal mask for the process is the intersection of its current signal mask and the complement of the signal set pointed to by *set*. That is, *set* contains the signals that we want to unblock.
SIG_SETMASK	The new signal mask for the process is replaced by the value of the signal set pointed to by *set*.

Ways to change current signal mask using sigprocmask

sigpending Function

The sigpending function returns the set of signals that are blocked from delivery and currently pending for the calling process. The set of signals is returned through the set argument.

```
#include <signal.h>
int sigpending(sigset_t *set);
Returns: 0 if OK, 1 on error
```

sigaction Function

The sigaction function allows us to examine or modify (or both) the action associated with a particular signal. This function supersedes the signal function from earlier releases of the UNIX System. Indeed, at the end of this section, show an implementation of signal using sigaction.

```
#include <signal.h>
int sigaction(int signo, const struct sigaction
*restrict act,
struct sigaction *restrict oact);
Returns: 0 if OK, 1 on error
```

The argument signo is the signal number whose action are examining or modifying.

sigsetjmp and siglongjmp Functions

The setjmp and longjmp functions, which can be used for nonlocal branching. The longjmp function is often called from a signal handler to return to the main loop of a program, instead of returning from the handler.

There is a problem in calling longjmp, however. When a signal is caught, the signal-catching function is entered with the current signal automatically being added to the signal mask of the process. This prevents subsequent occurrences of that signal from interrupting the signal handler. If longjmp out of the signal handler, what happens to the signal mask for the process?

Under FreeBSD 5.2.1 and Mac OS X 10.3, setjmp and longjmp save and restore the signal mask. Linux 2.4.22 and Solaris 9, however, do not do this. FreeBSD and Mac OS X provide the functions _setjmp and _longjmp, which do not save and restore the signal mask.

To allow either form of behavior, POSIX.1 does not specify the effect of setjmp and longjmp on signal masks. Instead, two new functions, sigsetjmp and siglongjmp, are defined by POSIX.1. These two functions should always be used when branching from a signal handler.

```
#include <setjmp.h>
int sigsetjmp(sigjmp_buf env, int savemask);
Returns: 0 if called directly, nonzero if returning from a call to siglongjmp
void siglongjmp(sigjmp_buf env, int val);
```

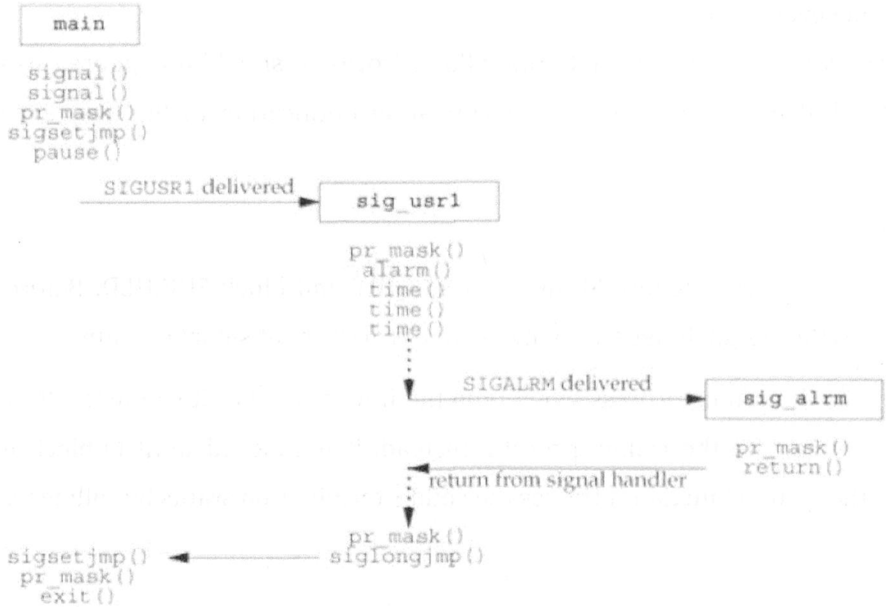

Time line for example program handling two signals

The only difference between these functions and the setjmp and longjmp functions is that sigsetjmp has an additional argument. If savemask is nonzero, then sigsetjmp also saves the current signal mask of the process in env. When siglongjmp is called, if the env argument was saved by a call to sigsetjmp with a nonzero savemask, then siglongjmp restores the saved signal mask.

sigsuspend Function

The signal mask for a process to block and unblock selected signals.

#include <signal.h>

int sigsuspend(const sigset_t *sigmask);

Returns: 1 with errno set to EINTR

The signal mask of the process is set to the value pointed to by sigmask. Then the process is suspended until a signal is caught or until a signal occurs that terminates the process. If a signal is caught and if the signal handler returns, then sigsuspend returns, and the signal mask of the process is set to its value before the call to sigsuspend.

abort Function

We mentioned earlier that the abort function causes abnormal program termination.

#include <stdlib.h>

void abort(void);

This function never returns

This function sends the SIGABRT signal to the caller. (Processes should not ignore this signal.) ISO C states that calling abort will deliver an unsuccessful termination notification to the host environment by calling raise(SIGABRT).

system Function

POSIX.1 requires that system ignore SIGINT and SIGQUIT and block SIGCHLD. Before showing a version that correctly handles these signals, let's see why need to worry about signal handling.

No signal is sent to the calling process when type the interrupt or quit character. When the ed command exits, SIGCHLD is not sent to the calling process. Instead, it is blocked until unblock it in the last call to sigprocmask, after the system function retrieves the child's termination status by calling waitpid.

sleep Function

#include <unistd.h>

unsigned int sleep(unsigned int seconds);

Returns: 0 or number of unslept seconds

This function causes the calling process to be suspended until either

- The amount of wall clock time specified by seconds has elapsed.
- A signal is caught by the process and the signal handler returns.

As with an alarm signal, the actual return may be at a time later than requested, because of other system activity.

Job-Control Signals

SIGCHLD Child process has stopped or terminated.

SIGCONT Continue process, if stopped.

SIGSTOP Stop signal (can't be caught or ignored).

SIGTSTP Interactive stop signal.

SIGTTIN Read from controlling terminal by member of a background process group.

SIGTTOU Write to controlling terminal by member of a background process group.

Except for SIGCHLD, most application programs don't handle these signals: interactive shells usually do all the work required to handle these signals. When we type the suspend character (usually Control-Z), SIGTSTP is sent to all processes in the foreground process group. When we tell the shell to resume a job in the foreground or background, the shell sends all the processes in the job the SIGCONT signal. Similarly, if SIGTTIN or SIGTTOU is delivered to a process, the process is stopped by default, and the job-control shell recognizes this and notifies us.

An exception is a process that is managing the terminal: the vi(1) editor, for example. It needs to know when the user wants to suspend it, so that it can restore the terminal's state to the way it was when vi was started.

There are some interactions between the job-control signals. When any of the four stop signals (SIGTSTP, SIGSTOP, SIGTTIN, or SIGTTOU) is generated for a process, any pending SIGCONT signal for that process is discarded. Similarly, when the SIGCONT signal is generated for a process, any pending stop signals for that same process are discarded.

Note that the default action for SIGCONT is to continue the process, if it is stopped; otherwise, the signal is ignored. Normally, we don't have to do anything with this signal. When SIGCONT is generated for a process that is stopped, the process is continued, even if the signal is blocked or ignored.

Additional Features

Signal Names

Some systems provide the array

extern char *sys_siglist[];

These systems normally provide the function psignal also.

```
#include <signal.h>
void psignal(int signo, const char *msg);
```

The string msg (which is normally the name of the program) is output to the standard error, followed by a colon and a space, followed by a description of the signal, followed by a newline.

Another common function is strsignal. This function is similar to strerror.

```
#include <string.h>
char *strsignal(int signo);
```

Returns: a pointer to a string describing the signal

Signal Mappings

Solaris provides a couple of functions to map a signal number to a signal name and vice versa.

```
#include <signal.h>
int sig2str(int signo, char *str);
int str2sig(const char *str, int *signop);
```

Both return: 0 if OK, 1 on error

These functions are useful when writing interactive programs that need to accept and print signal names and numbers.

The sig2str function translates the given signal number into a string and stores the result in the memory pointed to by str. The caller must ensure that the memory is large enough to hold the longest string, including the terminating null byte. Solaris provides the constant SIG2STR_MAX in <signal.h> to define the maximum string length. The string consists of the signal name without the "SIG" prefix. For example, translating SIGKILL would result in the string "KILL" being stored in the str memory buffer.

The str2sig function translates the given name into a signal number. The signal number is stored in the integer pointed to by signop. The name can be either the signal name without the "SIG" prefix or a string representation of the decimal signal number.

Interprocess Communication

Introduction

The process control primitives and saw how to invoke multiple processes. But the only way for these processes to exchange information is by passing open files across a fork or an exec or through the file system. The other techniques for processes to communicate with each other: IPC, or interprocess communication.

Pipes

Pipes are the oldest form of UNIX System IPC and are provided by all UNIX systems. Pipes have two limitations.

- Historically, they have been half duplex (i.e., data flows in only one direction). Some systems now provide full-duplex pipes, but for maximum portability, should never assume that this is the case.
- Pipes can be used only between processes that have a common ancestor. Normally, a pipe is created by a process, that process calls fork, and the pipe is used between the parent and the child.

A pipe is created by calling the pipe function.

```
#include <unistd.h>
int pipe(int filedes[2]);
Returns: 0 if OK, 1 on error
```

Two file descriptors are returned through the filedes argument: filedes[0] is open for reading, and filedes[1] is open for writing. The output of filedes[1] is the input for filedes[0].

- Pipes are implemented using UNIX domain sockets in 4.3BSD, 4.4BSD, and Mac OS X 10.3. Even though UNIX domain sockets are full duplex by default, these operating systems hobble the sockets used with pipes so that they operate in half-duplex mode only.
- POSIX.1 allows for an implementation to support full-duplex pipes. For these implementations, filedes[0] and filedes[1] are open for both reading and writing.

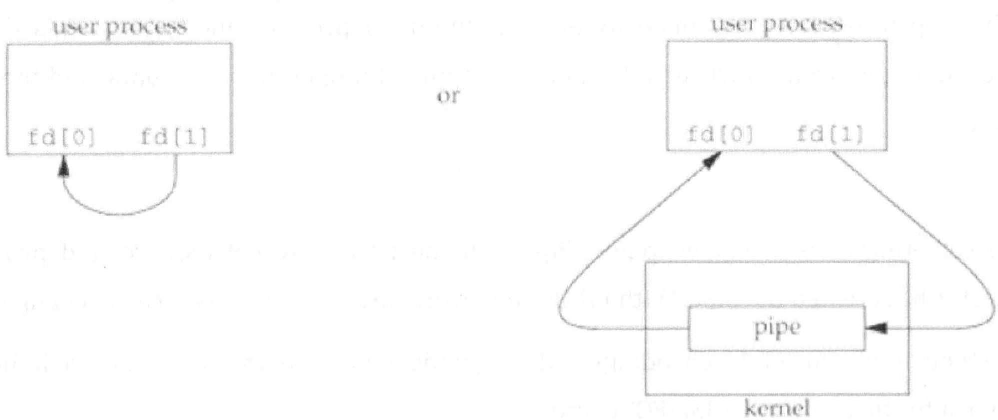

Two ways to view a half-duplex pipe

popen and pclose Functions

Since a common operation is to create a pipe to another process, to either read its output or send it input, the standard I/O library has historically provided the popen and pclose functions. These two functions handle all the dirty work that we've been doing ourselves: creating a pipe, forking a child, closing the unused ends of the pipe, executing a shell to run the command, and waiting for the command to terminate.

```
#include <stdio.h>
FILE *popen(const char *cmdstring, const char *type);
Returns: file pointer if OK, NULL on error
int pclose(FILE *fp);
Returns: termination status of cmdstring, or 1 on error
```

The function popen does a fork and exec to execute the cmdstring, and returns a standard I/O file pointer. If type is "r", the file pointer is connected to the standard output of cmdstring

Coprocesses

A UNIX system filter is a program that reads from standard input and writes to standard output. Filters are normally connected linearly in shell pipelines. A filter becomes a coprocess when the same program generates the filter's input and reads the filter's output.

The Korn shell provides coprocesses [Bolsky and Korn 1995]. The Bourne shell, the Bourne-again shell, and the C shell don't provide a way to connect processes together as coprocesses. A coprocess normally runs in the background from a shell, and its standard input and standard output are connected to another program using a pipe. Although the shell syntax required to initiate a coprocess and connect its input and output to other processes is quite contorted, coprocesses are also useful from a C program.

Whereas popen gives us a one-way pipe to the standard input or from the standard output of another process, with a coprocess, have two one-way pipes to the other process: one to its standard input and one from its standard output. want to write to its standard input, let it operate on the data, and then read from its standard output.

FIFOs

FIFOs are sometimes called named pipes. Pipes can be used only between related processes when a common ancestor has created the pipe. With FIFOs, however, unrelated processes can exchange data.

A FIFO is a type of file. One of the encodings of the st_mode member of the stat structure indicates that a file is a FIFO. can test for this with the S_ISFIFO macro.

Creating a FIFO is similar to creating a file. Indeed, the pathname for a FIFO exists in the file system.

```
#include <sys/stat.h>
int mkfifo(const char *pathname, mode_t mode);
Returns: 0 if OK, 1 on error
```

There are two uses for FIFOs.

- FIFOs are used by shell commands to pass data from one shell pipeline to another without creating intermediate temporary files.
- FIFOs are used as rendezvous points in clientserver applications to pass data between the clients and the servers.

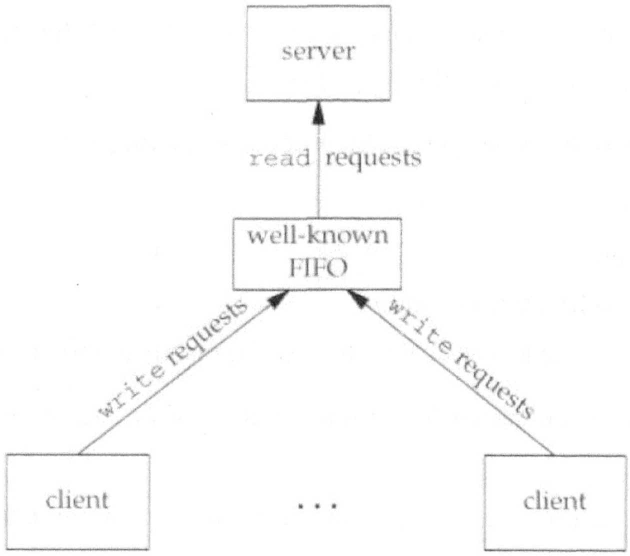

Clients sending requests to a server using a FIFO

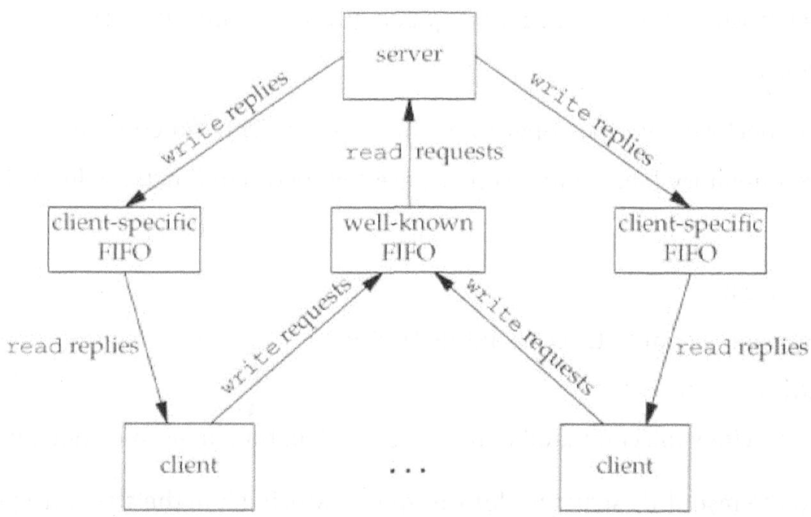

Clientserver communication using FIFOs

Message Queues

A message queue is a linked list of messages stored within the kernel and identified by a message queue identifier. We'll call the message queue just a queue and its identifier a queue ID.

The Single UNIX Specification includes an alternate IPC message queue implementation in the message-passing option of its real-time extensions. do not cover the real-time extensions in this text.

A new queue is created or an existing queue opened by msgget. New messages are added to the end of a queue by msgsnd. Every message has a positive long integer type field, a non-negative length, and the actual data bytes (corresponding to the length), all of which are specified to msgsnd when the message is added to a queue. Messages are fetched from a queue by msgrcv. don't have to fetch the messages in a first-in, first-out order. Instead, can fetch messages based on their type field.

The first function normally called is msgget to either open an existing queue or create a new queue.

```
#include <sys/msg.h>
int msgget(key_t key, int flag);
Returns: message queue ID if OK, 1 on error
```

When a new queue is created, the following members of the msqid_ds structure are initialized.

- The ipc_perm structure is initialized. The mode member of this structure is set to the corresponding permission bits of flag.
- msg_qnum, msg_lspid, msg_lrpid, msg_stime, and msg_rtime are all set to 0.
- msg_ctime is set to the current time.
- msg_qbytes is set to the system limit.

On success, msgget returns the non-negative queue ID. This value is then used with the other three message queue functions.

The msgctl function performs various operations on a queue. This function and the related functions for semaphores and shared memory (semctl and shmctl) are the ioctl-like functions for XSI IPC (i.e., the garbage-can functions).

```
#include <sys/msg.h>
int msgctl(int msqid, int cmd, struct msqid_ds *buf );
Returns: 0 if OK, 1 on error
```

The cmd argument specifies the command to be performed on the queue specified by msqid.

- IPC_STAT Fetch the msqid_ds structure for this queue, storing it in the structure pointed to by buf.
- IPC_SET Copy the following fields from the structure pointed to by buf to the msqid_ds structure associated with this queue: msg_perm.uid, msg_perm.gid, msg_perm.mode, and msg_qbytes. This command can be executed only by a process whose effective user ID equals msg_perm.cuid or msg_perm.uid or by a process with superuser privileges. Only the superuser can increase the value of msg_qbytes.

- IPC_RMID Remove the message queue from the system and any data still on the queue. This removal is immediate. Any other process still using the message queue will get an error of EIDRM on its next attempted operation on the queue. This command can be executed only by a process whose effective user ID equals msg_perm.cuid or msg_perm.uid or by a process with superuser privileges.

Data is placed onto a message queue by calling msgsnd.

```
#include <sys/msg.h>
int msgsnd(int msqid, const void *ptr, size_t
nbytes, int flag);
Returns: 0 if OK, 1 on error
```

Messages are retrieved from a queue by msgrcv.

```
#include <sys/msg.h>
ssize_t msgrcv(int msqid, void *ptr, size_t nbytes
, long type, int flag);
Returns: size of data portion of message if OK, 1 on error
```

The type argument lets us specify which message we want.

- type == 0 The first message on the queue is returned.
- type > 0 The first message on the queue whose message type equals type is returned.
- type < 0 The first message on the queue whose message type is the lowest value less than or equal to the absolute value of type is returned.

Semaphores

A semaphore isn't a form of IPC similar to the others that we've described (pipes, FIFOs, and message queues). A semaphore is a counter used to provide access to a shared data object for multiple processes.

The Single UNIX Specification includes an alternate set of semaphore interfaces in the semaphore option of its real-time extensions. do not discuss these interfaces in this text.

To obtain a shared resource, a process needs to do the following:

- Test the semaphore that controls the resource. If the value of the semaphore is positive, the process can use the resource. In this case, the process decrements the semaphore value by 1, indicating that it has used one unit of the resource.
- Otherwise, if the value of the semaphore is 0, the process goes to sleep until the semaphore value is greater than 0. When the process wakes up, it returns to step 1.
- When a process is done with a shared resource that is controlled by a semaphore, the semaphore value is incremented by 1. If any other processes are asleep, waiting for the semaphore, they are awakened.

XSI semaphores are, unfortunately, more complicated than this. Three features contribute to this unnecessary complication.

- A semaphore is not simply a single non-negative value. Instead, have to define a semaphore as a set of one or more semaphore values. When create a semaphore, specify the number of values in the set.
- The creation of a semaphore (semget) is independent of its initialization (semctl). This is a fatal flaw, since cannot atomically create a new semaphore set and initialize all the values in the set.
- Since all forms of XSI IPC remain in existence even when no process is using them, have to worry about a program that terminates without releasing the semaphores it has been allocated.

The first function to call is semget to obtain a semaphore ID.

```
#include <sys/sem.h>
int semget(key_t key, int nsems, int flag);
```

Returns: semaphore ID if OK, 1 on error

When a new set is created, the following members of the semid_ds structure are initialized.

- The ipc_perm structure is initialized. The mode member of this structure is set to the corresponding permission bits of flag. sem_otime is set to 0.
- sem_ctime is set to the current time.
- sem_nsems is set to nsems.

The semctl function is the catchall for various semaphore operations.

```
#include <sys/sem.h>
int semctl(int semid, int semnum, int cmd,
... /* union semun arg */);
```

The function semop atomically performs an array of operations on a semaphore set.

```
#include <sys/sem.h>
int semop(int semid, struct sembuf semoparray[],
size_t nops);
```

Returns: 0 if OK, 1 on error

Shared Memory

Shared memory allows two or more processes to share a given region of memory. This is the fastest form of IPC, because the data does not need to be copied between the client and the server. The only trick in using shared memory is synchronizing access to a given region among multiple processes. If the server is placing data into a shared memory region, the client shouldn't try to access the data until the server is done. Often, semaphores are used to synchronize shared memory access. (But as saw at the end of the previous section, record locking can also be used.)

The Single UNIX Specification includes an alternate set of interfaces to access shared memory in the shared memory objects option of its real-time extensions. do not cover the real-time extensions in this text.

The kernel maintains a structure with at least the following members for each shared memory segment:

```
struct shmid_ds {
struct ipc_perm shm_perm; /* see Section 15.6.2 */
size_t shm_segsz; /* size of segment in bytes */
pid_t shm_lpid; /* pid of last shmop() */
pid_t shm_cpid; /* pid of creator */
shmatt_t shm_nattch; /* number of current attaches */
time_t shm_atime; /* last-attach time */
time_t shm_dtime; /* last-detach time */
time_t shm_ctime; /* last-change time */
.
.
.
};
```

(Each implementation adds other structure members as needed to support shared memory segments.)

The first function called is usually shmget, to obtain a shared memory identifier.

```
#include <sys/shm.h>
int shmget(key_t key, size_t size, int flag);
Returns: shared memory ID if OK, 1 on error
```

The shmctl function is the catchall for various shared memory operations.

```
#include <sys/shm.h>
int shmctl(int shmid, int cmd, struct shmid_ds *buf);
Returns: 0 if OK, 1 on error
```

The cmd argument specifies one of the following five commands to be performed, on the segment specified by shmid.

Once a shared memory segment has been created, a process attaches it to its address space by calling shmat.

```
#include <sys/shm.h>
void *shmat(int shmid, const void *addr, int flag);
```

Returns: pointer to shared memory segment if OK, 1 on error

Overview of TCP/IP protocols

Application layer (telnet, ssh, http, ftp, etc)

- The things that we use daily.
- Main functionality: run application protocols

Transport layer (TCP, UDP)

- Allows processes (on different machines) to communicate (reliably or unreliably) with each other.
- Main functionality: reliability

Network layer (IPv4, IPv6)

- Allows machines to talk to one another
- Main functionality: routing/fragmentation/internetworking

Host to Network layer (Ethernet)

- Allows directly connected machines to talk to one another
- Main functionality: medium access, encoding
- The entities that implement each layer can be processes/system calls/hardware/etc.
- Protocol: rules that govern how peer entities in the same layer (on different machines) communicate.
- Each layer provides services to the upper layer defined by the service interface.

  e.g. tcp service interface is defined by a set of system calls: socket, bind, listen, accept, connect, read and write.

Some TCP/IP protocols:

- TCP: transmission control protocol

  connection-oriented, reliable, full duplex, byte stream service
- UDP: User datagram protocol

  Connectionless, unreliable
- IPv4: Internet Protocol, version 4.

  The protocol that glues the Internet together. Provides (unreliable) packet delivery service for TCP, UDP, ICMP, IGMP.
- IPv6: Internet Protocol, version 6.

  128 bits address, newer version of Internet Protocol.

  Will it ever happen?
- ICMP: Internet Control Message Protocol.

  Handles errors and control information for IP (ping, traceroute).

- IGMP: Internet Group Management Protocol.

  Used in IP multicast
- Socket Programming:

  The use of TCP and UDP

  Can also access the lower layers directly (raw socket)
- UDP: User Datagram Protocol

  Interface

  socket, bind, sendto, recvfrom

  Can also use the TCP interface (connect/read/write)
- Unreliable/connectionless service

  Data may be lost, duplicated and reordered.

  Client/server don't have any long term relation.

Can perform (unreliable) multicast.

TCP: Transmission control protocol.

Interface: socket, bind, listen, accept, connect, read, write, close.

An analogy:

Socket: telephone

Bind: assign telephone number to a telephone

Listen: turn on the ringer so that you can hear the phone call

Connect: dial a phone number

Accept: answer the phone

Read/write: talking

Close: ???

Realizing reliable communication means a lot:

- Sequence number, acknowledgement, retransmission, timeout (RTT)
- Sliding window protocol for efficiency
- Flow control
- Congestion control
- Connection establishment/release
- UDP for raw performance, TCP for enhanced functionality (with inherent lower performance).

Basic functionality of TCP and UDP: to allow processes on different machines to communicate.

- One crucial issue: addressing
  1. how to identify your peer?

2. Two components: identifying the peer machine and identifying the peer process.
    - Identifying peer machine: IP address
    - A unique identifier for each network interface connected to an IP network.

      A machine may have multiple IP addresses, one for each interface.

- IP address (IPv4):
  1. 32 bit binary number (IPv4)
  2. Represented as "dotted decimal" notation:
      - 4 decimal values, each representing 8 bits (octet), in the range 0 to 255.
      - Example:

        Dotted Decimal: 140 .179 .220 .200

        Binary: 10001100.10110011.11011100.11001000

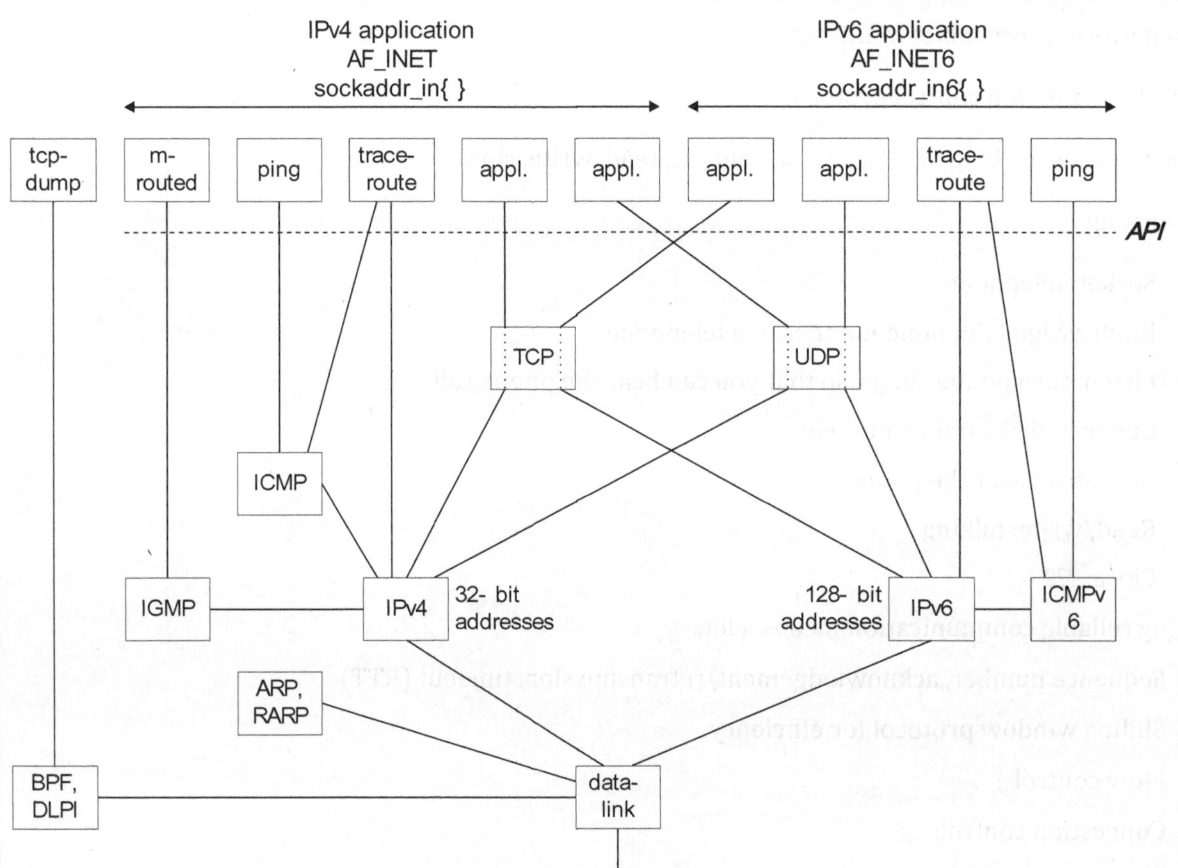

Figure 2.1 Overview of TCP/IP protocols

UNIT- I

QUESTION BANK

PART-A

1. Define File Descriptors

All the open files are referred by the file descriptors. The descriptor 0 refers the standard input, file descriptor 1 refers the standard output and file descriptor 2 refers the standard error. File descriptors ranges from 0 through OPEN_MAX.

2. Clearly explain the open( ) including headers, function parameters in detail and return values.

```
#include<sys/types.h>
#include<sys/stat.h>
#include<fcntl.h>
int open(const char *path_name, int oflag, ....../* , mode_t mode */);
```

Access modes:

O_RDONLY, O_WRONLY, O_RDWR

Access modifier:

O_CREAT, O_EXCL, O_APPEND, etc.,

Permissions: Read, Write and Execute permissions (0777)

3. Briefly explain lseek function

```
#include<sys/types.h>
#include<unistd.h>
off_t lseek(int filedes, off_t offset,int whence);
```

If whence is SEEK_SET , the file's offset is set to offset bytes from the beginning of the file.

If whence is SEEK_CUR , the file's offset is set to its current value plus the offset. The offset can be positive or negative.

If whence is SEEK_END , the file's offset is set to the size of the file plus the offset. The offset can be positive or negative.

4. Mention the Kernel data structures for open files

- Process table
- File table
- V-node table

5. Define atomic operations

Assume 2 processes A and B are appending to a same file. Assume the file is created without O_APPEND flag. Hence overwriting occurs. Atomic operation positions to eof and then writes. Unix provides an atomic way to do this operation using O_APPEND flag.

6. Mention the use of fstat function

int fstat(int filedes, struct stat *buf)

This function returns the structure of information for the given file descriptor.

7. Mention some of the fields used to describe the information about a file.

mode_t st_mode – file type and mode

ino_t st_ino – i-node number

dev_t st_dev – device number

long st_blksize – best I/O block size

off_t st_size – size in bytes, for regular files.

8. List the macros for the various file types

- S_ISREG( )
- S_ISDIR( )
- S_ISCHR( )
- S_ISBLK( )
- S_ISFIFO( )
- S_ISLINK ( )
- S_ISSOCK( )

9. What are the components of file system?

Boot block

Super block

Inode block

Data block

10. Compare hard links and soft links

Hard Link	Symbolic Link
Does not create a new inode	Create a new inode
Can't link directories, unless this is done by root	Can link directories
Can't link files across file systems	Can link files across file systems
Increase the hard link count of the linked inode	Does not change the hard link count of the linked inode

11. What are the limitations of Hard link

- Hard links normally require that the link and the file reside in the same file system
- Only the superuser can create a hardlink to a directory

12. What are the components of i-node

The i-node contains the following

- Size of the file
- Pointers to the datablocks for the file
- File type
- File access permission bits
- Link count

13. Define Sticky Bit

One of the mode is S_ISVTX. If this bit is set, for an executable program file, then the first time the program was executed, a copy of the program's text was saved in the swap area when the process terminated. In this swap area, the copy is saved as a contiguous file.

Adv: Next time when that program is used, it will be executed very faster since we need not search in a random location for the file.

14. What is the use of ioctl function

```
#include<unistd.h>
#include<sys/ioctl.h>
int ioctl(int filedes, int request,.....);
```

The ioctl function is included in the Single UNIX Specification only as an extension for dealing with STREAMS devices

15. Differentiate chmod and fchmod function

```
#include <sys/types.h>
#include< sys/stat.h>
int chmod( const char *pathname, mode_t mode);
int fchmod( int filedes, mode_t mode) ;
```

The chmod function operates on the specified file while the fchmod function operates on a file that has already been opened.

16. What are the functions used to fetch entries from the password file

```
#include<sys/types.h>
#include<pwd.h>
struct passwd *getpwuid(uid_t uid);
struct passwd *getpwname(const char *name);
```

17. Define Password aging

Password aging occurs in systems supporting shadow password. ie, users have to choose a new password at certain intervals.

In SVR4 the shadow password file is /etc/shadow

In 4.3+BSD the encrypted passwords are stored in /etc/master.passwd

18. What are the fields present in the Group File

- group name
- encrypted password
- numerical group ID
- Array of pointers to individual user names

19. Mention any 4 conversion specifiers for strftime

%a abbreviated weekday name

%A full weekday name

%b abbreviated month name

%B full month name

20. Define the structure utmp

```
struct utmp {
char ut_line[8] ;       /* tty line: ttyh0, ttyd0, ttyp0   */
char ut_name[8] ;   /* login name */
long ut_time;                    /* seconds */};
```

UNIT- I

PART-B (16 MARKS)

Explain with a block diagram how a C program is started and terminated with necessary function calls required.

1. Write a note on the following with examples
   - Unreliable signals (5)
   - Reentrant functions (5)
   - System ( ) function (6)
2. Discuss the memory layout of C Program
3. (i) Write short notes on terminal logins. (8)

   (ii) Discuss unreliable signals (8)
4. Explain process termination and command line arguments.
5. Explain the implementation details of fork( ) and vfork( ) function.
6. Write a note on the following functions : (i)wait( ) (ii)exit( ) (iii)exec()

   (iv) signal( ).
7. Explain any 5 signals with example
8. (i) Discuss on the set of states a process undergoes during its lifetime.(6)

   (ii) What 2 kernel data structures describe the state of a process? (4)

   (iii) Illustrate any 3 situations when the kernel saves the context of a process. (6)
9. (i) What are real and effective user-ids? Why are they necessary? (2)

   (ii) Why does a parent await the termination of a child? What happens during this wait? (8)

   (iii) What system call terminates a process? What winding up operations are carried out here? (6)
10. (i) Describe Environment List (6)

    (ii) Explain Environment Variables (10)
11. Give a detailed note on Threads
12. Explain the Lifecycle of a Process.

UNIT-II

ELEMENTARY TCP SOCKETS

Introduction

The description of the sockets API. begin with socket address structures, which will be found in almost every example in the text. These structures can be passed in two directions: from the process to the kernel, and from the kernel to the process. The latter case is an example of a value-result argument, and will encounter other examples of these arguments throughout the text.

The address conversion functions convert between a text representation of an address and the binary value that goes into a socket address structure. Most existing IPv4 code uses inet_addr and inet_ntoa, but two new functions, inet_pton and inet_ntop, handle both IPv4 and IPv6. One problem with these address conversion functions is that they are dependent on the type of address being converted: IPv4 or IPv6. will develop a set of functions whose names begin with sock_ that work with socket address structures in a protocol-independent fashion. will use these throughout the text to make our code protocol-independent.

Socket Address Structures

Most socket functions require a pointer to a socket address structure as an argument. Each supported protocol suite defines its own socket address structure. The names of these structures begin with sockaddr_ and end with a unique suffix for each protocol suite.

IPv4 Socket Address Structure

An IPv4 socket address structure, commonly called an "Internet socket address structure," is named sockaddr_in and is defined by including the <netinet/in.h> header. Figure 3.1 shows the POSIX definition.

```
struct in_addr {
in_addr_t s_addr; /* 32-bit IPv4 address */
/* network byte ordered */
};
struct sockaddr_in {
uint8_t sin_len; /* length of structure (16) */
sa_family_t sin_family; /* AF_INET */
in_port_t sin_port; /* 16-bit TCP or UDP port number */
/* network byte ordered */
struct in_addr sin_addr; /* 32-bit IPv4 address */
/* network byte ordered */
```

```
char sin_zero[8]; /* unused */
};
```

There are several points need to make about socket address structures in general using this example:

The length member, sin_len , was added with 4.3BSD-Reno, when support for the OSI protocols was added. Before this release, the first member was sin_family , which was historically an unsigned short . Not all vendors support a length field for socket address structures and the POSIX specification does not require this member. The datatype that show, uint8_t , is typical, and POSIX-compliant systems provide datatypes of this form.

Having a length field simplifies the handling of variable-length socket address structures. Even if the length field is present, need never set it and need never examine it, unless are dealing with routing sockets. It is used within the kernel by the routines that deal with socket address structures from various protocol families (e.g., the routing table code).

The four socket functions that pass a socket address structure from the process to the kernel, bind , connect , sendto , and sendmsg , all go through the sockargs function in a Berkeley-derived implementation (p. 452 of TCPv2). This function copies the socket address structure from the process and explicitly sets its sin_len member to the size of the structure that was passed as an argument to these four functions. The five socket functions that pass a socket address structure from the kernel to the process, accept , recvfrom , recvmsg , getpeername , and getsockname , all set the sin_len member before returning to the process.

Unfortunately, there is normally no simple compile-time test to determine whether an implementation defines a length field for its socket address structures. In our code, test our own HAVE_SOCKADDR_SA_LEN constant (Figure D.2), but whether to define this constant or not requires trying to compile a simple test program that uses this optional structure member and seeing if the compilation succeeds or not. will see in Figure 3.4 that IPv6 implementations are required to define SIN6_LEN if socket address structures have a length field. Some IPv4 implementations provide the length field of the socket address structure to the application based on a compile-time option (e.g., _SOCKADDR_LEN). This feature provides compatibility for older programs.

The POSIX specification requires only three members in the structure: sin_family , sin_addr , and sin_port . It is acceptable for a POSIX-compliant implementation to define additional structure members, and this is normal for an Internet socket address structure. Almost all implementations add the sin_zero member so that all socket address structures are at least 16 bytes in size.

The POSIX datatypes for the s_addr , sin_family , and sin_port members. The in_addr_t datatype must be an unsigned integer type of at least 32 bits, in_port_t must be an unsigned integer type of at least 16 bits, and sa_family_t can be any unsigned integer type. The latter is normally an 8-bit unsigned integer if the implementation supports the length field, or an unsigned 16-bit integer if the length field is not supported. Figure 3.2 lists these three POSIX-defined datatypes, along with some other POSIX datatypes that will encounter.

Also encounter the datatypes u_char , u_short , u_int , and u_long , which are all unsigned. The POSIX specification defines these with a note that they are obsolete. They are provided for backward compatibility.

Both the IPv4 address and the TCP or UDP port number are always stored in the structure in network byte order. must be cognizant of this when using these members. will say more about the difference between host byte order and network byte order.

The 32-bit IPv4 address can be accessed in two different ways. For example, if serv is defined as an Internet socket address structure, then serv.sin_addr references the 32-bit IPv4 address as an in_addr structure, while serv.sin_addr.s_addr references the same 32-bit IPv4 address as an in_addr_t (typically an unsigned 32-bit integer). must be certain that are referencing the IPv4 address correctly, especially when it is used as an argument to a function, because compilers often pass structures differently from integers.

The reason the sin_addr member is a structure, and not just an in_addr_t , is historical. Earlier releases (4.2BSD) defined the in_addr structure as a union of various structures, to allow access to each of the 4 bytes and to both of the 16-bit values contained within the 32-bit IPv4 address. This was used with class A, B, and C addresses to fetch the appropriate bytes of the address. But with the advent of subnetting and then the disappearance of the various address classes with classless addressing (Section A.4), the need for the union disappeared. Most systems today have done away with the union and just define in_addr as a structure with a single in_addr_t member.

The sin_zero member is unused, but always set it to 0 when filling in one of these structures. By convention, always set the entire structure to 0 before filling it in, not just the sin_zero member.

Although most uses of the structure do not require that this member be 0, when binding a non-wildcard IPv4 address, this member must be 0 (pp. 731–732 of TCPv2).

Socket address structures are used only on a given host: The structure itself is not communicated between different hosts, although certain fields (e.g., the IP address and port) are used for communication.

Generic Socket Address Structure

A socket address structures is always passed by reference when passed as an argument to any socket functions. But any socket function that takes one of these pointers as an argument must deal with socket address structures from any of the supported protocol families.

A problem arises in how to declare the type of pointer that is passed. With ANSI C, the solution is simple: void * is the generic pointer type. But, the socket functions predate ANSI C and the solution chosen in 1982 was to define a generic socket address structure in the <sys/socket.h> header.

***The generic socket address structure: sockaddr*.**

```
struct sockaddr {
uint8_t sa_len;
sa_family_t sa_family; /* address family: AF_xxx value */
char sa_data[14]; /* protocol-specific address */
};
```

The socket functions are then defined as taking a pointer to the generic socket address structure, as shown here in the ANSI C function prototype for the bind function:

```
int bind(int, struct sockaddr *, socklen_t);
```

This requires that any calls to these functions must cast the pointer to the protocol-specific socket address structure to be a pointer to a generic socket address structure. For example,

```
struct sockaddr_in serv; /* IPv4 socket address structure */
/* fill in serv{} */
bind(sockfd, (struct sockaddr *) &serv, sizeof(serv));
```

If omit the cast "(struct sockaddr *)," the C compiler generates a warning of the form "warning: passing arg 2 of 'bind' from incompatible pointer type," assuming the system's headers have an ANSI C prototype for the bind function.

From an application programmer's point of view, the only use of these generic socket address structures is to cast pointers to protocol-specific structures.

The unp.h header, define SA to be the string "struct sockaddr " just to shorten the code that must write to cast these pointers. From the kernel's perspective, another reason for using pointers to generic socket address structures as arguments is that the kernel must take the caller's pointer, cast it to a struct sockaddr * , and then look at the value of sa_family to determine the type of the structure. But from an application programmer's perspective, it would be simpler if the pointer type was void * , omitting the need for the explicit cast.

IPv6 Socket Address Structure

The IPv6 socket address is defined by including the <netinet/in.h> header.

IPv6 socket address structure: sockaddr_in6

```
struct in6_addr {
uint8_t s6_addr[16]; /* 128-bit IPv6 address */
/* network byte ordered */
};
#define SIN6_LEN /* required for compile-time tests */
struct sockaddr_in6 {
uint8_t sin6_len; /* length of this struct (28) */
sa_family_t sin6_family; /* AF_INET6 */
in_port_t sin6_port; /* transport layer port# */
/* network byte ordered */
uint32_t sin6_flowinfo; /* flow information, undefined */
struct in6_addr sin6_addr; /* IPv6 address */
/* network byte ordered */
uint32_t sin6_scope_id; /* set of interfaces for a scope */
};
```

The extensions to the sockets API for IPv6 are defined in RFC 3493.

- The SIN6_LEN constant must be defined if the system supports the length member for socket address structures.
- The IPv6 family is AF_INET6 , whereas the IPv4 family is AF_INET .
- The members in this structure are ordered so that if the sockaddr_in6 structure is 64-bit aligned, so is the 128-bit sin6_addr member. On some 64-bit processors, data accesses of 64-bit values are optimized if stored on a 64-bit boundary.
- The sin6_flowinfo member is divided into two fields:
  1. The low-order 20 bits are the flow label
  2. The high-order 12 bits are reserved

New Generic Socket Address Structure

A new generic socket address structure was defined as part of the IPv6 sockets API, to overcome some of the shortcomings of the existing struct sockaddr . Unlike the struct sockaddr, the new struct sockaddr_storage is large enough to hold any socket address type supported by the system. The sockaddr_storage structure is defined by including the <netinet/in.h> header

The storage socket address structure: sockaddr_storage .

```
struct sockaddr_storage {
uint8_t ss_len; /* length of this struct (implementation dependent) */
sa_family_t ss_family; /* address family: AF_xxx value */
/* implementation-dependent elements to provide:
* a) alignment sufficient to fulfill the alignment requirements of
* all socket address types that the system supports.
* b) enough storage to hold any type of socket address that the
* system supports.
*/
};
```

The sockaddr_storage type provides a generic socket address structure that is different from struct sockaddr in two ways:

- If any socket address structures that the system supports have alignment requirements, the sockaddr_storage provides the strictest alignment requirement.
- The sockaddr_storage is large enough to contain any socket address structure that the system supports.

Note that the fields of the sockaddr_storage structure are opaque to the user, except for ss_family and ss_len (if present). The sockaddr_storage must be cast or copied to the appropriate socket address structure for the address given in ss_family to access any other fields.

Comparison of Socket Address Structures

A comparison of the five socket address structures that will encounter in this text: IPv4, IPv6, Unix domain, datalink, and storage. In this figure, assume that the socket address structures all contain a one-byte length field, that the family field also occupies one byte, and that any field that must be at least some number of bits is exactly that number of bits.

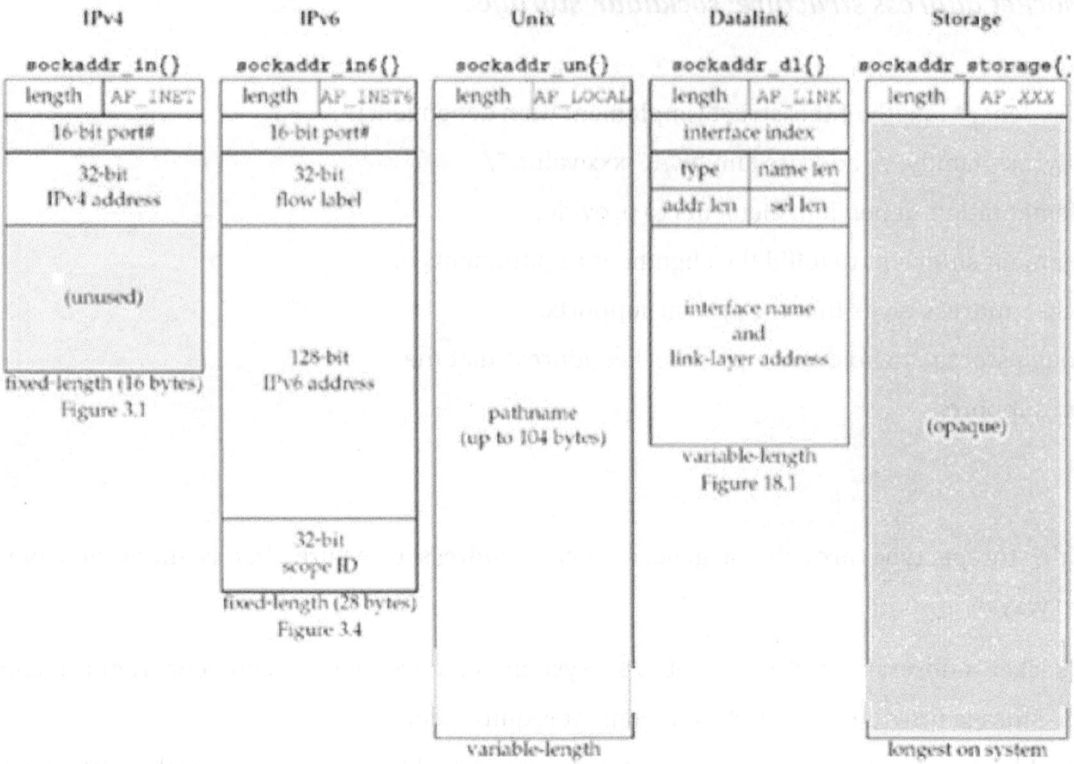

Comparison of various socket address structures.

Two of the socket address structures are fixed-length, while the Unix domain structure and the datalink structure are variable-length. To handle variable-length structures, whenever pass a pointer to a socket address structure as an argument to one of the socket functions, pass its length as another argument. show the size in bytes (for the 4.4BSD implementation) of the fixed-length structures beneath each structure.

The sockaddr_un structure itself is not variable-length (Figure 15.1), but the amount of information—the pathname within the structure—is variable-length. When passing pointers to these structures, must be careful how handle the length field, both the length field in the socket address structure itself (if supported by the implementation) and the length to and from the kernel.

This figure shows the style that follow throughout the text: structure names are always shown in a bolder font, followed by braces, as in sockaddr_in{} . noted earlier that the length field was added to all the socket address structures with the 4.3BSD Reno release. Had the length field been present with the original release of sockets, there would be no need for the length argument to all the socket functions: the third argument to bind and connect , for example. Instead, the size of the structure could be contained in the length field of the structure.

Byte Ordering Functions

A 16-bit integer that is made up of 2 bytes. There are two ways to store the two bytes in memory: with the low-order byte at the starting address, known as little-endian byte order, or with the high-order byte at the starting address, known as big-endian byte order.

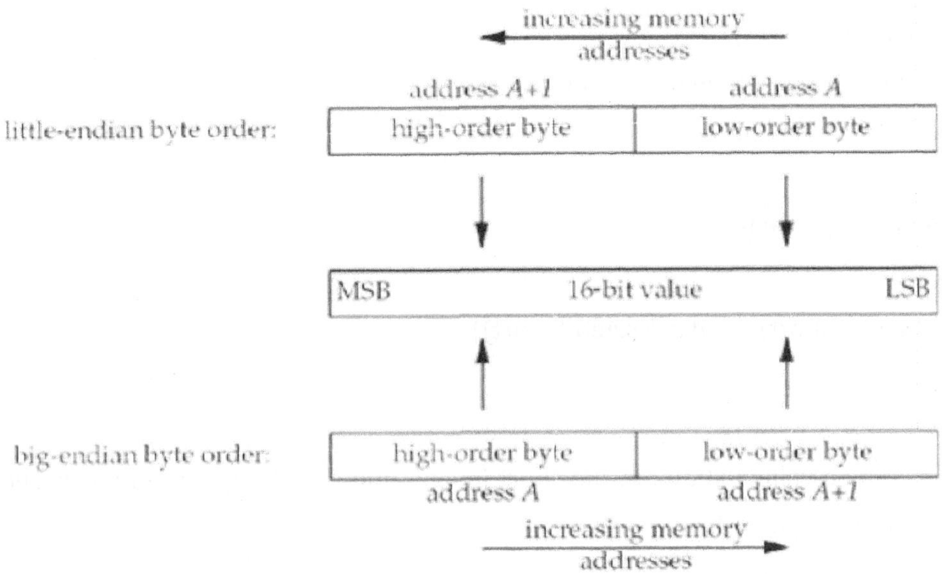

Little-endian byte order and big-endian byte order for a 16- bit integer

In this figure, increasing memory addresses going from right to left in the top, and from left to right in the bottom. also show the most significant bit (MSB) as the leftmost bit of the 16-bit value and the least significant bit (LSB) as the rightmost bit.

The terms "little-endian" and "big-endian" indicate which end of the multibyte value, the little end or the big end, is stored at the starting address of the value. Unfortunately, there is no standard between these two byte orderings and encounter systems that use both formats. Refer to the byte ordering used by a given system as the host byte order.

Program to determine host byte order

intro/byteorder.c

```
#include "unp.h"
int
main(int argc, char **argv)
{
union {
short s;
char c[sizeof(short)];
```

```
} un;
un.s = 0x0102;
printf("%s: ", CPU_VENDOR_OS);
if (sizeof(short) == 2) {
if (un.c[0] == 1 && un.c[1] == 2)
printf("big-endian\n");
else if (un.c[0] == 2 && un.c[1] == 1)
printf("little-endian\n");
else
printf("unknown\n");
} else
printf("sizeof(short) = %d\n", sizeof(short));
exit(0);
}
```

We store the two-byte value 0x0102 in the short integer and then look at the two consecutive bytes, c[0] and c[1], to determine the byte order.

The string CPU_VENDOR_OS is determined by the GNU autoconf program when the software in this book is configured, and it identifies the CPU type, vendor, and OS release. show some examples here in the output from this program when run on the various systems.

```
reebsd4 % byteorder
i386-unknown-freebsd4.8: little-endian
macosx % byteorder
powerpc-apple-darwin6.6: big-endian
freebsd5 % byteorder
sparc64-unknown-freebsd5.1: big-endian
aix % byteorder
powerpc-ibm-aix5.1.0.0: big-endian
hpux % byteorder
hppa1.1-hp-hpux11.11: big-endian
linux % byteorder
i586-pc-linux-gnu: little-endian
solaris % byteorder
sparc-sun-solaris2.9: big-endian
```

There are currently a variety of systems that can change between little-endian and big-endian byte ordering, sometimes at system reset, sometimes at run-time.

These byte ordering differences as network programmers because networking protocols must specify a network byte order. For example, in a TCP segment, there is a 16-bit port number and a 32-bit IPv4 address. The sending protocol stack and the receiving protocol stack must agree on the order in which the bytes of these multibyte fields will be transmitted. The Internet protocols use big-endian byte ordering for these multibyte integers.

In theory, an implementation could store the fields in a socket address structure in host byte order and then convert to and from the network byte order when moving the fields to and from the protocol headers, saving us from having to worry about this detail. But, both history and the POSIX specification say that certain fields in the socket address structures must be maintained in network byte order. Our concern is therefore converting between host byte order and network byte order. use the following four functions to convert between these two byte orders.

```
#include <netinet/in.h>
uint16_t htons(uint16_t host16bitvalue) ;
uint32_t htonl(uint32_t host32bitvalue) ;
Both return: value in network byte order
uint16_t ntohs(uint16_t net16bitvalue) ;
uint32_t ntohl(uint32_t net32bitvalue) ;
Both return: value in host byte order
```

Address Conversion Function

inet_aton, inet_addr, and inet_ntoa Functions

Two groups of address conversion functions. They convert Internet addresses between ASCII strings (what humans prefer to use) and network byte ordered binary values (values that are stored in socket address structures).

inet_aton, inet_ntoa, and inet_addr convert an IPv4 address from a dotted-decimal string (e.g., "206.168.112.96") to its 32-bit network byte ordered binary value.

The newer functions, inet_pton and inet_ntop, handle both IPv4 and IPv6 addresses.

```
#include <arpa/inet.h>
int inet_aton(const char *strptr, struct in_addr *addrptr);
Returns: 1 if string was valid, 0 on error
in_addr_t inet_addr(const char *strptr);
```

Returns: 32-bit binary network byte ordered IPv4 address; INADDR_NONE if error

char *inet_ntoa(struct in_addr inaddr);

Returns: pointer to dotted-decimal string

The first of these, inet_aton, converts the C character string pointed to by strptr into its 32-bit binary network byte ordered value, which is stored through the pointer addrptr. If successful, 1 is returned; otherwise, 0 is returned.

An undocumented feature of inet_aton is that if addrptr is a null pointer, the function still performs its validation of the input string but does not store any result.

inet_addr does the same conversion, returning the 32-bit binary network byte ordered value as the return value. The problem with this function is that all 232 possible binary values are valid IP addresses (0.0.0.0 through 255.255.255.255), but the function returns the constant INADDR_NONE (typically 32 one-bits) on an error. This means the dotted-decimal string 255.255.255.255 (the IPv4 limited broadcast address) cannot be handled by this function since its binary value appears to indicate failure of the function.

A potential problem with inet_addr is that some man pages state that it returns –1 on an error, instead of INADDR_NONE. This can lead to problems, depending on the C compiler, when comparing the return value of the function (an unsigned value) to a negative constant. Today, inet_addr is deprecated and any new code should use inet_aton instead. Better still is to use the newer functions described in the next section, which handle both IPv4 and IPv6.

The inet_ntoa function converts a 32-bit binary network byte ordered IPv4 address into its corresponding dotted-decimal string. The string pointed to by the return value of the function resides in static memory. This means the function is not reentrant This function takes a structure as its argument, not a pointer to a structure.

Functions that take actual structures as arguments are rare. It is more common to pass a pointer to the structure.

Elementary TCP Sockets

Introduction

The concurrent servers, a common Unix technique for providing concurrency when numerous clients are connected to the same server at the same time. Each client connection causes the server to fork a new process just for that client. In this chapter, consider only the oneprocess- per-client model using fork, but will consider a different one-thread-per-client model when describe threads.

A timeline of the typical scenario that takes place between a TCP client and server. First, the server is started, then sometime later, a client is started that connects to the server. assume that the client sends a request to the server, the server processes the request, and the server sends a reply back to the client. This continues until the client closes its end of the connection, which sends an end-of-file notification to the server. The server then closes its end of the connection and either terminates or waits for a new client connection.

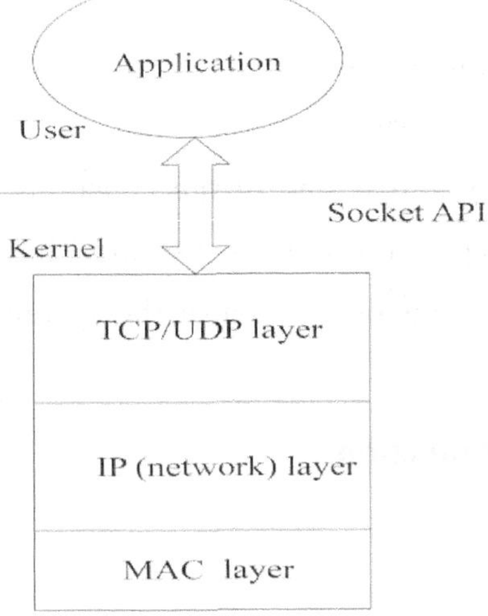

Socket Architecture

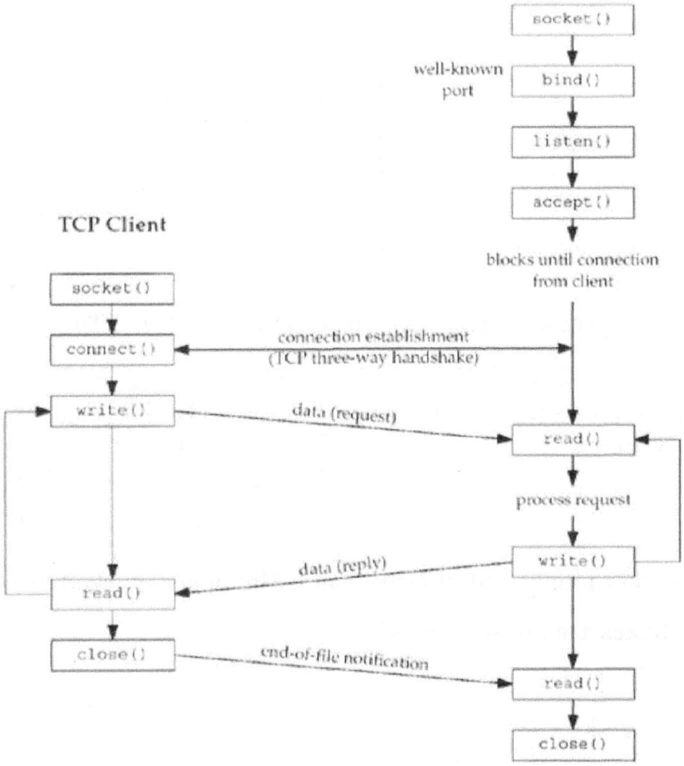

Socket functions for elementary TCP client/server

socket Function

To perform network I/O, the first thing a process must do is call the socket function, specifying the type of communication protocol desired (TCP using IPv4, UDP using IPv6, Unix domain stream protocol, etc.).

```
#include <sys/socket.h>
int socket (int family, int type, int protocol);
Returns: non-negative descriptor if OK, -1 on error
```

family specifies the protocol family and is one of the constants. This argument is often referred to as domain instead of family. The socket type is one of the constants. The protocol argument to the socket function should be set to the specific protocol type, or 0 to select the system's default for the given combination of family and type.

Protocol family constants for socket function

- AF_INET - IPv4 protocols
- AF_INET6 - IPv6 protocols
- AF_LOCAL (AF_UNIX) - Unix domain protocols

type of socket for socket function

type	Description
SOCK_STREAM	stream socket
SOCK_DGRAM	datagram socket
SOCK_SEQPACKET	sequenced packet socket
SOCK_RAW	raw socket

protocol of sockets for AF_INET or AF_INET6

Protocol	Description
IPPROTO_TCP	TCP transport protocol
IPPROTO_UDP	UDP transport protocol
IPPROTO_SCTP	SCTP transport protocol

Not all combinations of socket family and type are valid. The boxes marked "Yes" are valid but do not have handy acronyms. The blank boxes are not supported.

Combinations of family and type for the socket function

	AF_INET	AF_INET6	AF_LOCAL	AF_ROUTE	AF_KEY
SOCK_STREAM	TCP|SCTP	TCP|SCTP	Yes		
SOCK_DGRAM	UDP	UDP	Yes		
SOCK_SEQPACKET	SCTP	SCTP	Yes		
SOCK_RAW	IPv4	IPv6		Yes	Yes

There are other values for the family and type arguments. For example, 4.4BSD supports both AF_NS (the Xerox NS protocols, often called XNS) and AF_ISO (the OSI protocols). Similarly, the type of SOCK_SEQPACKET, a sequenced-packet socket, is implemented by both the Xerox NS protocols and the OSI protocols, and will describe its use with SCTP. But, TCP is a byte stream protocol, and supports only SOCK_STREAM sockets.

Linux supports a new socket type, SOCK_PACKET, that provides access to the datalink, similar to BPF and DLPI.

The key socket, AF_KEY, is newer than the others. It provides support for cryptographic security. Similar to the way that a routing socket (AF_ROUTE) is an interface to the kernel's routing table, the key socket is an interface into the kernel's key table.

On success, the socket function returns a small non-negative integer value, similar to a file descriptor. call this a socket descriptor, or a sockfd. To obtain this socket descriptor, all have specified is a protocol family (IPv4, IPv6, or Unix) and the socket type (stream, datagram, or raw). have not yet specified either the local protocol address or the foreign protocol address.

connect Function

The connect function is used by a TCP client to establish a connection with a TCP server.

```
#include <sys/socket.h>
int connect(int sockfd, const struct sockaddr *servaddr, socklen_t addrlen);
Returns: 0 if OK, -1 on error
```

sockfd is a socket descriptor returned by the socket function. The second and third arguments are a pointer to a socket address structure and its size. The socket address structure must contain the IP address and port number of the server.

The client does not have to call bind (which will describe in the next section) before calling connect: the kernel will choose both an ephemeral port and the source IP address if necessary.

In the case of a TCP socket, the connect function initiates TCP's three-way handshake. The function returns only when the connection is established or an error occurs. There are several different error returns possible.

- If the client TCP receives no response to its SYN segment, ETIMEDOUT is returned. 4.4BSD, for example, sends one SYN when connect is called, another 6 seconds later, and another 24 seconds later (p. 828 of TCPv2). If no response is received after a total of 75 seconds, the error is returned. Some systems provide administrative control over this timeout; see Appendix E of TCPv1.
- If the server's response to the client's SYN is a reset (RST), this indicates that no process is waiting for connections on the server host at the port specified (i.e., the server process is probably not running). This is a hard error and the error ECONNREFUSED is retrned to the client as soon as the RST is received. An RST is a type of TCP segment that is sent by TCP when something is wrong. Three conditions that generate an RST are: when a SYN arrives for a port that has no listening server (what just described), when TCP wants to abort an existing connection, and when TCP receives a segment for a connection that does not exist. (TCPv1 [pp. 246–250] contains additional information.)
- If the client's SYN elicits an ICMP "destination unreachable" from some intermediate router, this is considered a soft error. The client kernel saves the message but keeps sending SYNs with the same time between each SYN as in the first scenario. If no response is received after some fixed amount of time (75 seconds for 4.4BSD), the saved ICMP error is returned to the process as either EHOSTUNREACH or ENETUNREACH. It is also possible that the remote system is not reachable by any route in the local system's forwarding table, or that the connect call returns without waiting at all.

Many earlier systems, such as 4.2BSD, incorrectly aborted the connection establishment attempt when the ICMP "destination unreachable" was received. This is wrong because this ICMP error can indicate a transient condition. For example, it could be that the condition is caused by a routing problem that will be corrected. Network unreachables are considered obsolete, and applications should just treat ENETUNREACH and EHOSTUNREACH as the same error.

To specify the local host (127.0.0.1), which is running the daytime server, and see the output.

```
solaris % daytimetcpcli 127.0.0.1
Sun Jul 27 22:01:51 2003
```

To see a different format for the returned reply, specify a different machine's IP address (in this example, the IP address of the HP-UX machine).

```
solaris % daytimetcpcli 192.6.38.100
Sun Jul 27 22:04:59 PDT 2003
```

Next, specify an IP address that is on the local subnet (192.168.1/24) but the host ID (100) is nonexistent. That is, there is no host on the subnet with a host ID of 100, so when the client host sends out ARP requests (asking for that host to respond with its hardware address), it will never receive an ARP reply.

```
solaris % daytimetcpcli 192.168.1.100
```

connect error: Connection timed out

To get the error after the connect times out (around four minutes with Solaris 9). Notice that our err_sys function prints the human-readable string associated with the ETIMEDOUT error.

Our next example is to specify a host (a local router) that is not running a daytime server.

```
solaris % daytimetcpcli 192.168.1.5
connect error: Connection refused
```

The server responds immediately with an RST. Our final example specifies an IP address that is not reachable on the Internet. If watch the packets with tcpdump, see that a router six hops away returns an ICMP host unreachable error.

```
solaris % daytimetcpcli 192.3.4.5
connect error: No route to host
```

As with the ETIMEDOUT error, in this example, connect returns the EHOSTUNREACH error only after waiting its specified amount of time.

In terms of the TCP state transition diagram, connect moves from the CLOSED state (the state in which a socket begins when it is created by the socket function) to the SYN_SENT state, and then, on success, to the ESTABLISHED state. If connect fails, the socket is no longer usable and must be closed. cannot call connect again on the socket. When call connect in a loop, trying each IP address for a given host until one works, each time connect fails, must close the socket descriptor and call socket again.

bind Function

The bind function assigns a local protocol address to a socket. With the Internet protocols, the protocol address is the combination of either a 32-bit IPv4 address or a 128-bit IPv6 address, along with a 16-bit TCP or UDP port number.

```
#include <sys/socket.h>
int bind (int sockfd, const struct sockaddr *myaddr, socklen_t addrlen);
Returns: 0 if OK,-1 on error
```

Historically, the man page description of bind has said "bind assigns a name to an unnamed socket." The use of the term "name" is confusing and gives the connotation of domain names such as foo.bar.com. The bind function has nothing to do with names. Bind assigns a protocol address to a socket, and what that protocol address means depends on the protocol.

The second argument is a pointer to a protocol-specific address, and the third argument is the size of this address structure. With TCP, calling bind lets us specify a port number, an IP address, both, or neither.

Servers bind their well-known port when they start. If a TCP client or server does not do this, the kernel chooses an ephemeral port for the socket when either connect or listen is called. It is normal for a TCP client to let the kernel choose an ephemeral port, unless the application requires a reserved port, but it is rare for a TCP server to let the kernel choose an ephemeral port, since servers are known by their well-known port.

Exceptions to this rule are Remote Procedure Call (RPC) servers. They normally let the kernel choose an ephemeral port for their listening socket since this port is then registered with the RPC port mapper. Clients have to contact the port mapper to obtain the ephemeral port before they can connect to the server. This also applies to RPC servers using UDP.

A process can bind a specific IP address to its socket. The IP address must belong to an interface on the host. For a TCP client, this assigns the source IP address that will be used for IP datagrams sent on the socket. For a TCP server, this restricts the socket to receive incoming client connections destined only to that IP address.

Normally, a TCP client does not bind an IP address to its socket. The kernel chooses the source IP address when the socket is connected, based on the outgoing interface that is used, which in turn is based on the route required to reach the server (p. 737 of TCPv2).

If a TCP server does not bind an IP address to its socket, the kernel uses the destination IP address of the client's SYN as the server's source IP address (p. 943 of TCPv2).

As said, calling bind lets us specify the IP address, the port, both, or neither. The values to which set sin_addr and sin_port, or sin6_addr and sin6_port, depending on the desired result.

Result when specifying IP address and/or port number to bind

Process specifies		Result
IP address	port	
Wildcard	0	Kernel chooses IP address and port
Wildcard	nonzero	Kernel chooses IP address, process specifies port
Local IP address	0	Process specifies IP address, kernel chooses port
Local IP address	nonzero	Process specifies IP address and port

If specify a port number of 0, the kernel chooses an ephemeral port when bind is called. But if specify a wildcard IP address, the kernel does not choose the local IP address until either the socket is connected (TCP) or a datagram is sent on the socket (UDP).

With IPv4, the wildcard address is specified by the constant INADDR_ANY, whose value is normally 0. This tells the kernel to choose the IP address.

```
struct sockaddr_in servaddr;
```

```
servaddr.sin_addr.s_addr = htonl (INADDR_ANY); /* wildcard */
```

While this works with IPv4, where an IP address is a 32-bit value that can be represented as a simple numeric constant (0 in this case), cannot use this technique with IPv6, since the 128-bit IPv6 address is stored in a structure. (In C cannot represent a constant structure on the righthand side of an assignment.) To solve this problem, write

```
struct sockaddr_in6 serv;
serv.sin6_addr = in6addr_any; /* wildcard */
```

The system allocates and initializes the in6addr_any variable to the constant IN6ADDR_ANY_INIT.

The <netinet/in.h> header contains the extern declaration for in6addr_any. The value of INADDR_ANY (0) is the same in either network or host byte order, so the use of htonl is not really required. But, since all the INADDR_constants defined by the <netinet/in.h> header are defined in host byte order, should use htonl with any of these constants.

If tell the kernel to choose an ephemeral port number for our socket, notice that bind does not return the chosen value. Indeed, it cannot return this value since the second argument to bind has the const qualifier. To obtain the value of the ephemeral port assigned by the kernel, must call getsockname to return the protocol address.

A common example of a process binding a non-wildcard IP address to a socket is a host that provides Web servers to multiple organizations (Section 14.2 of TCPv3). First, each organization has its own domain name, such as www.organization.com. Each organization's domain name maps into a different IP address, but typically on the same subnet. For example, if the subnet is 198.69.10, the first organization's IP address could be 198.69.10.128, the next 198.69.10.129, and so on. All these IP addresses are then aliased onto a single network interface (using the alias option of the ifconfig command on 4.4BSD, for example) so that the IP layer will accept incoming datagrams destined for any of the aliased addresses. Finally, one copy of the HTTP server is started for each organization and each copy binds only the IP address for that organization.

An alternative technique is to run a single server that binds the wildcard address. When a connection arrives, the server calls getsockname to obtain the destination IP address from the client, which in our discussion above could be 198.69.10.128, 198.69.10.129, and so on. The server then handles the client request based on the IP address to which the connection was issued.

One advantage in binding a non-wildcard IP address is that the demultiplexing of a given destination IP address to a given server process is then done by the kernel. must be careful to distinguish between the interface on which a packet arrives versus the destination IP address of that packet. The weak end system model and the strong end system model. Most implementations employ the former, meaning it is okay for a packet to arrive with a destination IP address that identifies an interface other than the interface on which the packet arrives. (This assumes a multihomed host.) Binding a non-wildcard IP address restricts the datagrams that will be delivered to the socket based only on the destination IP address. It says nothing about the arriving interface, unless the host employs the strong end system model.

A common error from bind is EADDRINUSE ("Address already in use"). When talk about the SO_REUSEADDR and SO_REUSEPORT socket options.

listen Function

The listen function is called only by a TCP server and it performs two actions:

- When a socket is created by the socket function, it is assumed to be an active socket, that is, a client socket that will issue a connect. The listen function converts an unconnected socket into a passive socket, indicating that the kernel should accept incoming connection requests directed to this socket. In terms of the TCP state transition diagram, the call to listen moves the socket from the CLOSED state to the LISTEN state.
- The second argument to this function specifies the maximum number of connections the kernel should queue for this socket.

```
#include <sys/socket.h>
#int listen (int sockfd, int backlog);
Returns: 0 if OK, -1 on error
```

This function is normally called after both the socket and bind functions and must be called before calling the accept function. To understand the backlog argument, must realize that for a given listening socket, the kernel maintains two queues:

- An incomplete connection queue, which contains an entry for each SYN that has arrived from a client for which the server is awaiting completion of the TCP three-way handshake. These sockets are in the SYN_RCVD state.
- A completed connection queue, which contains an entry for each client with whom the TCP three-way handshake has completed. These sockets are in the ESTABLISHED state.

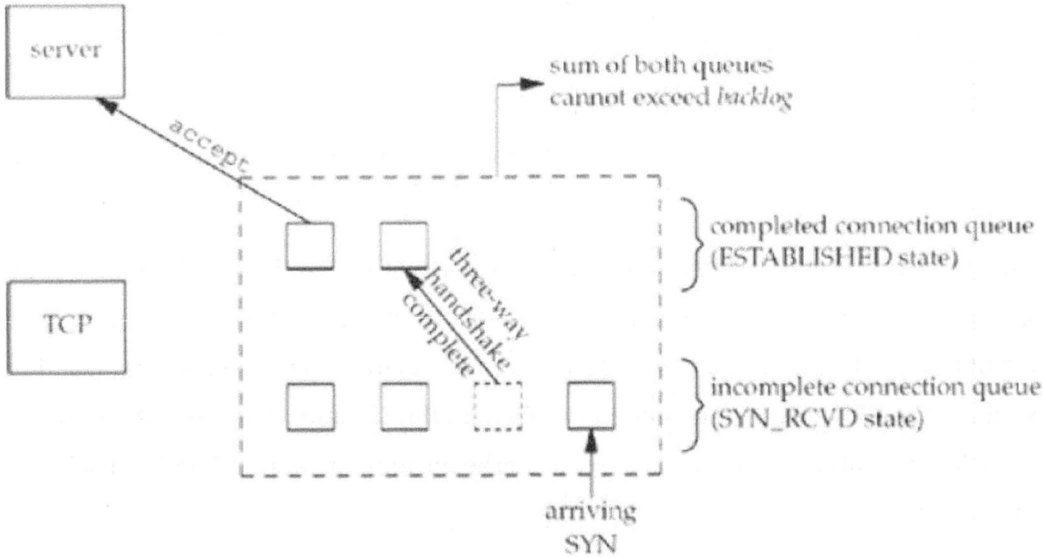

The two queues maintained by TCP for a listening socket

When an entry is created on the incomplete queue, the parameters from the listen socket are copied over to the newly created connection. The connection creation mechanism is completely automatic; the server process is not involved. The packets exchanged during the connection establishment with these two queues.

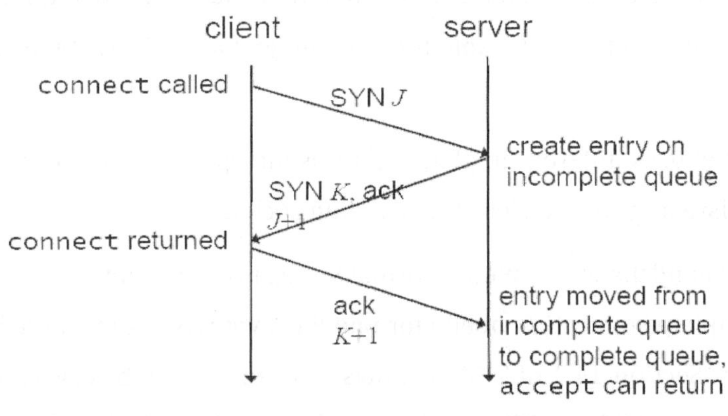

TCP three-way handshake and the two queues for a listening socket

When a SYN arrives from a client, TCP creates a new entry on the incomplete queue and then responds with the second segment of the three-way handshake: the server's SYN with an ACK of the client's SYN. This entry will remain on the incomplete queue until the third segment of the three-way handshake arrives (the client's ACK of the server's SYN), or until the entry times out. (Berkeley-derived implementations have a timeout of 75 seconds for these incomplete entries.) If the three-way handshake completes normally, the entry moves from the incomplete queue to the end of the completed queue. When the process calls accept, which will describe in the next section, the first entry on the completed queue is returned to the process, or if the queue is empty, the process is put to sleep until an entry is placed onto the completed queue.

There are several points to consider regarding the handling of these two queues.

The backlog argument to the listen function has historically specified the maximum value for the sum of both queues.

There has never been a formal definition of what the backlog means. The 4.2BSD man page says that it "defines the maximum length the queue of pending connections may grow to." Many man pages and even the POSIX specification copy this definition verbatim, but this definition does not say whether a pending connection is one in the SYN_RCVD state, one in the ESTABLISHED state that has not yet been accepted, or either. The historical definition in this bullet is the Berkeley implementation, dating back to 4.2BSD, and copied by many others.

Berkeley-derived implementations add a fudge factor to the backlog: It is multiplied by 1.5 (p. 257 of TCPv1 and p. 462 of TCPV2). For example, the commonly specified backlog of 5 really allows up to 8 queued entries on these systems.

The reason for adding this fudge factor appears lost to history [Joy 1994]. But if consider the backlog as specifying the maximum number of completed connections that the kernel will queue for a socket ([Borman 1997b], as discussed shortly), then the reason for the fudge factor is to take into account incomplete connections on the queue.

Do not specify a backlog of 0, as different implementations interpret this differently. If you do not want any clients connecting to your listening socket, close the listening socket.

Assuming the three-way handshake completes normally (i.e., no lost segments and no retransmissions), an entry remains on the incomplete connection queue for one RTT, whatever that value happens to be between a particular client and server. Section 14.4 of TCPv3 shows that for one Web server, the median RTT between many clients and the server was 187 ms. (The median is often used for this statistic, since a few large values can noticeably skew the mean.)

Historically, sample code always shows a backlog of 5, as that was the maximum value supported by 4.2BSD. This was adequate in the 1980s when busy servers would handle only a few hundred connections per day. But with the growth of the World Wide Web (WWW), where busy servers handle millions of connections per day, this small number is completely inadequate (pp. 187–192 of TCPv3). Busy HTTP servers must specify a much larger backlog, and newer kernels must support larger values.

Many current systems allow the administrator to modify the maximum value for the backlog. A problem is: What value should the application specify for the backlog, since 5 is often inadequate? There is no easy answer to this. HTTP servers now specify a larger value, but if the value specified is a constant in the source code, to increase the constant requires recompiling the server. Another method is to assume some default but allow a command-line option or an environment variable to override the default. It is always acceptable to specify a value that is larger than supported by the kernel, as the kernel should silently truncate the value to the maximum value that it supports, without returning an error (p. 456 of TCPv2).

We can provide a simple solution to this problem by modifying our wrapper function for the listen function. To allow the environment variable LISTENQ to override the value specified by the caller.

Wrapper function for listen that allows an environment variable to specify backlog

lib/wrapsock.c

```
void
Listen (int fd, int backlog)
{
char *ptr;
/* can override 2nd argument with environment variable */
if ( (ptr = getenv("LISTENQ")) != NULL)
backlog = atoi (ptr);
if (listen (fd, backlog) < 0)
err_sys ("listen error");
}
```

Manuals and books have historically said that the reason for queuing a fixed number of connections is to handle the case of the server process being busy between successive calls to accept. This implies that of the two queues, the completed queue should normally have more entries than the incomplete queue. Again, busy Web servers have shown that this is false. The reason for specifying a large backlog is because the incomplete connection queue can grow as client SYNs arrive, waiting for completion of the three-way handshake.

If the queues are full when a client SYN arrives, TCP ignores the arriving SYN (pp. 930–931 of TCPv2); it does not send an RST. This is because the condition is considered temporary, and the client TCP will retransmit its SYN, hopefully finding room on the queue in the near future.

If the server TCP immediately responded with an RST, the client's connect would return an error, forcing the application to handle this condition instead of letting TCP's normal retransmission take over. Also, the client could not differentiate between an RST in response to a SYN meaning "there is no server at this port" versus "there is a server at this port but its queues are full."

Some implementations do send an RST when the queue is full. This behavior is incorrect for the reasons stated above, and unless your client specifically needs to interact with such a server, it's best to ignore this possibility. Coding to handle this case reduces the robustness of the client and puts more load on the network in the normal RST case, where the port really has no server listening on it.

Data that arrives after the three-way handshake completes, but before the server calls accept, should be queued by the server TCP, up to the size of the connected socket's receive buffer.

The actual number of queued connections provided for different values of the backlog argument for the various operating systems. For seven different operating systems there are five distinct columns.

Actual number of queued connections for values of backlog.

	Maximum actual number of queued connections				
backlog	MacOS 10.2.6 AIX 5.1	Linux 2.4.7	HP-UX 11.11	FreeBSD 4.8 FreeBSD 5.1	Solaris 2.9
0	1	3	1	1	1
1	2	4	1	2	2
2	4	5	3	3	4
3	5	6	4	4	5
4	7	7	6	5	6
5	8	8	7	6	8
6	10	9	9	7	10
7	11	10	10	8	11
8	13	11	12	9	13
9	14	12	13	10	14
10	16	13	15	11	16
11	17	14	16	12	17
12	19	15	18	13	19
13	20	16	19	14	20
14	22	17	21	15	22

AIX and MacOS have the traditional Berkeley algorithm, and Solaris seems very close to that algorithm as well. FreeBSD just adds one to backlog.

The purpose of having a limit on these completed connections is to stop the kernel from accepting new connection requests for a given socket when the application is not accepting them (for whatever reason). If a system implements this interpretation, as does BSD/OS 3.0, then the application need not specify huge backlog values just because the server handles lots of client requests (e.g., a busy Web server) or to provide protection against SYN flooding. The kernel handles lots of incomplete connections, regardless of whether they are legitimate or from a hacker. But even with this interpretation, scenarios do occur where the traditional value of 5 is inadequate.

accept Function

accept is called by a TCP server to return the next completed connection from the front of the completed connection queue. If the completed connection queue is empty, the process is put to sleep (assuming the default of a blocking socket).

```
#include <sys/socket.h>
int accept (int sockfd, struct sockaddr *cliaddr, socklen_t *addrlen);
Returns: non-negative descriptor if OK, -1 on error
```

The cliaddr and addrlen arguments are used to return the protocol address of the connected peer process (the client). addrlen is a value-result argument: Before the call, set the integer value referenced by *addrlen to the size of the socket address structure pointed to by cliaddr; on return, this integer value contains the actual number of bytes stored by the kernel in the socket address structure.

If accept is successful, its return value is a brand-new descriptor automatically created by the kernel. This new descriptor refers to the TCP connection with the client. When discussing accept, call the first argument to accept the listening socket (the descriptor created by socket and then used as the first argument to both bind and listen), and call the return value from accept the connected socket. It is important to differentiate between these two sockets. A given server normally creates only one listening socket, which then exists for the lifetime of the server. The kernel creates one connected socket for each client connection that is accepted (i.e., for which the TCP three-way handshake completes). When the server is finished serving a given client, the connected socket is closed.

This function returns up to three values: an integer return code that is either a new socket descriptor or an error indication, the protocol address of the client process (through the cliaddr pointer), and the size of this address (through the addrlen pointer). If are not interested in having the protocol address of the client returned, set both cliaddr and addrlen to null pointers.

The connected socket is closed each time through the loop, but the listening socket remains open for the life of the server. also see that the second and third arguments to accept are null pointers, since were not interested in the identity of the client.

fork and exec Functions

Before describing how to write a concurrent server in the next section, must describe the Unix fork function. This function (including the variants of it provided by some systems) is the only way in Unix to create a new process.

```
#include <unistd.h>
pid_t fork(void);
Returns: 0 in child, process ID of child in parent, -1 on error
```

If you have never seen this function before, the hard part in understanding fork is that it is called once but it returns twice. It returns once in the calling process (called the parent) with a return value that is the process ID of the newly created process (the child). It also returns once in the child, with a return value of 0. Hence, the return value tells the process whether it is the parent or the child.

The reason fork returns 0 in the child, instead of the parent's process ID, is because a child has only one parent and it can always obtain the parent's process ID by calling getppid. A parent, on the other hand, can have any number of children, and there is no way to obtain the process IDs of its children. If a parent wants to keep track of the process IDs of all its children, it must record the return values from fork.

All descriptors open in the parent before the call to fork are shared with the child after fork returns. The parent calls accept and then calls fork. The connected socket is then shared between the parent and child. Normally, the child then reads and writes the connected socket and the parent closes the connected socket.

There are two typical uses of fork:

- A process makes a copy of itself so that one copy can handle one operation while the other copy does another task. This is typical for network servers. will see many examples of this later in the text.
- A process wants to execute another program. Since the only way to create a new process is by calling fork, the process first calls fork to make a copy of itself, and then one of the copies (typically the child process) calls exec (described next) to replace itself with the new program. This is typical for programs such as shells.

The only way in which an executable program file on disk can be executed by Unix is for an existing process to call one of the six exec functions. (We will often refer generically to "the exec function" when it does not matter which of the six is called.) exec replaces the current process image with the new program file, and this new program normally starts at the main function. The process ID does not change. refer to the process that calls exec as the calling process and the newly executed program as the new program.

The differences in the six exec functions are: (a) whether the program file to execute is specified by a filename or a pathname; (b) whether the arguments to the new program are listed one by one or referenced through an array of pointers; and (c) whether the environment of the calling process is passed to the new program or whether a new environment is specified.

```
#include <unistd.h>
int execl (const char *pathname, const char *arg0, ... /* (char *) 0 */ );
int execv (const char *pathname, char *const argv[]);
int execle (const char *pathname, const char *arg0, ...
/* (char *) 0, char *const envp[] */ );
int execve (const char *pathname, char *const argv[], char *const envp[]);
int execlp (const char *filename, const char *arg0, ... /* (char *) 0 */ );
int execvp (const char *filename, char *const argv[]);
All six return: -1 on error, no return on success
```

These functions return to the caller only if an error occurs. Otherwise, control passes to the start of the new program, normally the main function.

The execve is a system call within the kernel and the other five are library functions that call execve.

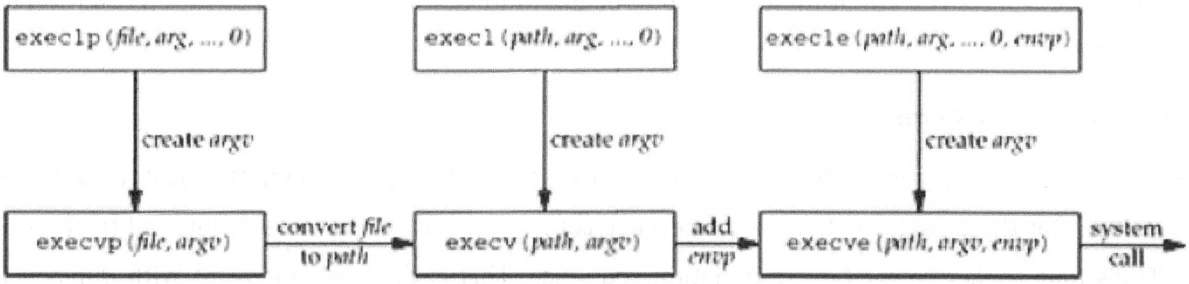

Relationship among the six exec functions

Note the following differences among these six functions:

- The three functions in the top row specify each argument string as a separate argument to the exec function, with a null pointer terminating the variable number of arguments. The three functions in the second row have an argv array, containing pointers to the argument strings. This argv array must contain a null pointer to specify its end, since a count is not specified.
- The two functions in the left column specify a filename argument. This is converted into a pathname using the current PATH environment variable. If the filename argument to execlp or execvp contains a slash (/) anywhere in the string, the PATH variable is not used. The four functions in the right two columns specify a fully qualified pathname argument.
- The four functions in the left two columns do not specify an explicit environment pointer. Instead, the current value of the external variable environ is used for building an environment list that is passed to the new program. The two functions in the right column specify an explicit environment list. The envp array of pointers must be terminated by a null pointer.

Descriptors open in the process before calling exec normally remain open across the exec. use the qualifier "normally" because this can be disabled using fcntl to set the FD_CLOEXEC descriptor flag.

close Function

The normal Unix close function is also used to close a socket and terminate a TCP connection.

```
#include <unistd.h>
int close (int sockfd);
Returns: 0 if OK, -1 on error
```

The default action of close with a TCP socket is to mark the socket as closed and return to the process immediately. The socket descriptor is no longer usable by the process: It cannot be used as an argument to read or write. But, TCP will try to send any data that is already queued to be sent to the other end, and after this occurs, the normal TCP connection termination sequence takes place.

The SO_LINGER socket option, which lets us change this default action with a TCP socket. In that section, will also describe what a TCP application must do to be guaranteed that the peer application has received any outstanding data.

Descriptor Reference Counts

The parent process in our concurrent server closes the connected socket, this just decrements the reference count for the descriptor. Since the reference count was still greater than 0, this call to close did not initiate TCP's four-packet connection termination sequence. This is the behavior want with our concurrent server with the connected socket that is shared between the parent and child.

If really want to send a FIN on a TCP connection, the shutdown function can be used instead of close. The parent will eventually run out of descriptors, as there is usually a limit to the number of descriptors that any process can have open at any time. But more importantly, none of the client connections will be terminated. When the child closes the connected socket, its reference count will go from 2 to 1 and it will remain at 1 since the parent never closes the connected socket. This will prevent TCP's connection termination sequence from occurring, and the connection will remain open.

Concurrent Servers

The server is an iterative server. For something as simple as a daytime server, this is fine. But when a client request can take longer to service, do not want to tie up a single server with one client; want to handle multiple clients at the same time. The simplest way to write a concurrent server under Unix is to fork a child process to handle each client.

Outline for typical concurrent server

```
pid_t pid;
    int listenfd, connfd;
    listenfd = Socket( ... );
    /* fill in sockaddr_in{} with server's well-known port */
    Bind(listenfd, ... );
    Listen(listenfd, LISTENQ);
    for ( ; ; ) {
    connfd = Accept (listenfd, ... ); /* probably blocks */
    if( (pid = Fork()) == 0) {
    Close(listenfd); /* child closes listening socket */
```

```
doit(connfd); /* process the request */
Close(connfd); /* done with this client */
exit(0); /* child terminates */
}
Close(connfd); /* parent closes connected socket */
}
```

When a connection is established, accept returns, the server calls fork, and the child process services the client (on connfd, the connected socket) and the parent process waits for another connection (on listenfd, the listening socket). The parent closes the connected socket since the child handles the new client.

When this function returns, explicitly close the connected socket in the child. This is not required since the next statement calls exit, and part of process termination is to close all open descriptors by the kernel. Whether to include this explicit call to close or not is a matter of personal programming taste.

The close on a TCP socket causes a FIN to be sent, followed by the normal TCP connection termination sequence. The reference count is maintained in the file table entry (pp. 57–60 of APUE). This is a count of the number of descriptors that are currently open that refer to this file or socket. After socket returns, the file table entry associated with listenfd has a reference count of 1. After accept returns, the file table entry associated with connfd has a reference count of 1. But, after fork returns, both descriptors are shared (i.e., duplicated) between the parent and child, so the file table entries associated with both sockets now have a reference count of 2. Therefore, when the parent closes connfd, it just decrements the reference count from 2 to 1 and that is all. The actual cleanup and de-allocation of the socket does not happen until the reference count reaches 0. This will occur at some time later when the child closes connfd.

Status of client/server before call to accept returns

Immediately after accept returns, the connection is accepted by the kernel and a new socket, connfd, is created. This is a connected socket and data can now be read and written across the connection.

Status of client/server after return from accept

The next step in the concurrent server is to call fork.

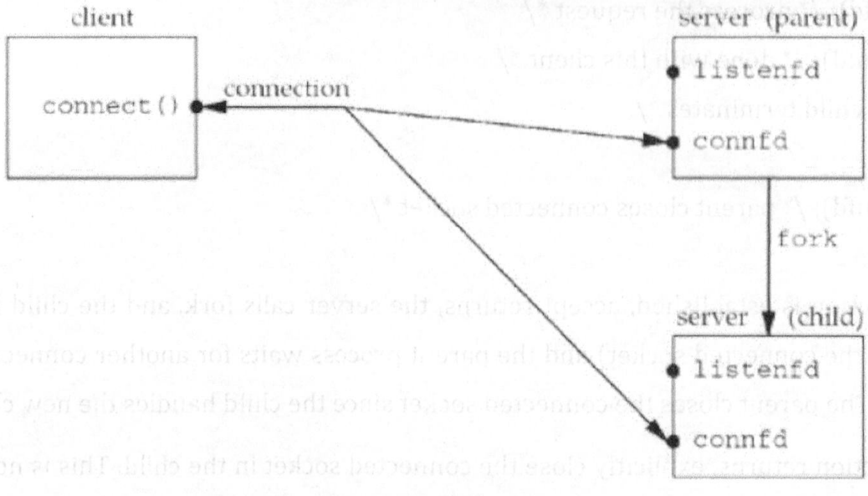

Status of client/server after fork returns

The both descriptors, listenfd and connfd, are shared (duplicated) between the parent and child.

The next step is for the parent to close the connected socket and the child to close the listening socket.

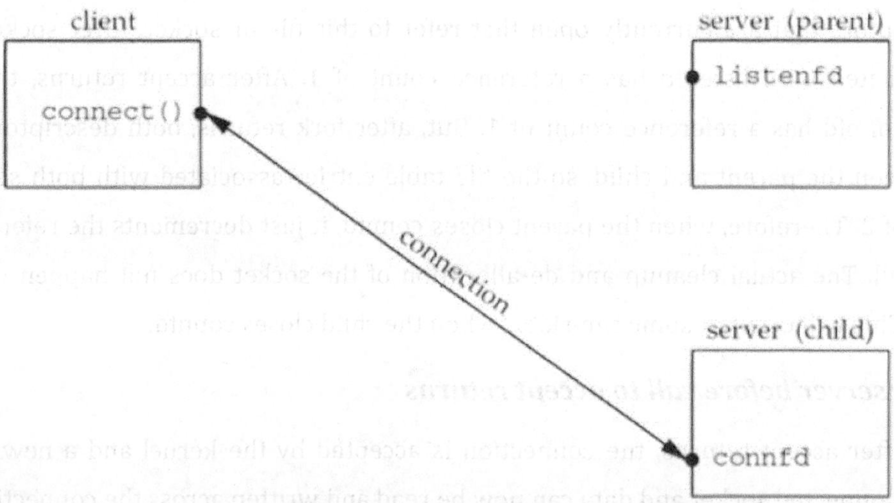

Status of client/server after parent and child close appropriate sockets

This is the desired final state of the sockets. The child is handling the connection with the client and the parent can call accept again on the listening socket, to handle the next client connection.

UNIT-II

QUESTION BANK

PART-A

1. **What are the ways for Normal Termination**

- return from main
- calling exit
- calling _exit

Differentiate exit and _exit function

- exit performs certain cleanup processing and then returns to the kernel. It performs a clean shutdown of the standard I/O library. All buffered output data will be flushed.
- _exit returns to the kernel immediately

2. **Define command line arguments**

When a program is executed, the process that does the 'exec' can pass command-line arguments to the new program. This is a part of the normal operation of the Unix shells.

Prototype is

int main (int argc,char *argv[ ]);

argc => number of command line arguments

argv => array of pointers to the arguments

3. **Define Environment List**

Environment List is an array of character pointers, with each pointer containing the address of a null terminated C string. The address of the array of pointers is contained in the global variable environ.

4. **If you are adding /deleting a new name to a value in an environment string, what are the steps you should follow?**

```
#include<stdlib.h>
int putenv(const char *str);
int setenv(const char *name, const char *value, int rewrite);
void unsetenv(const char *name);
```

putenv – takes a string of the form name=value and places it in the environment list. If the name already exists, its old definition is first removed.

setenv – sets name to value. If name already exists in the environment then (a) if rewrite is nonzero, the existing definition for name is first removed; (b) if rewrite is 0, an existing definition for name is not removed.

unsetenv – removes any definition of name. It is not an error if such a definition does not exist.

5. Define heap

Heap is the area where dynamic memory allocation takes place. Heap lies between the stack and uninitialized data.

6. Define Shared Libraries

Shared Libraries remove the common library routines from the executable file, instead maintaining a single copy of the library routine in the memory that all the processes reference.

Adv: reduces the size of the executable files

7. List the functions used for memory allocation

- malloc
- calloc
- realloc

8. Define init process

- It is invoked by the kernel at the end of the bootstrap procedure
- init process never dies
- It is a normal user process

9. Define Copy-On-Write

Instead of making a complete copy of parent's dataspace, heap, stack,parent & child can share these regions(read-only copy). If either of the process tries to modify this region, the kernel then makes a copy of that memory alone.

10. Write the two option constants for waitpid with its descriptors.

Two option constants in waitpid() are,

- WNOHANG – waitpid will not block if a child specified by pids is not immediately available. In this case the return value is 0.
- WUNTRACED – If the implementation supports job control, the status of any child specified by pid that has stopped, and whose status has not been reported since it has stopped, is returned.

11. What are the differences between wait and waitpid function

- The wait function can block the caller until a child process terminates, whereas waitpid has an option that prevents it from blocking.
- The waitpid function doesn't wait for the child that terminates first; it has a number of options that control which process it waits for.

12. Define the macros WIFEXITED and WIFSIGNALED

WIFEXITED(status)	True if status was returned for a child that terminated normally. In this case, we can execute WEXITSTATUS (status) to fetch the low-order 8 bits of the argument that the child passed to exit, _exit, or _Exit.
WIFSIGNALED (status)	True if status was returned for a child that terminated abnormally, by receipt of a signal that it didn't catch. In this case, we can execute WTERMSIG (status) to fetch the signal number that caused the termination.

13. Differentiate Thread from a Process

Process	Thread
Active entity	Light weight process
Context switching is difficult	Context switching is easy
Has process lifecycle	Has thread lifecycle (thread creation, termination, suspension)
Each process has its own address space	Threads share the address space (code, data, files)

14. Give a brief note on Multithreaded environment

In a multithreaded environment, all the threads share the same code, data and files. But each thread has its own registers, stack and program counter. The program counter contains the address of the next instruction to be executed.

15. Define Hybrid Threads

Multiplexing of user level threads with kernel threads is termed Hybrid threads.

16. What are the functionalities of Login

- Fetches the password file entry, prompt the password and encrypt the password that we entered.
- If the login is correct, then login changes to home directory using chdir( ) and ownership is changed using chown( )

- Access permissions are changed
- The environment is initialized
- Prints the message of day-to-day life
- checks for new e-mail

17. What are the functions of getty program

- getty calls 'open' for terminal device. The device is opened if it is a local and if it is a modem, the open may delay in device driver until the terminal answers.
- getty outputs something like Login:
- getty creates an environment for login.

18. Mention the signals that cannot be caught or ignored

- SIGKILL
- SIGSTOP

19. Define Unreliable signals

Unreliable signals means, the signal could get lost. A signal could occur and the process would never know about it.

UNIT- II

PART-B (16 MARKS)

1. Compare the implementation details of concurrent and iterative server.
2. Discuss the syntactical issues of various address conversion function.
3. Compare the IPV4, IPV6. State your assumptions.
4. Write notes on byte ordering functions.
5. Explain in detail about TCP/IP protocols for internetworking and management.
6. Explain about socket, connect, bind, listen and accept functions.
7. Explain TCP/IP layering in detail with neat sketch.
8. Explain in detail about address conversion functions.
9. Unix domain and data link socket address structures. State your assumptions.
10. Explain about concurrent server.

UNIT- III

APPLICATION DEVELOPMENT

Introduction

An echo server that performs the following steps:

- The client reads a line of text from its standard input and writes the line to the server.
- The server reads the line from its network input and echoes the line back to the client.
- The client reads the echoed line and prints it on its standard output.

The client/server along with the functions used for input and output.

Simple echo client and server

The two arrows between the client and server, but this is really one full-duplex TCP connection. The fgets and fputs functions are from the standard I/O library.

While develop the implementation of an echo server, most TCP/IP implementations provide such a server, using both TCP and UDP.

A client/server that echoes input lines is a valid, yet simple, example of a network application. All the basic steps required to implement any client/server are illustrated by this example. To expand this example into your own application, all you need to do is change what the server does with the input it receives from its clients.

Besides running our client and server in their normal mode (type in a line and watch it echo), examine lots of boundary conditions for this example: what happens when the client and server are started; what happens when the client terminates normally; what happens to the client if the server process terminates before the client is done; what happens to the client if the server host crashes; and so on. By looking at all these scenarios and understanding what happens at the network level, and how this appears to the sockets API, will understand more about what goes on at these levels and how to code our applications to handle these scenarios.

In all these examples, have "hard-coded" protocol-specific constants such as addresses and ports. There are two reasons for this. First, must understand exactly what needs to be stored in the protocol-specific address structures. Second, have not yet covered the library functions that can make this more portable.

TCP Echo Server

TCP Echo Server: main Function

Create socket, bind server's well-known port

9–15 A TCP socket is created. An Internet socket address structure is filled in with the wildcard address (INADDR_ANY) and the server's well-known port (SERV_PORT, which is defined as 9877 in our unp.h header). Binding the wildcard address tells the system that will accept a connection destined for any local interface, in case the system is multihomed. It should be greater than 1023 (we do not need a reserved port), greater than 5000 (to avoid conflict with the ephemeral ports allocated by many Berkeley-derived implementations), less than 49152 (to avoid conflict with the "correct" range of ephemeral ports), and it should not conflict with any registered port. The socket is converted into a listening socket by listen.

Wait for client connection to complete

17–18 The server blocks in the call to accept, waiting for a client connection to complete.

Concurrent server

19–24 For each client, fork spawns a child, and the child handles the new client. The child closes the listening socket and the parent closes the connected socket. The child then calls str_echo to handle the client.

TCP echo server

tcpdiserv/tcpserv01.c

```
1 #include "unp.h"
2 int
3 main(int argc, char **argv)
4 {
5 int listenfd, connfd;
6 pid_t childpid;
7 socklen_t clilen;
8 struct sockaddr_in cliaddr, servaddr;
9 listenfd = Socket (AF_INET, SOCK_STREAM, 0);
10 bzero(&servaddr, sizeof(servaddr));
11 servaddr.sin_family = AF_INET;
```

```
12 servaddr.sin_addr.s_addr = htonl (INADDR_ANY);
13 servaddr.sin_port = htons (SERV_PORT);
14 Bind(listenfd, (SA *) &servaddr, sizeof(servaddr));
15 Listen(listenfd, LISTENQ);
16 for ( ; ; ) {
17 clilen = sizeof(cliaddr);
18 connfd = Accept(listenfd, (SA *) &cliaddr, &clilen);
19 if ( (childpid = Fork()) == 0) { /* child process */
20 Close(listenfd); /* close listening socket */
21 str_echo(connfd); /* process the request */
22 exit (0);
23 }
24 Close(connfd); /* parent closes connected socket */
25 }
26 }
```

TCP Echo Server: str_echo Function

The function str_echo, performs the server processing for each client: It reads data from the client and echoes it back to the client.

Read a buffer and echo the buffer

8–9 read reads data from the socket and the line is echoed back to the client by writen. If the client closes the connection (the normal scenario), the receipt of the client's FIN causes the child's read to return 0. This causes the str_echo function to return, which terminates the child.

TCP Echo Client

TCP Echo Client: main Function

str_echo function: echoes data on a socket

lib/str_echo.c

```
1 #include "unp.h"
2 void
3 str_echo(int sockfd)
4 {
5 ssize_t n;
6 char buf[MAXLINE];
```

```
again:
while ( (n = read(sockfd, buf, MAXLINE)) > 0)
Writen(sockfd, buf, n);
if (n < 0 && errno == EINTR)
goto again;
else if (n < 0)
err_sys("str_echo: read error");
}
```

TCP echo client

tcpcliserv/tcpli01.c

```
1 #include "unp.h"
2 int
3 main(int argc, char **argv)
4 {
5 int sockfd;
6 struct sockaddr_in servaddr;
7 if (argc != 2)
8 err_quit("usage: tcpcli <IPaddress>");
9 sockfd = Socket(AF_INET, SOCK_STREAM, 0);
10 bzero(&servaddr, sizeof(servaddr));
11 servaddr.sin_family = AF_INET;
12 servaddr.sin_port = htons(SERV_PORT);
13 Inet_pton(AF_INET, argv[1], &servaddr.sin_addr);
14 Connect(sockfd, (SA *) &servaddr, sizeof(servaddr));
15 str_cli(stdin, sockfd); /* do it all */
16 exit(0);
17 }
```

Create socket, fill in Internet socket address structure

9–13 A TCP socket is created and an Internet socket address structure is filled in with the server's IP address and port number. take the server's IP address from the command-line argument and the server's well-known port (SERV_PORT) is from our unp.h header.

Connect to server

14–15 connect establishes the connection with the server. The function str_cli handles the rest of the client processing.

TCP Echo Client: str_cli Function

This function, handles the client processing loop: It reads a line of text from standard input, writes it to the server, reads back the server's echo of the line, and outputs the echoed line to standard output.

str_cli function: client processing loop

lib/str_cli.c

```
1 #include "unp.h"
2 void
3 str_cli(FILE *fp, int sockfd)
4 {
5 char sendline[MAXLINE], recvline[MAXLINE];
6 while (Fgets(sendline, MAXLINE, fp) != NULL) {
7 Writen(sockfd, sendline, strlen (sendline));
8 if (Readline(sockfd, recvline, MAXLINE) == 0)
9 err_quit("str_cli: server terminated prematurely");
10 Fputs(recvline, stdout);
11 }
12 }
```

Read a line, write to server

6–7 fgets reads a line of text and writen sends the line to the server.

Read echoed line from server, write to standard output

8–10 readline reads the line echoed back from the server and fputs writes it to standard output.

Return to main

11–12 The loop terminates when fgets returns a null pointer, which occurs when it encounters either an end-of-file (EOF) or an error. Our Fgets wrapper function checks for an error and aborts if one occurs, so Fgets returns a null pointer only when an end-of-file is encountered.

POSIX Signal Handling

A signal is a notification to a process that an event has occurred. Signals are sometimes called software interrupts. Signals usually occur asynchronously. By this mean that a process doesn't know ahead of time exactly when a signal will occur.

Signals can be sent

- By one process to another process (or to itself)
- By the kernel to a process

The SIGCHLD signal that described at the end of the previous section is one that is sent by the kernel whenever a process terminates, to the parent of the terminating process.

Every signal has a disposition, which is also called the action associated with the signal. set the disposition of a signal by calling the sigaction function (described shortly) and have three choices for the disposition:

- We can provide a function that is called whenever a specific signal occurs. This function is called a signal handler and this action is called catching a signal. The two signals SIGKILL and SIGSTOP cannot be caught. Our function is called with a single integer argument that is the signal number and the function returns nothing. Its function prototype is therefore
  void handler (int signo);
- For most signals, calling sigaction and specifying a function to be called when the signal occurs is all that is required to catch a signal. But will see later that a few signals, SIGIO, SIGPOLL, and SIGURG, all require additional actions on the part of the process to catch the signal.
- We can ignore a signal by setting its disposition to SIG_IGN. The two signals SIGKILL and SIGSTOP cannot be ignored.
- We can set the default disposition for a signal by setting its disposition to SIG_DFL. The default is normally to terminate a process on receipt of a signal, with certain signals also generating a core image of the process in its current working directory. There are a few signals whose default disposition is to be ignored: SIGCHLD and SIGURG (sent on the arrival of out-of-band data, are two that will encounter in this text.

signal Function

The POSIX way to establish the disposition of a signal is to call the sigaction function. This gets complicated, however, as one argument to the function is a structure that must allocate and fill in. An easier way to set the disposition of a signal is to call the signal function. The first argument is the signal name and the second argument is either a pointer to a function or one of the constants SIG_IGN or SIG_DFL. But, signal is an historical function that predates POSIX. Different implementations provide different signal semantics when it is called, providing backward compatibility, whereas POSIX explicitly spells out the semantics when sigaction is called. The solution is to define our own function named signal that just calls the POSIX sigaction function.

This provides a simple interface with the desired POSIX semantics. include this function in our own library, along with our err_XXX functions and our wrapper functions, for example, that specify when building any of our programs in this text.

signal function that calls the POSIX sigaction function

lib/signal.c

```
1 #include "unp.h"
2 Sigfunc *
3 signal (int signo, Sigfunc *func)
4 {
5 struct sigaction act, oact;
6 act.sa_handler = func;
7 sigemptyset (&act.sa_mask);
8 act.sa_flags = 0;
9 if (signo == SIGALRM) {
10 #ifdef SA_INTERRUPT
11 act.sa_flags |= SA_INTERRUPT; /* SunOS 4.x */
12 #endif
13 } else {
14 #ifdef SA_RESTART
15 act.sa_flags |= SA_RESTART; /* SVR4, 4.4BSD */
16 #endif
17 }
18 if (sigaction (signo, &act, &oact) < 0)
19 return (SIG_ERR);
20 return (oact.sa_handler);
21 }
```

Simplify function prototype using typedef

2–3 The normal function prototype for signal is complicated by the level of nested parentheses.

```
void (*signal (int signo, void (*func) (int))) (int);
```

To simplify this, define the Sigfunc type in our unp.h header as typedef void Sigfunc(int);

stating that signal handlers are functions with an integer argument and the function returns nothing (void). The function prototype then becomes Sigfunc *signal (int signo, Sigfunc *func);

A pointer to a signal handling function is the second argument to the function, as well as the return value from the function.

Set handler

6 The sa_handler member of the sigaction structure is set to the func argument.

Set signal mask for handler

7 POSIX allows us to specify a set of signals that will be blocked when our signal handler is called.

Any signal that is blocked cannot be delivered to a process. set the sa_mask member to the empty set, which means that no additional signals will be blocked while our signal handler is running. POSIX guarantees that the signal being caught is always blocked while its handler is executing.

Set SA_RESTART flag

8–17 SA_RESTART is an optional flag. When the flag is set, a system call interrupted by this signal will be automatically restarted by the kernel. (We will talk more about interrupted system calls in the next section when continue our example.) If the signal being caught is not SIGALRM, specify the SA_RESTART flag, if defined. (The reason for making a special case for SIGALRM is that the purpose of generating this signal is normally to place a timeout on an I/O operation, in which case, want the blocked system call to be interrupted by the signal.) Some older systems, notably SunOS 4.x, automatically restart an interrupted system call by default and then define the complement of this flag as SA_INTERRUPT. If this flag is defined, set it if the signal being caught is SIGALRM.

Call sigaction

18–20 call sigaction and then return the old action for the signal as the return value of the signal function.

POSIX Signal Semantics

The following points about signal handling on a POSIX-compliant system:

- Once a signal handler is installed, it remains installed. (Older systems removed the signal handler each time it was executed.)
- While a signal handler is executing, the signal being delivered is blocked. Furthermore, any additional signals that were specified in the sa_mask signal set passed to sigaction when the handler was installed are also blocked. Set sa_mask to the empty set, meaning no additional signals are blocked other than the signal being caught.

- If a signal is generated one or more times while it is blocked, it is normally delivered only one time after the signal is unblocked. That is, by default, Unix signals are not queued. will see an example of this in the next section. The POSIX real-time standard, 1003.1b, defines some reliable signals that are queued, but do not use them in this text.
- It is possible to selectively block and unblock a set of signals using the sigprocmask function.

This lets us protect a critical region of code by preventing certain signals from being caught while that region of code is executing.

Boundary Conditions

Termination of Server Process

Now start our client/server and then kill the server child process. This simulates the crashing of the server process, so can see what happens to the client. To distinguish between the crashing of the server process, which are about to describe, and the crashing of the server host. The following steps take place:

- To start the server and client and type one line to the client to verify that all is okay. That line is echoed normally by the server child.
- To find the process ID of the server child and kill it. As part of process termination, all open descriptors in the child are closed. This causes a FIN to be sent to the client, and the client TCP responds with an ACK. This is the first half of the TCP connection termination.
- The SIGCHLD signal is sent to the server parent and handled correctly.
- Nothing happens at the client. The client TCP receives the FIN from the server TCP and responds with an ACK, but the problem is that the client process is blocked in the call to fgets waiting for a line from the terminal.
- Running netstat at this point shows the state of the sockets.

  ```
  linux % netstat -a | grep 9877
  tcp 0 0 *:9877 *:* LISTEN
  tcp 0 0 localhost:9877 localhost:43604 FIN_WAIT2
  tcp 1 0 localhost:43604 localhost:9877 CLOSE_WAIT
  ```

  That half of the TCP connection termination sequence has taken place.
- Still type a line of input to the client. Here is the client starting from Step 1:

  ```
  linux % tcpcli01 127.0.0.1 start client
  hello the first line that type
  hello is echoed correctly here kill the server child
  on the server host
  another line then type a second line to the client
  ```

str_cli : server terminated

prematurely

When type "another line," str_cli calls writen and the client TCP sends the data to the server. This is allowed by TCP because the receipt of the FIN by the client TCP only indicates that the server process has closed its end of the connection and will not be sending any more data. The receipt of the FIN does not tell the client TCP that the server process has terminated.

When the server TCP receives the data from the client, it responds with an RST since the process that had that socket open has terminated. can verify that the RST was sent by watching the packets with tcpdump.

- The client process will not see the RST because it calls readline immediately after the call to writen and readline returns 0 (EOF) immediately because of the FIN that was received in Step 2. Our client is not expecting to receive an EOF at this point, so it quits with the error message "server terminated prematurely."
- When the client terminates, all its open descriptors are closed.

What have described also depends on the timing of the example. The client's call to readline may happen before the server's RST is received by the client, or it may happen after. If the readline happens before the RST is received, as we've shown in our example, the result is an unexpected EOF in the client. But if the RST arrives first, the result is an ECONNRESET ("Connection reset by peer") error return from readline.

The problem in this example is that the client is blocked in the call to fgets when the FIN arrives on the socket. The client is really working with two descriptors—the socket and the user input—and instead of blocking on input from only one of the two sources (as str_cli is currently coded), it should block on input from either source. Indeed, this is one purpose of the select and poll functions. When recode the str_cli function, as soon as kill the server child, the client is notified of the received FIN.

Crashing of Server Host

This scenario will test to see what happens when the server host crashes. To simulate this, must run the client and server on different hosts. then start the server, start the client, type in a line to the client to verify that the connection is up, disconnect the server host from the network, and type in another line at the client. This also covers the scenario of the server host being unreachable when the client sends data (i.e., some intermediate router goes down after the connection has been established).

The following steps take place:

- When the server host crashes, nothing is sent out on the existing network connections. Thatis, are assuming the host crashes and is not shut down by an operator.

- We type a line of input to the client, it is written by writen, and is sent by the client TCP as a data segment. The client then blocks in the call to readline, waiting for the echoed reply.
- If watch the network with tcpdump, will see the client TCP continually retransmitting the data segment, trying to receive an ACK from the server. Section 25.11 of TCPv2 shows a typical pattern for TCP retransmissions: Berkeley-derived implementations retransmit the data segment 12 times, waiting for around 9 minutes before giving up. When the client TCP finally gives up (assuming the server host has not been rebooted during this time, or if the server host has not crashed but was unreachable on the network, assuming the host was still unreachable), an error is returned to the client process. Since the client is blocked in the call to readline, it returns an error. Assuming the server host crashed and there were no responses at all to the client's data segments, the error is ETIMEDOUT. But if some intermediate router determined that the server host was unreachable and responded with an ICMP "destination unreachable' message, the error is either EHOSTUNREACH or ENETUNREACH.

Although our client discovers (eventually) that the peer is down or unreachable, there are times when want to detect this quicker than having to wait nine minutes. The solution is to place a timeout on the call to readline.

The server host has crashed only when send data to that host. If want to detect the crashing of the server host even if are not actively sending it data, another technique is required. will discuss the SO_KEEPALIVE socket option.

Crashing and Rebooting of Server Host

To establish a connection between the client and server and then assume the server host crashes and reboots. In the previous section, the server host was still down when sent it data. Here, will let the server host reboot before sending it data. The easiest way to simulate this is to establish the connection, disconnect the server from the network, shut down the server host and then reboot it, and then reconnect the server host to the network. do not want the client to see the server host shut down.

As stated in the previous section, if the client is not actively sending data to the server when the server host crashes, the client is not aware that the server host has crashed. (This assumes are not using the SO_KEEPALIVE socket option.) The following steps take place:

- We start the server and then the client. type a line to verify that the connection is established.
- The server host crashes and reboots.
- We type a line of input to the client, which is sent as a TCP data segment to the server host.
- When the server host reboots after crashing, its TCP loses all information about connections that existed before the crash. Therefore, the server TCP responds to the received data segment from the client with an RST.

- Our client is blocked in the call to readline when the RST is received, causing readline to return the error ECONNRESET.

If it is important for our client to detect the crashing of the server host, even if the client is not actively sending data, then some other technique (such as the SO_KEEPALIVE socket option or some client/server heartbeat function) is required.

Shutdown of Server Host

When a Unix system is shut down, the init process normally sends the SIGTERM signal to all processes (we can catch this signal), waits some fixed amount of time (often between 5 and 20 seconds), and then sends the SIGKILL signal (which cannot catch) to any processes still running. This gives all running processes a short amount of time to clean up and terminate. If do not catch SIGTERM and terminate, our server will be terminated by the SIGKILL signal. When the process terminates, all open descriptors are closed. As stated there, must use the select or poll function in our client to have the client detect the termination of the server process as soon as it occurs.

I/O Multiplexing: The select and poll Functions

Introduction

The TCP client handling two inputs at the same time: standard input and a TCP socket. encountered a problem when the client was blocked in a call to fgets (on standard input) and the server process was killed. The server TCP correctly sent a FIN to the client TCP, but since the client process was blocked reading from standard input, it never saw the EOF until it read from the socket (possibly much later). What need is the capability to tell the kernel that want to be notified if one or more I/O conditions are ready (i.e., input is ready to be read, or the descriptor is capable of taking more output). This capability is called I/O multiplexing and is provided by the select and poll functions. will also cover a newer POSIX variation of the former, called pselect.

Some systems provide more advanced ways for processes to wait for a list of events. A poll device is one mechanism provided in different forms by different vendors.

I/O multiplexing is typically used in networking applications in the following scenarios:

- When a client is handling multiple descriptors (normally interactive input and a network socket), I/O multiplexing should be used. This is the scenario described previously.
- It is possible, but rare, for a client to handle multiple sockets at the same time. will show an example of this using select in the context of a Web client.
- If a TCP server handles both a listening socket and its connected sockets, I/O multiplexing is normally used.
- If a server handles both TCP and UDP, I/O multiplexing is normally used.

- If a server handles multiple services and perhaps multiple protocols, I/O multiplexing is normally used.

I/O multiplexing is not limited to network programming. Many nontrivial applications find a need for these techniques.

I/O Models

The basic differences in the five I/O models that are available to us under Unix:

- blocking I/O
- nonblocking I/O
- I/O multiplexing (select and poll)
- signal driven I/O (SIGIO)
- asynchronous I/O (the POSIX aio_functions)

To encounter the different I/O models described in more detail in later chapters. As show in all the examples in this section, there are normally two distinct phases for an input operation:

- Waiting for the data to be ready
- Copying the data from the kernel to the process

For an input operation on a socket, the first step normally involves waiting for data to arrive on the network. When the packet arrives, it is copied into a buffer within the kernel. The second step is copying this data from the kernel's buffer into our application buffer.

Blocking I/O Model

The most prevalent model for I/O is the blocking I/O model, which have used for all our examples so far in the text. By default, all sockets are blocking. Using a datagram socket for our examples.

The UDP instead of TCP because with UDP, the concept of data being "ready" to read is simple: either an entire datagram has been received or it has not. With TCP it gets more complicated, as additional variables such as the socket's low-water mark come into play.

The recvfrom as a system call because are differentiating between our application and the kernel. Regardless of how recvfrom is implemented (as a system call on a Berkeley-derived kernel or as a function that invokes the getmsg system call on a System V kernel), there is normally a switch from running in the application to running in the kernel, followed at some time later by a return to the application.

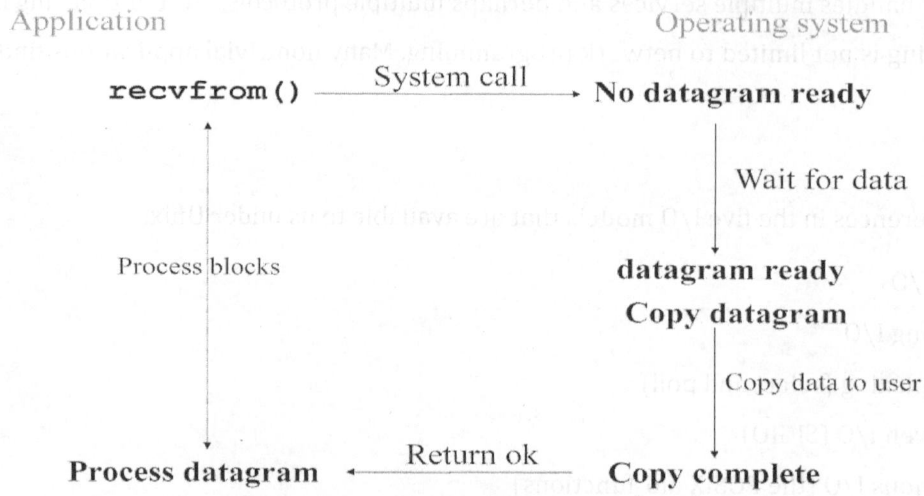

Blocking I/O model

The process calls recvfrom and the system call does not return until the datagram arrives and is copied into our application buffer, or an error occurs. The most common error is the system call being interrupted by a signal. The process is blocked the entire time from when it calls recvfrom until it returns. When recvfrom returns successfully, our application processes the datagram.

Nonblocking I/O Model

When set a socket to be nonblocking, are telling the kernel "when an I/O operation that I request cannot be completed without putting the process to sleep, do not put the process to sleep, but return an error instead." will describe nonblocking I/O.

The first three times that call recvfrom, there is no data to return, so the kernel immediately returns an error of EWOULDBLOCK instead. The fourth time call recvfrom, a datagram is ready, it is copied into our application buffer, and recvfrom returns successfully. then process the data. When an application sits in a loop calling recvfrom on a nonblocking descriptor like this, it is called polling. The application is continually polling the kernel to see if some operation is ready. This is often a waste of CPU time, but this model is occasionally encountered, normally on systems dedicated to one function.

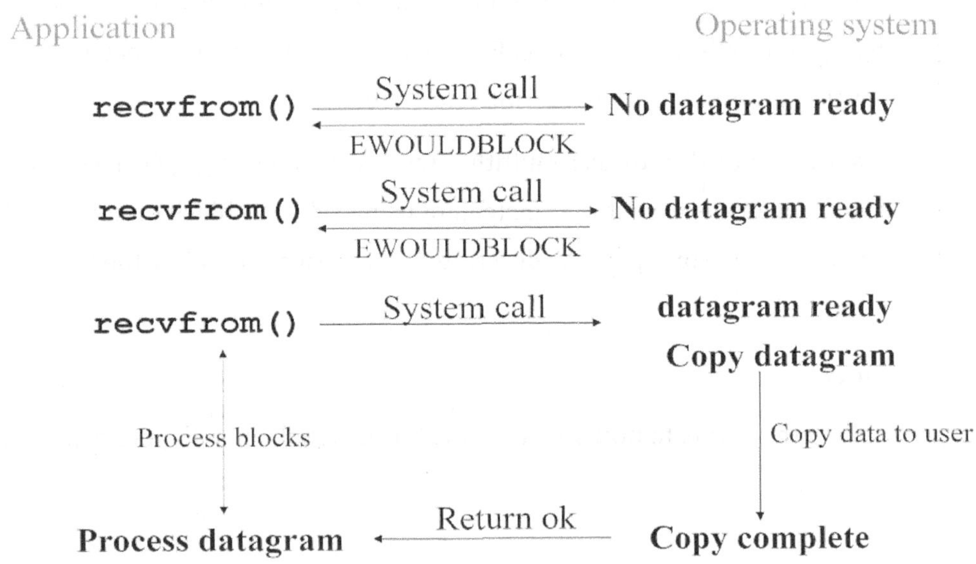

Nonblocking I/O model

I/O Multiplexing Model

With I/O multiplexing, call select or poll and block in one of these two system calls, instead of blocking in the actual I/O system call. el.

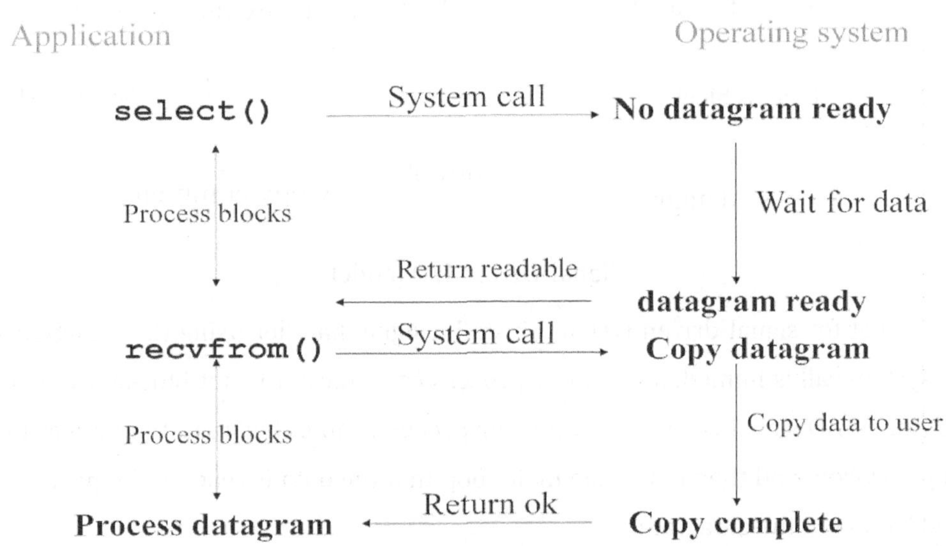

I/O multiplexing model

To block in a call to select, waiting for the datagram socket to be readable. When select returns that the socket is readable, then call recvfrom to copy the datagram into our application buffer.

Comparing, there does not appear to be any advantage, and in fact, there is a slight disadvantage because using select requires two system calls instead of one. But the advantage in using select, which will see later in this chapter, is that can wait for more than one descriptor to be ready.

Another closely related I/O model is to use multithreading with blocking I/O. That model very closely resembles the model described above, except that instead of using select to block on multiple file descriptors, the program uses multiple threads (one per file descriptor), and each thread is then free to call blocking system calls like recvfrom.

Signal-Driven I/O Model

To use signals, telling the kernel to notify us with the SIGIO signal when the descriptor is ready.

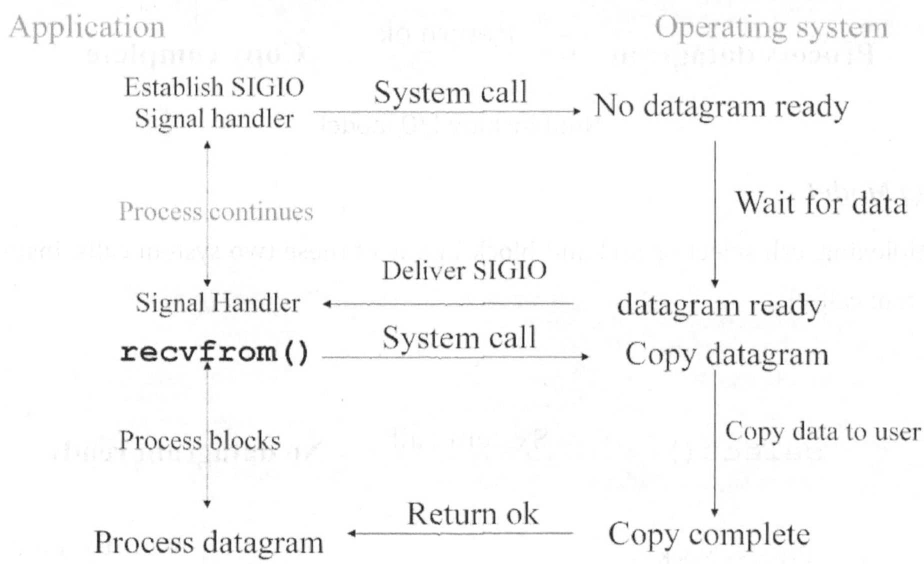

Signal-Driven I/O model

To enable the socket for signal-driven I/O and install a signal handler using the sigaction system call. The return from this system call is immediate and our process continues; it is not blocked. When the datagram is ready to be read, the SIGIO signal is generated for our process. can either read the datagram from the signal handler by calling recvfrom and then notify the main loop that the data is ready to be processed, or can notify the main loop and let it read the datagram.

Regardless of how handle the signal, the advantage to this model is that are not blocked while waiting for the datagram to arrive. The main loop can continue executing and just wait to be notified by the signal handler that either the data is ready to process or the datagram is ready to be read.

Asynchronous I/O Model

Asynchronous I/O is defined by the POSIX specification, and various differences in the real-time functions that appeared in the various standards which came together to form the current POSIX specification have been reconciled. In general, these functions work by telling the kernel to start the operation and to notify us when the entire operation (including the copy of the data from the kernel to our buffer) is complete. The main difference between this model and the signal-driven I/O model in the previous section is that with signal-driven I/O, the kernel tells us when an I/O operation can be initiated, but with asynchronous I/O, the kernel tells us when an I/O operation is complete.

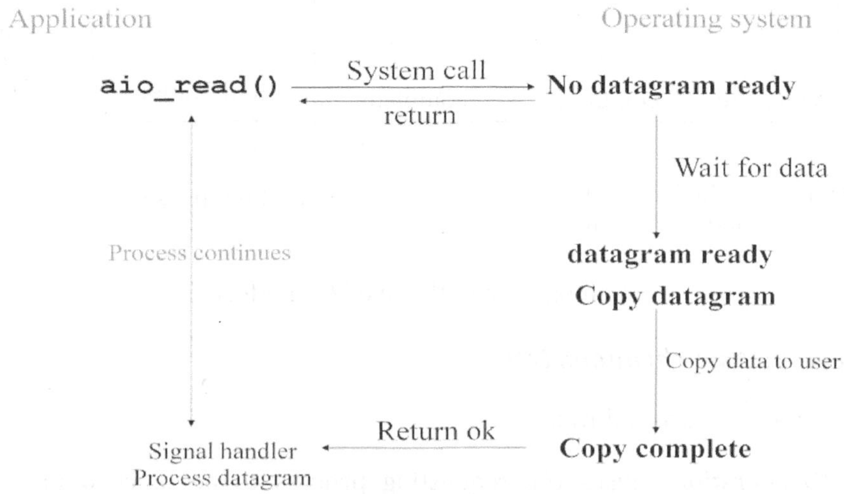

Asynchronous I/O model

To call aio_read (the POSIX asynchronous I/O functions begin with aio_ or lio_) and pass the kernel the descriptor, buffer pointer, buffer size (the same three arguments for read), file offset (similar to lseek), and how to notify us when the entire operation is complete. This system call returns immediately and our process is not blocked while waiting for the I/O to complete. assume in this example that ask the kernel to generate some signal when the operation is complete. This signal is not generated until the data has been copied into our application buffer, which is different from the signal-driven I/O model.

As of this writing, few systems support POSIX asynchronous I/O. are not certain, for example, if systems will support it for sockets. Our use of it here is as an example to compare against the signal-driven I/O model.

Comparison of the I/O Models

A comparison of the five different I/O models. It shows that the main difference between the first four models is the first phase, as the second phase in the first four models is the same: the process is blocked in a call to recvfrom while the data is copied from the kernel to the caller's buffer. Asynchronous I/O, however, handles both phases and is different from the first four.

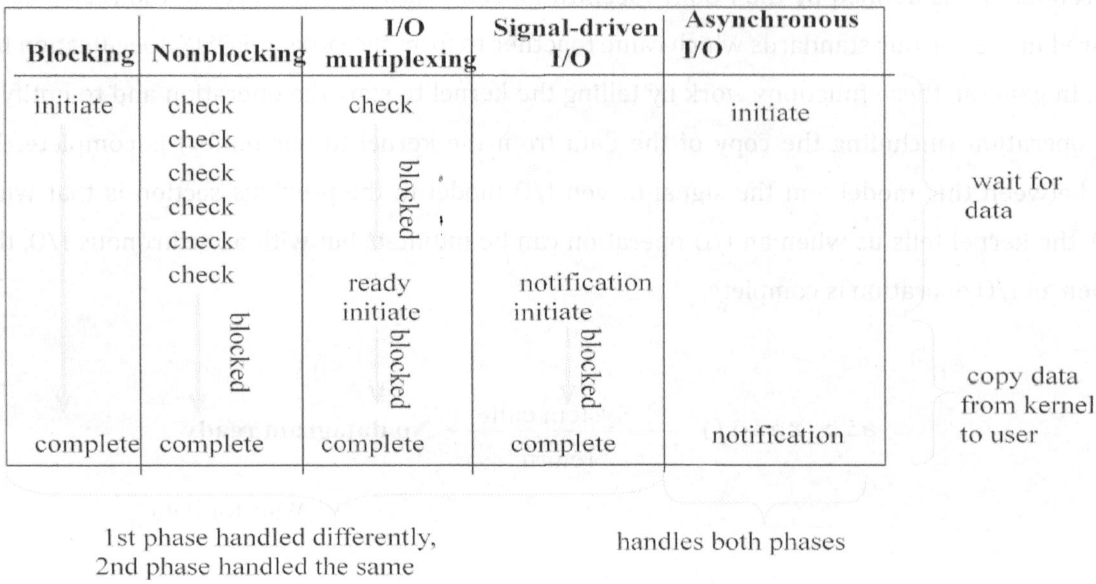

Comparison of the five I/O models

Synchronous I/O versus Asynchronous I/O

POSIX defines these two terms as follows:

A synchronous I/O operation causes the requesting process to be blocked until that I/O operation completes.

An asynchronous I/O operation does not cause the requesting process to be blocked. Using these definitions, the first four I/O models—blocking, nonblocking, I/O multiplexing, and signal-driven I/O—are all synchronous because the actual I/O operation (recvfrom) blocks the process. Only the asynchronous I/O model matches the asynchronous I/O definition.

select Function

This function allows the process to instruct the kernel to wait for any one of multiple events to occur and to wake up the process only when one or more of these events occurs or when a specified amount of time has passed.

As an example, can call select and tell the kernel to return only when:

- Any of the descriptors in the set {1, 4, 5} are ready for reading
- Any of the descriptors in the set {2, 7} are ready for writing
- Any of the descriptors in the set {1, 4} have an exception condition pending 10.2 seconds have elapsed

That is, tell the kernel what descriptors are interested in (for reading, writing, or an exception condition) and how long to wait. The descriptors in which are interested are not restricted to sockets; any descriptor can be tested using select.

Berkeley-derived implementations have always allowed I/O multiplexing with any descriptor. SVR3 originally limited I/O multiplexing to descriptors that were STREAMS devices, but this limitation was removed with SVR4.

```
#include <sys/select.h>
#include <sys/time.h>
int select(int maxfdp1, fd_set *readset, fd_set *writeset, fd_set *exceptset, const
struct timeval *timeout);
Returns: positive count of ready descriptors, 0 on timeout, –1 on error
```

A timeval structure specifies the number of seconds and microseconds.

```
struct timeval {
long tv_sec; /* seconds */
long tv_usec; /* microseconds */
};
```

There are three possibilities

- Wait forever— Return only when one of the specified descriptors is ready for I/O. For this, specify the timeout argument as a null pointer.
- Wait up to a fixed amount of time— Return when one of the specified descriptors is ready for I/O, but do not wait beyond the number of seconds and microseconds specified in the timeval structure pointed to by the timeout argument.
- Do not wait at all— Return immediately after checking the descriptors. This is called polling. To specify this, the timeout argument must point to a timeval structure and the timer value (the number of seconds and microseconds specified by the structure) must be 0.

The wait in the first two scenarios is normally interrupted if the process catches a signal and returns from the signal handler.

Berkeley-derived kernels never automatically restart select (p. 527 of TCPv2), while SVR4 will if the SA_RESTART flag is specified when the signal handler is installed. This means that for portability, must be prepared for select to return an error of EINTR if are catching signals.

Although the timeval structure lets us specify a resolution in microseconds, the actual resolution supported by the kernel is often more coarse. For example, many Unix kernels round the timeout value up to a multiple of

10 ms. There is also a scheduling latency involved, meaning it takes some time after the timer expires before the kernel schedules this process to run.

On some systems, select will fail with EINVAL if the tv_sec field in the timeout is over 100 million seconds. Of course, that's a very large timeout (over three years) and likely not very useful, but the point is that the timeval structure can represent values that are not supported by select.

The const qualifier on the timeout argument means it is not modified by select on return. For example, if specify a time limit of 10 seconds, and select returns before the timer expires with one or more of the descriptors ready or with an error of EINTR, the timeval structure is not updated with the number of seconds remaining when the function returns. If wish to know this value, must obtain the system time before calling select, and then again when it returns, and subtract the two (any robust program will take into account that the system time may be adjusted by either the administrator or by a daemon like ntpd occasionally).

Some Linux versions modify the timeval structure. Therefore, for portability, assume the timeval structure is undefined upon return, and initialize it before each call to select. POSIX specifies the const qualifier.

The three middle arguments, readset, writeset, and exceptset, specify the descriptors that want the kernel to test for reading, writing, and exception conditions. There are only two exception conditions currently supported:

The arrival of out-of-band data for a socket.

The presence of control status information to be read from the master side of a pseudo terminal that has been put into packet mode. do not talk about pseudo-terminals in this book.

A design problem is how to specify one or more descriptor values for each of these three

arguments. select uses descriptor sets, typically an array of integers, with each bit in each integer corresponding to a descriptor. For example, using 32-bit integers, the first element of the array corresponds to descriptors 0 through 31, the second element of the array corresponds to descriptors 32 through 63, and so on. All the implementation details are irrelevant to the application and are hidden in the fd_set datatype and the following four macros:

```
void FD_ZERO(fd_set *fdset); /* clear all bits in fdset */
void FD_SET(int fd, fd_set *fdset); /* turn on the bit for fd in fdset */
void FD_CLR(int fd, fd_set *fdset); /* turn off the bit for fd in fdset */
int FD_ISSET(int fd, fd_set *fdset); /* is the bit for fd on in fdset ? */
```

To allocate a descriptor set of the fd_set datatype, set and test the bits in the set using these macros, and can also assign it to another descriptor set across an equals sign (=) in C.

An array of integers using one bit per descriptor, is just one possible way to implement select. Nevertheless, it is common to refer to the individual descriptors within a descriptor set as bits, as in "turn on the bit for the listening descriptor in the read set."

The poll function uses a completely different representation: a variable-length array of structures with one structure per descriptor. For example, to define a variable of type fd_set and then turn on the bits for descriptors 1, 4, and 5, write

```
fd_set rset;
FD_ZERO(&rset); /* initialize the set: all bits off */
FD_SET(1, &rset); /* turn on bit for fd 1 */
FD_SET(4, &rset); /* turn on bit for fd 4 */
FD_SET(5, &rset); /* turn on bit for fd 5 */
```

It is important to initialize the set, since unpredictable results can occur if the set is allocated as an automatic variable and not initialized.

Any of the middle three arguments to select, readset, writeset, or exceptset, can be specified as a null pointer if are not interested in that condition. Indeed, if all three pointers are null, then have a higher precision timer than the normal Unix sleep function (which sleeps for multiples of a second). The poll function provides similar functionality. Figures C.9 and C.10 of APUE show a sleep_us function implemented using both select and poll that sleeps for multiples of a microsecond.

The maxfdp1 argument specifies the number of descriptors to be tested. Its value is the maximum descriptor to be tested plus one (hence our name of maxfdp1). The descriptors 0, 1, 2, up through and including maxfdp1-1 are tested.

The constant FD_SETSIZE, defined by including <sys/select.h>, is the number of descriptors in the fd_set datatype. Its value is often 1024, but few programs use that many descriptors. The maxfdp1 argument forces us to calculate the largest descriptor that are interested in and then tell the kernel this value. For example, given the previous code that turns on the indicators for descriptors 1, 4, and 5, the maxfdp1 value is 6. The reason it is 6 and not 5 is that are specifying the number of descriptors, not the largest value, and descriptors start at 0.

The reason this argument exists, along with the burden of calculating its value, is purely for efficiency. Although each fd_set has room for many descriptors, typically 1,024, this is much more than the number used by a typical process. The kernel gains efficiency by not copying unneeded portions of the descriptor set between the process and the kernel, and by not testing bits that are always 0.

Select modifies the descriptor sets pointed to by the readset, writeset, and exceptset pointers.

These three arguments are value-result arguments. When call the function, specify the values of the descriptors that are interested in, and on return, the result indicates which descriptors are ready. use the FD_ISSET macro on return to test a specific descriptor in an fd_set structure. Any descriptor that is not ready on return will have its corresponding bit cleared in the descriptor set. To handle this, turn on all the bits in which are interested in all the descriptor sets each time call select.

The two most common programming errors when using select are to forget to add one to the largest descriptor number and to forget that the descriptor sets are value-result arguments.

The second error results in select being called with a bit set to 0 in the descriptor set, when think that bit is 1.

The return value from this function indicates the total number of bits that are ready across all the descriptor sets. If the timer value expires before any of the descriptors are ready, a value of 0 is returned. A return value of –1 indicates an error (which can happen, for example, if the function is interrupted by a caught signal).

Early releases of SVR4 had a bug in their implementation of select: If the same bit was on in multiple sets, say a descriptor was ready for both reading and writing, it was counted only once.

Under What Conditions Is a Descriptor Ready?

The waiting for a descriptor to become ready for I/O (reading or writing) or to have an exception condition pending on it (out-of-band data). While readability and writ ability are obvious for descriptors such as regular files, must be more specific about the conditions that cause select to return "ready" for sockets.

1. A socket is ready for reading if any of the following four conditions is true:
   - The number of bytes of data in the socket receive buffer is greater than or equal to the current size of the low-water mark for the socket receive buffer. A read operation on the socket will not block and will return a value greater than 0 (i.e., the data that is ready to be read). can set this low-water mark using the SO_RCVLOWAT socket option. It defaults to 1 for TCP and UDP sockets.
   - The read half of the connection is closed (i.e., a TCP connection that has received a FIN). A read operation on the socket will not block and will return 0 (i.e., EOF).
   - The socket is a listening socket and the number of completed connections is nonzero. An accept on the listening socket will normally not block, although will describe a timing condition under which the accept can block.

- A socket error is pending. A read operation on the socket will not block and will return an error (–1) with errno set to the specific error condition. These pending errors can also be fetched and cleared by calling getsockopt and specifying the SO_ERROR socket option.

2. A socket is ready for writing if any of the following four conditions is true:
   - The number of bytes of available space in the socket send buffer is greater than or equal to the current size of the low-water mark for the socket send buffer and either: (i) the socket is connected, or (ii) the socket does not require a connection (e.g., UDP). This means that if set the socket to nonblocking, a write operation will not block and will return a positive value (e.g., the number of bytes accepted by the transport layer). can set this low-water mark using the SO_SNDLOWAT socket option. This low-water mark normally defaults to 2048 for TCP and UDP sockets.
   - The write half of the connection is closed. A write operation on the socket will generate SIGPIPE.
   - A socket using a non-blocking connect has completed the connection, or the connect has failed.
   - A socket error is pending. A write operation on the socket will not block and will return an error (–1) with errno set to the specific error condition. These pending errors can also be fetched and cleared by calling getsockopt with the SO_ERROR socket option.
3. A socket has an exception condition pending if there is out-of-band data for the socket or the socket is still at the out-of-band mark. (We will describe out-of-band data.

Our definitions of "readable" and "writable" are taken directly from the kernel's soreadable and sowriteable macros on pp. 530–531 of TCPv2. Similarly, our definition of the "exception condition" for a socket is from the soo_select function on these same pages.

Notice that when an error occurs on a socket, it is marked as both readable and writable by select.

The purpose of the receive and send low-water marks is to give the application control over how much data must be available for reading or how much space must be available for writing before select returns a readable or writable status. For example, if know that our application has nothing productive to do unless at least 64 bytes of data are present, can set the receive lowwater mark to 64 to prevent select from waking us up if less than 64 bytes are ready for reading.

As long as the send low-water mark for a UDP socket is less than the send buffer size (which should always be the default relationship), the UDP socket is always writable, since a connection is not required.

Maximum Number of Descriptors for select

That most applications do not use lots of descriptors. It is rare, for example, to find an application that uses hundreds of descriptors. But, such applications do exist, and they often use select to multiplex the descriptors.

When select was originally designed, the OS normally had an upper limit on the maximum number of descriptors per process and select just used this same limit.

Many implementations have declarations similar to the following, which are taken from the 4.4BSD <sys/types.h> header:

```
/*
 * Select uses bitmasks of file descriptors in longs. These macros
 * manipulate such bit fields (the filesystem macros use chars).
 * FD_SETSIZE may be defined by the user, but the default here should
 * be enough for most uses.
 */
#ifndef FD_SETSIZE
#define FD_SETSIZE 256
#endif
```

This makes us think that can just #define FD_SETSIZE to some larger value before including this header to increase the size of the descriptor sets used by select. Unfortunately, this normally does not work.

To see what is wrong, notice that Figure 16.53 of TCPv2 declares three descriptor sets within the kernel and also uses the kernel's definition of FD_SETSIZE as the upper limit. The only way to increase the size of the descriptor sets is to increase the value of FD_SETSIZE and then recompile the kernel. Changing the value without recompiling the kernel is inadequate.

Some vendors are changing their implementation of select to allow the process to define FD_SETSIZE to a larger value than the default. BSD/OS has changed the kernel implementation to allow larger descriptor sets, and it also provides four new FD_xxx macros to dynamically allocate and manipulate these larger sets. From a portability standpoint, however, beware of using large descriptor sets.

shutdown Function

The normal way to terminate a network connection is to call the close function. But, there are two limitations with close that can be avoided with shutdown:

- close decrements the descriptor's reference count and closes the socket only if the count reaches 0. With shutdown, can initiate TCP's normal connection termination sequence.
- close terminates both directions of data transfer, reading and writing. Since a TCP connection is full-duplex, there are times when want to tell the other end that have finished sending, even though that end might have more data to send us. This is the scenario encountered in the previous section with batch input to our str_cli function.

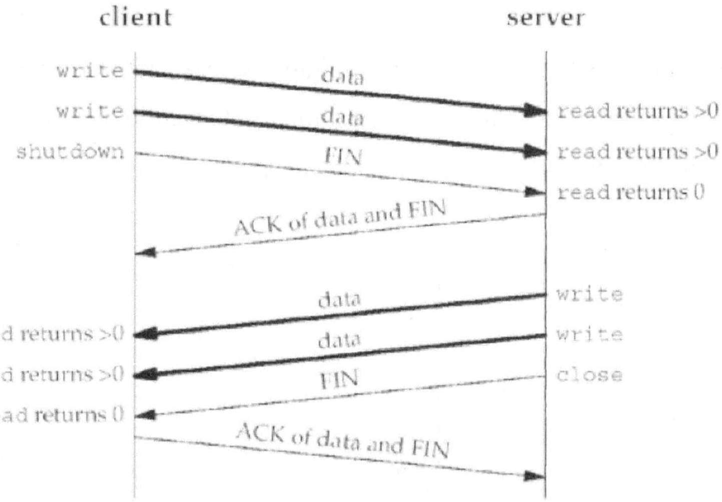

Calling shutdown to close half of a TCP connection

```
#include <sys/socket.h>
int shutdown(int sockfd, int howto);
Returns: 0 if OK, -1 on error
```

The action of the function depends on the value of the howto argument.

SHUT_RD The read half of the connection is closed— No more data can be received on the socket and any data currently in the socket receive buffer is discarded. The process can no longer issue any of the read functions on the socket. Any data received after this call for a TCP socket is acknowledged and then silently discarded. By default, everything written to a routing socket loops back as possible input to all routing sockets on the host. Some programs call shutdown with a second argument of SHUT_RD to prevent the loopback copy. An alternative way to prevent this loopback copy is to clear the SO_USELOOPBACK socket option.

SHUT_WR The write half of the connection is closed— In the case of TCP, this is called a halfclose (Section 18.5 of TCPv1). Any data currently in the socket send buffer will be sent, followed by TCP's normal connection termination sequence. As mentioned earlier, this closing of the write half is done regardless of whether or not the socket descriptor's reference count is currently greater than 0. The process can no longer issue any of the write functions on the socket.

SHUT_RDWR The read half and the write half of the connection are both closed— This is equivalent to calling shutdown twice: first with SHUT_RD and then with SHUT_WR.

The three SHUT_xxx names are defined by the POSIX specification. Typical values for the howto argument that you will encounter will be 0 (close the read half), 1 (close the write half), and 2 (close the read half and the write half).

TCP Echo Server

The TCP echo server and rewrite the server as a single process that uses select to handle any number of clients, instead of forking one child per client. Before showing the code, let's look at the data structures that will use to keep track of the clients.

TCP server before first client has established a connection

The server has a single listening descriptor, which show as a bullet. The server maintains only a read descriptor set. The server is started in the foreground, so descriptors 0, 1, and 2 are set to standard input, output, and error. Therefore, the first available descriptor for the listening socket is 3. also show an array of integers named client that contains the connected socket descriptor for each client. All elements in this array are initialized to –1.

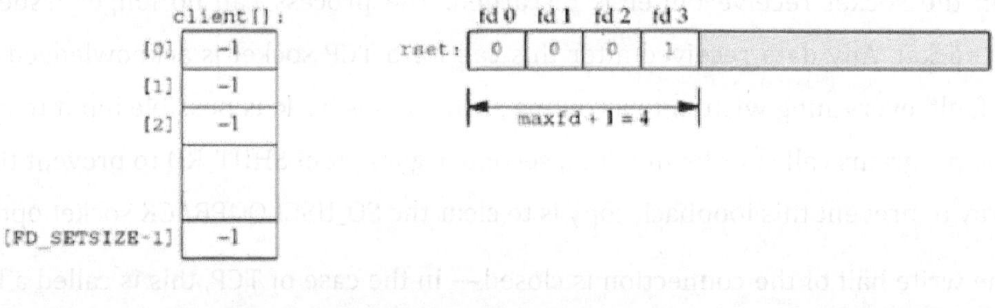

Data structures for TCP server with just a listening socket

The only nonzero entry in the descriptor set is the entry for the listening sockets and the first argument to select will be 4. When the first client establishes a connection with our server, the listening descriptor becomes readable and our server calls accept.

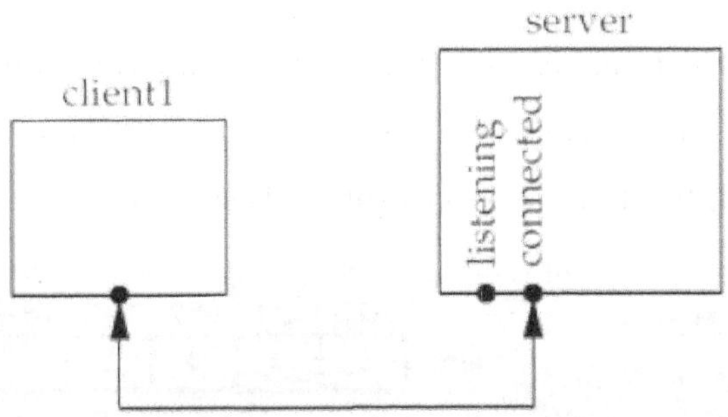

TCP server after first client establishes connection

The server must remember the new connected socket in its client array, and the connected socket must be added to the descriptor set.

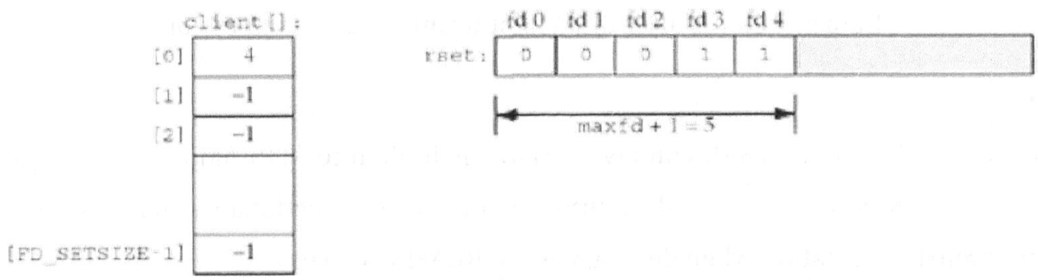

Data structures after first client connection is established

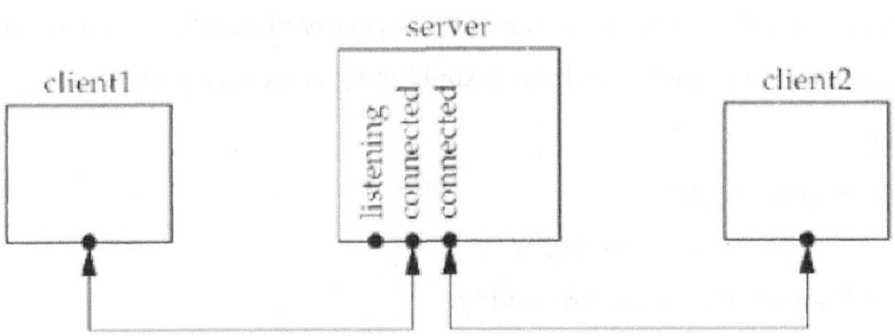

TCP server after second client connection is established

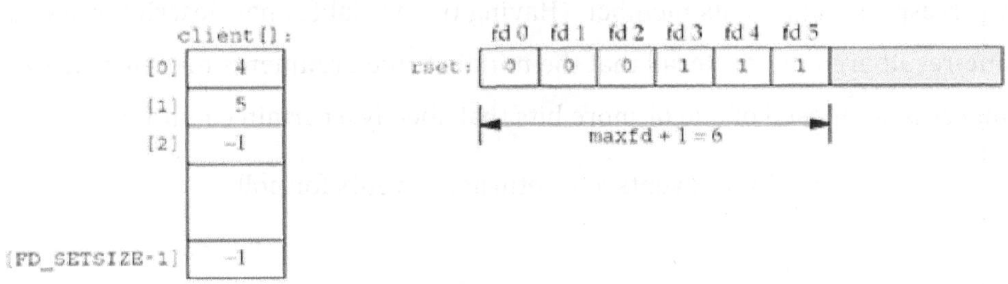

Data structures after second client connection is established

The client TCP sends a FIN, which makes descriptor 4 in the server readable. When our server reads this connected socket, read returns 0. then close this socket and update our data structures accordingly. The value of client [0] is set to –1 and descriptor 4 in the descriptor set is set to 0.

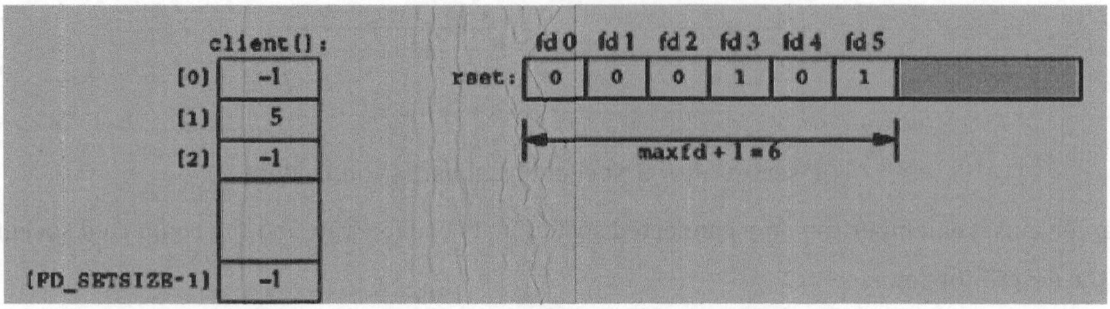

Data structures after first client terminates its connection

poll Function

The poll function originated with SVR3 and was originally limited to STREAMS devices. SVR4 removed this limitation, allowing poll to work with any descriptor. poll provides functionality that is similar to select, but poll provides additional information when dealing with STREAMS devices.

```
#include <poll.h>
int poll (struct pollfd *fdarray, unsigned long nfds, int timeout);
Returns: count of ready descriptors, 0 on timeout, –1 on error
```

The first argument is a pointer to the first element of an array of structures. Each element of the array is a pollfd structure that specifies the conditions to be tested for a given descriptor, fd.

```
struct pollfd {
int fd; /* descriptor to check */
short events; /* events of interest on fd */
short revents; /* events that occurred on fd */
};
```

The conditions to be tested are specified by the events member, and the function returns the status for that descriptor in the corresponding revents member. (Having two variables per descriptor, one a value and one a result, avoids value-result arguments. Recall that the middle three arguments for select are value-result.) Each of these two members is composed of one or more bits that specify a certain condition.

Input events and returned revents for poll

Constant	Input to *events* ?	Result from *revents* ?	Description
POLLIN	•	•	Normal or priority band data can be read
POLLRDNORM	•	•	Normal data can be read
POLLRDBAND	•	•	Priority band data can be read
POLLPRI	•	•	High-priority data can be read
POLLOUT	•	•	Normal data can be written
POLLWRNORM	•	•	Normal data can be written
POLLWRBAND	•	•	Priority band data can be written
POLLERR		•	Error has occurred
POLLHUP		•	Hangup has occurred
POLLNVAL		•	Descriptor is not an open file

The first four constants deal with input, the next three deal with output, and the final three deal with errors. Notice that the final three cannot be set in events, but are always returned in revents when the corresponding condition exists.

There are three classes of data identified by poll: normal, priority band, and high-priority. These terms come from the STREAMS-based implementations. POLLIN can be defined as the logical OR of POLLRDNORM and POLLRDBAND. The POLLIN constant exists from SVR3 implementations that predated the priority bands in SVR4, so the constant remains for backward compatibility. Similarly, POLLOUT is equivalent to POLLWRNORM, with the former predating the latter.

With regard to TCP and UDP sockets, the following conditions cause poll to return the specified revent. Unfortunately, POSIX leaves many holes (i.e., optional ways to return the same condition) in its definition of poll.

- All regular TCP data and all UDP data is considered normal.
- TCP's out-of-band data is considered priority band.
- When the read half of a TCP connection is closed (e.g., a FIN is received), this is also considered normal data and a subsequent read operation will return 0.
- The presence of an error for a TCP connection can be considered either normal data or an error (POLLERR). In either case, a subsequent read will return –1 with errno set to the appropriate value. This handles conditions such as the receipt of an RST or a timeout.
- The availability of a new connection on a listening socket can be considered either normal data or priority data. Most implementations consider this normal data.
- The completion of a nonblocking connect is considered to make a socket writable.

The number of elements in the array of structures is specified by the nfds argument. This argument has been an unsigned long, which seems excessive. An unsigned int would be adequate. Unix 98 defines a new datatype for this argument: nfds_t. The timeout argument specifies how long the function is to wait before returning. A positive value specifies the number of milliseconds to wait.

Timeout values for poll

timeout value	Description
INFTIM	Wait forever
0	Return immediately, do not block
>0	Wait specified number of milliseconds

The constant INFTIM is defined to be a negative value. If the system does not provide a timer with millisecond accuracy, the value is rounded up to the nearest supported value. The POSIX specification requires that INFTIM be defined by including <poll.h>, but many systems still define it in <sys/stropts.h>.

As with select, any timeout set for poll is limited by the implementation's clock resolution (often 10 ms). The return value from poll is –1 if an error occurred, 0 if no descriptors are ready before the timer expires, otherwise it is the number of descriptors that have a nonzero revents member. If are no longer interested in a particular descriptor, just set the fd member of the pollfd structure to a negative value. Then the events member is ignored and the revents member is set to 0 on return.

The FD_SETSIZE and the maximum number of descriptors per descriptor set versus the maximum number of descriptors per process. do not have that problem with poll since it is the caller's responsibility to allocate an array of pollfd structures and then tell the kernel the number of elements in the array. There is no fixed-size datatype similar to fd_set that the kernel knows about. The POSIX specification requires both select and poll. But, from a portability perspective today, more systems support select than poll. Also, POSIX defines pselect, an enhanced version of select that handles signal blocking and provides increased time resolution. Nothing similar is defined for poll.

UNIT-III

QUESTION BANK

PART-A

1. What are the main mechanisms of an IPC package of UNIX?

The main mechanism of an IPC package is to create a communication link between both the related and unrelated processes.

4 mechanisms,

pipes

semaphore

message queue

shared memory

2. What are the limitations of Pipes

- They are half duplex (i.e., data flows in only one direction)
- Pipes can be used only between processes that have a common ancestor. Normally, a pipe is created by a process, that process calls fork, and the pipe is used between the parent and the child.

How is a Pipe created

A pipe is created by calling the pipe function.

```
# include <unistd.h>

int pipe(int filedes[2]);
```

Two file descriptors are returned through the filedes argument: filedes[0] is open for reading, and filedes[1] is open for writing. The output of filedes[1] is the input for filedes[0].

3. How do you create a named pipe

FIFOs are called named pipes. Creating a FIFO is similar to creating a file. Indeed, the pathname for a FIFO exists in the file system.

```
#include <sys/stat.h>

int mkfifo(const char *pathname, mode_t mode);
```

4. What are the uses of FIFOs

- FIFOs are used by shell commands to pass data from one shell pipeline to another without creating intermediate temporary files.
- FIFOs are used as rendezvous points in client-server applications to pass data between the clients and the servers.

5. Mention the use of specifying O_NONBLOCK in a FIFO

- No blocking occurs
- Returns an error ENXIO in case of blocking

6. Define Semaphore

A Semaphore is a counter used to provide access to a shared data object for multiple processes.

7. Define Binary Semaphore

A common form of semaphore is called a Binary semaphore. It controls a single resource and its value is initialized to 1.

8. Define the structure semid_ds

```
struct semid_ds
{
        struct ipc_perm  sem_perm;
        unsigned short  sem_nsems;  /* # of semaphores in set */
        time_t       sem_otime;     /* last-semop() time */
        time_t       sem_ctime;     /* last-change time */
};
```

9. Give the syntax of semctl( ) function and explain its use

semctl( ) function is used to perform various semaphore operations.

```
int  semctl(int semid, int semnum, int cmd, union semun arg);
```

Define Synchronization

Synchronization is needed to allow the sharing of data between threads or processes. The building blocks of Synchronization are

- Mutex
- condition variables

10. Define Condition Variables

A mutex is for locking and a condition variable is for waiting.

```
# include<pthread.h>

int pthread_cond_wait (pthread_cond_t *cptr, pthread_mutex_t *mptr);
```

11. Define granularity in Record Locking

It denotes the size of the object that can be locked. In Posix Record Locking , granularity is single byte.

12. Define Cooperating Processes

Cooperating Processes are processes that work together in some well-defined fashion to accomplish the tasks at hand.

13. Define Message Queue

Message Queues are a linked list of messages stored within the kernel and identified by a message queue identifier.

14. Differentiate msgsnd( ) and msgrcv( )

```
#include <sys/types.h>

#include <sys/ipc.h>

#include <sys/msg.h>
```

Data is placed onto a message queue by calling msgsnd.

```
int msgsnd (int msqid, const void *ptr, SIZE_t nbytes, int flag);
```

Messages are retrieved from a queue by msgrcv.

```
int msgrcv(int msqid, void *ptr,size_t nbytes,long type,int flag);
```

15. What is the use of an identifier in the IPC structure

- The non-negative integer identifier is used to send or fetch a message to or from an IPC structure(message queue, semaphore or shared memory segment)
- The identifier associated with the IPC structure increases until it reaches the maximum positive value for an integer and then wraps around to 0

16. Define Shared Memory

Shared Memory allows two or more processes to share a given region of memory. This is the fastest form of IPC because the data does not need to be copied between the client and server.

17. Give the syntax of shmat( ) function and explain its use

Once a shared memory segment has been created, a process attaches it to its address space by calling shmat.

include <sys/shm.h>

void *shmat (int shmid, void *addr, int flag);

18. What is the need of a key in the IPC structure

Whenever an IPC structure is being created a key must be specified. The data type of this key is the primitive system data type Key_t which is included in the header <sys/types.h>. The key is converted into an identifier by the kernel.

UNIT-III

PART-B (16 MARKS)

1. Write a TCP socket program to implement an Echo server/Echo client.
2. Explain the following concept with suitable example

   i) Shutdown function ii) Server host crashes
3. Explain the following concept with suitable example

   i) Input output models ii) Posix signal
4. Discuss the following scenario of server operations

   i) Crashing of server host ii) Shutdown of server host
5. Expalin about Crashing and rebooting of server host
6. Explain in detail about the various I/O models in Unix operating system
7. Explain in detail about
8. Explain with an example POSIX signal handling
9. Write a note on Boundary conduction
10. Explain in detail about I/O multiplexing

UNIT-IV

SOCKET OPTIONS, ELEMENTARY UDP SOCKETS

Socket Options

Introduction

There are various ways to get and set the options that affect a socket:

- The getsockopt and setsockopt functions
- The fcntl function
- The ioctl function

The setsockopt and getsockopt functions, followed by an example that prints the default value of all the options, and then a detailed description of all the socket options. divide the detailed descriptions into the following categories: generic, IPv4, IPv6, TCP, and SCTP. This detailed coverage can be skipped during a first reading of this chapter, and the individual sections referred to when needed. A few options are discussed in detail in a later chapter, such as the IPv4 and IPv6 multicasting options.

The fcntl function, because it is the POSIX way to set a socket for nonblocking I/O, signal-driven I/O, and to set the owner of a socket.

getsockopt and setsockopt Functions

These two functions apply only to sockets.

```
#include <sys/socket.h>
int getsockopt(int sockfd, int level, int optname, void *optval, socklen_t *optlen);
int setsockopt(int sockfd, int level, int optname, const void *optval socklen_t optlen);
Both return: 0 if OK,–1 on error
```

sockfd must refer to an open socket descriptor. level specifies the code in the system that interprets the option: the general socket code or some protocol-specific code (e.g., IPv4, IPv6, TCP, or SCTP).

optval is a pointer to a variable from which the new value of the option is fetched by setsockopt, or into which the current value of the option is stored by getsockopt. The size of this variable is specified by the final argument, as a value for setsockopt and as a value-result for getsockopt.

There are two basic types of options: binary options that enable or disable a certain feature (flags), and options that fetch and return specific values that can either set or examine (values). The column labeled "Flag" specifies if the option is a flag option. When calling getsockopt for these flag options, *optval is an integer. The value returned in *optval is zero if the option is disabled, or nonzero if the option is enabled. Similarly, setsockopt requires a nonzero *optval to turn the option on, and a zero value to turn the option off. If the

"Flag" column does not contain a "•," then the option is used to pass a value of the specified datatype between the user process and the system. Subsequent sections of this chapter will give additional details on the options that affect a socket.

Generic Socket Options

These options are protocol-independent (that is, they are handled by the protocol-independent code within the kernel, not by one particular protocol module such as IPv4), but some of the options apply to only certain types of sockets. For example, even though the SO_BROADCAST socket option is called "generic," it applies only to datagram sockets.

SO_BROADCAST Socket Option

This option enables or disables the ability of the process to send broadcast messages. Broadcasting is supported for only datagram sockets and only on networks that support the concept of a broadcast message (e.g., Ethernet, token ring, etc.). You cannot broadcast on a point-to-point link or any connection-based transport protocol such as SCTP or TCP.

Since an application must set this socket option before sending a broadcast datagram, it prevents a process from sending a broadcast when the application was never designed to broadcast. For example, a UDP application might take the destination IP address as a command-line argument, but the application never intended for a user to type in a broadcast address. Rather than forcing the application to try to determine if a given address is a broadcast address or not, the test is in the kernel: If the destination address is a broadcast address and this socket option is not set, EACCES is returned.

SO_DEBUG Socket Option

This option is supported only by TCP. When enabled for a TCP socket, the kernel keeps track of detailed information about all the packets sent or received by TCP for the socket. These are kept in a circular buffer within the kernel that can be examined with the trpt program. Pages 916–920 of TCPv2 provide additional details and an example that uses this option.

SO_DONTROUTE Socket Option

This option specifies that outgoing packets are to bypass the normal routing mechanisms of the underlying protocol. For example, with IPv4, the packet is directed to the appropriate local interface, as specified by the network and subnet portions of the destination address. If the local interface cannot be determined from the destination address (e.g., the destination is not on the other end of a point-to-point link, or is not on a shared network), ENETUNREACH is returned. The equivalent of this option can also be applied to individual datagrams using the MSG_DONTROUTE flag with the send, sendto, or sendmsg functions.

This option is often used by routing daemons (e.g., routed and gated) to bypass the routing table and force a packet to be sent out a particular interface.

SO_ERROR Socket Option

When an error occurs on a socket, the protocol module in a Berkeley-derived kernel sets a variable named so_error for that socket to one of the standard Unix Exxx values. This is called the pending error for the socket. The process can be immediately notified of the error in one of two ways:

1. If the process is blocked in a call to select on the socket, for either readability or writability, select returns with either or both conditions set.
2. If the process is using signal-driven I/O, the SIGIO signal is generated for either the process or the process group.

The process can then obtain the value of so_error by fetching the SO_ERROR socket option. The integer value returned by getsockopt is the pending error for the socket. The value of so_error is then reset to 0 by the kernel.

If so_error is nonzero when the process calls read and there is no data to return, read returns–1 with errno set to the value of so_error. The value of so_error is then reset to 0. If there is data queued for the socket, that data is returned by read instead of the error condition. If so_error is nonzero when the process calls write, -1 is returned with errno set to the value of so_error and so_error is reset to 0.

There is a bug in the code in that so_error is not reset to 0. This has been fixed in most modern releases. Anytime the pending error for a socket is returned, it must be reset to 0.

SO_KEEPALIVE Socket Option

When the keep-alive option is set for a TCP socket and no data has been exchanged across the socket in either direction for two hours, TCP automatically sends a keep-alive probe to the peer.

This probe is a TCP segment to which the peer must respond. One of three scenarios results:

1. The peer responds with the expected ACK. The application is not notified. TCP will send another probe following another two hours of inactivity.
2. The peer responds with an RST, which tells the local TCP that the peer host has crashed and rebooted. The socket's pending error is set to ECONNRESET and the socket is closed.
3. There is no response from the peer to the keep-alive probe. Berkeley-derived TCPs send 8 additional probes, 75 seconds apart, trying to elicit a response. TCP will give up if there is no response within 11 minutes and 15 seconds after sending the first probe.

SO_LINGER Socket Option

This option specifies how the close function operates for a connection-oriented protocol (e.g., for TCP and SCTP, but not for UDP). By default, close returns immediately, but if there is any data still remaining in the socket send buffer, the system will try to deliver the data to the peer.

The SO_LINGER socket option lets us change this default. This option requires the following structure to be passed between the user process and the kernel. It is defined by including

```
<sys/socket.h>.
struct linger {
int l_onoff; /* 0=off, nonzero=on */
int l_linger; /* linger time, POSIX specifies units as seconds */
};
```

Calling setsockopt leads to one of the following three scenarios, depending on the values of the two structure members:

If l_onoff is 0, the option is turned off. The value of l_linger is ignored and the previously discussed TCP default applies: close returns immediately.

If l_onoff is nonzero and l_linger is zero, TCP aborts the connection when it is closed (pp. 1019–1020 of TCPv2). That is, TCP discards any data still remaining in the socket send buffer and sends an RST to the peer, not the normal four-packet connection termination sequence. This avoids TCP's TIME_WAIT state, but in doing so, leaves open the possibility of another incarnation of this connection being created within 2MSL seconds and having old duplicate segments from the just-terminated connection being incorrectly delivered to the new incarnation.

SCTP will also do an abortive close of the socket by sending an ABORT chunk to the peer (see Section 9.2 of [Stewart and Xie 2001]) when l_onoff is nonzero and l_linger is zero.

Occasional USENET postings advocate the use of this feature just to avoid the TIME_WAIT state and to be able to restart a listening server even if connections are still in use with the server's well-known port. This should NOT be done and could lead to data corruption, as detailed in RFC 1337 [Braden 1992]. Instead, the SO_REUSEADDR socket option should always be used in the server before the call to bind, as will describe shortly. The TIME_WAIT state is our friend and is there to help us (i.e., to let old duplicate segments expire in the network).

There are certain circumstances which warrant using this feature to send an abortive close. One example is an RS-232 terminal server, which might hang forever in CLOSE_WAIT trying to deliver data to a struck terminal port, but would properly reset the stuck port if it got an RST to discard the pending data.

If l_onoff is nonzero and l_linger is nonzero, then the kernel will linger when the socket is closed (p. 472 of TCPv2). That is, if there is any data still remaining in the socket send buffer, the process is put to sleep until either: (i) all the data is sent and acknowledged by the peer TCP, or (ii) the linger time expires. If the socket has been set to nonblocking, it will not wait for the close to complete, even if the linger time is nonzero. When using this feature of the SO_LINGER option, it is important for the application to check the return value from close, because if the linger time expires before the remaining data is sent and acknowledged, close returns EWOULDBLOCK and any remaining data in the send buffer is discarded.

We now need to see exactly when a close on a socket returns given the various scenarios looked at. assume that the client writes data to the socket and then calls close.

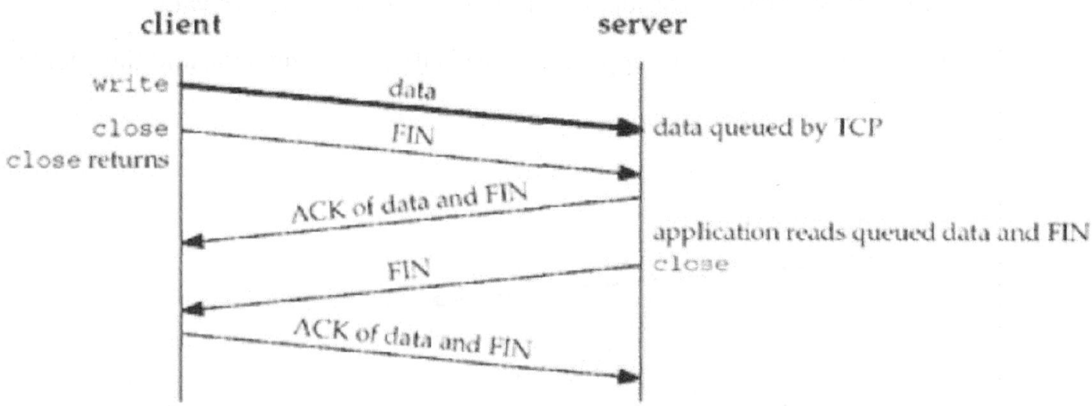

Default operation of close: it returns immediately

When the client's data arrives, the server is temporarily busy, so the data is added to the socket receive buffer by its TCP. Similarly, the next segment, the client's FIN, is also added to the socket receive buffer (in whatever manner the implementation records that a FIN has been received on the connection). But by default, the client's close returns immediately. As show in this scenario, the client's close can return before the server reads the remaining data in its socket receive buffer. Therefore, it is possible for the server host to crash before the server application reads this remaining data, and the client application will never know.

The client can set the SO_LINGER socket option, specifying some positive linger time. When this occurs, the client's close does not return until all the client's data and its FIN have been acknowledged by the server TCP.

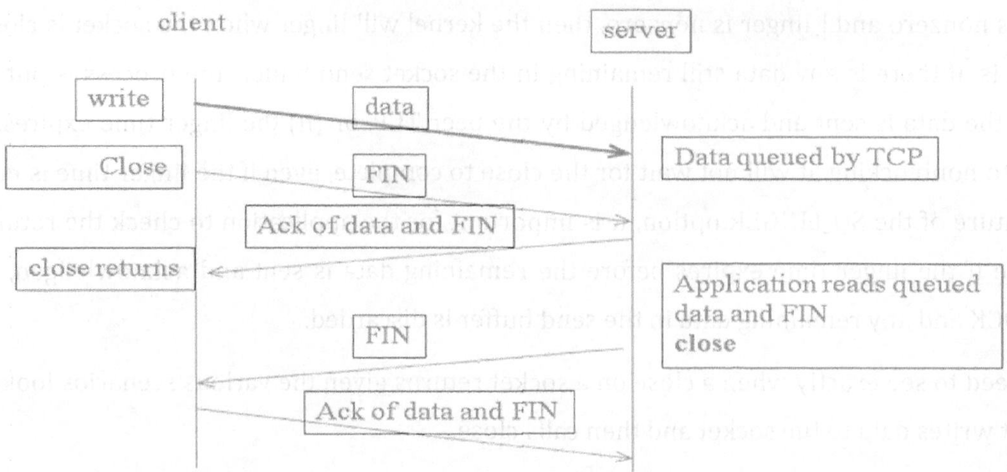

close with SO_LINGER socket option set and l_linger a positive value

The server host can crash before the server application reads its remaining data, and the client application will never know.

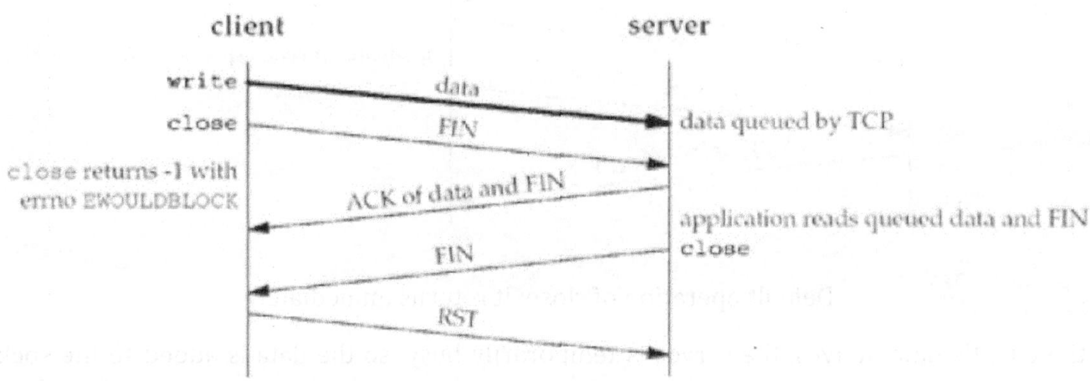

close with SO_LINGER socket option set and l_linger a small positive value

The basic principle here is that a successful return from close, with the SO_LINGER socket option set, only tells us that the data sent (and our FIN) have been acknowledged by the peer TCP.

This does not tell us whether the peer application has read the data. If do not set the SO_LINGER socket option, do not know whether the peer TCP has acknowledged the data.

One way for the client to know that the server has read its data is to call shutdown (with a second argument of SHUT_WR) instead of close and wait for the peer to close its end of the connection.

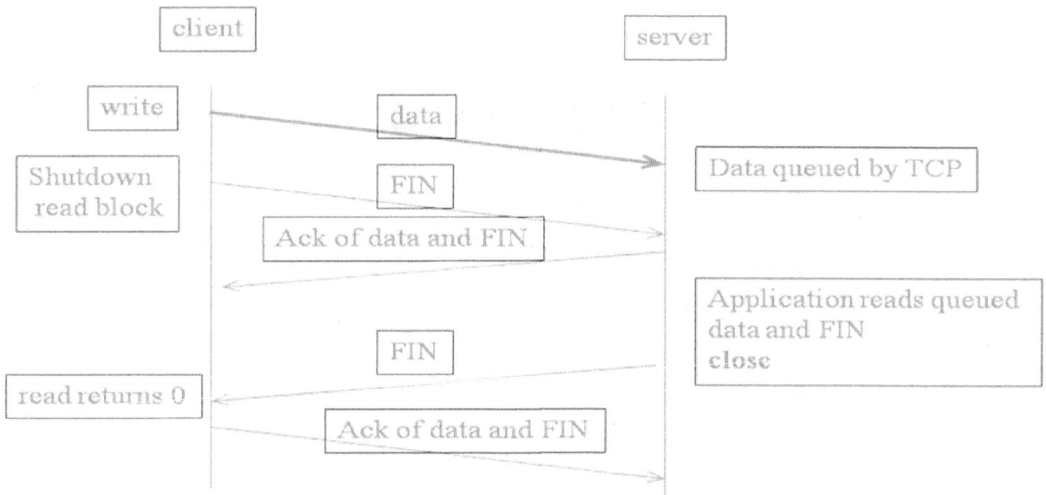

Using shutdown to know that peer has received our data

When close our end of the connection, depending on the function called (close or shutdown) and whether the SO_LINGER socket option is set, the return can occur at three different times:

1. close returns immediately, without waiting at all.
2. close lingers until the ACK of our FIN is received.
3. shutdown followed by a read waits until receive the peer's FIN.

The peer application has read our data is to use an application-level acknowledgment, or application ACK. For example, in the following, the client sends its data to the server and then calls read for one byte of data:

```
char ack;
Write(sockfd, data, nbytes); /* data from client to server */
n = Read(sockfd, &ack, 1); /* wait for application-level ACK */
```

The server reads the data from the client and then sends back the one-byte application-level ACK:

```
nbytes = Read(sockfd, buff, sizeof(buff)); /* data from client */
/* server verifies it received correct
amount of data from client */
Write(sockfd, "", 1); /* server's ACK back to client */
```

When the read in the client returns, the server process has read the data sent. (This assumes that either the server knows how much data the client is sending, or there is some application-defined end-of-record marker, which do not show here.) Here, the application-level ACK is a byte of 0, but the contents of this byte could be used to signal other conditions from the server to the client.

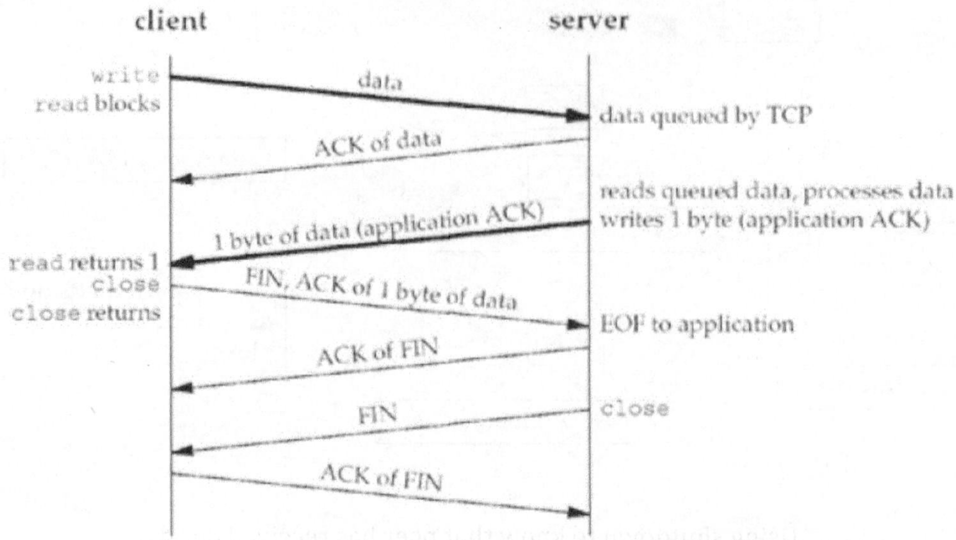

Application ACK

Function	Description
`shutdown, SHUT_RD`	No more receives can be issued on socket; process can still send on socket; socket receive buffer discarded; any further data received is discarded by TCP (Exercise 6.5); no effect on socket send buffer.
`shutdown, SHUT_WR`	No more sends can be issued on socket; process can still receive on socket; contents of socket send buffer sent to other end, followed by normal TCP connection termination (FIN); no effect on socket receive buffer.
`close, l_onoff = 0` (default)	No more receives or sends can be issued on socket; contents of socket send buffer sent to other end. If descriptor reference count becomes 0: normal TCP connection termination (FIN) sent following data in send buffer and socket receive buffer discarded.
`close, l_onoff = 1` `l_linger = 0`	No more receives or sends can be issued on socket. If descriptor reference count becomes 0: RST sent to other end, connection state set to CLOSED (no TIME_WAIT state), socket send buffer and socket receive buffer discarded.
`close, l_onoff = 1` `l_linger != 0`	No more receives or sends can be issued on socket; contents of socket send buffer sent to other end. If descriptor reference count becomes 0: normal TCP connection termination (FIN) sent following data in send buffer, socket receive buffer discarded, and if linger time expires before connection CLOSED, `close` returns EWOULDBLOCK.

Summary of shutdown and SO_LINGER scenarios

SO_OOBINLINE Socket Option

When this option is set, out-of-band data will be placed in the normal input queue (i.e., inline). When this occurs, the MSG_OOB flag to the receive functions cannot be used to read the out-of-band data.

SO_RCVBUF and SO_SNDBUF Socket Options

Every socket has a send buffer and a receive buffer. The receive buffers are used by TCP, UDP, and SCTP to hold received data until it is read by the application. With TCP, the available room in the socket receive buffer limits the window that TCP can advertise to the other end. The TCP socket receive buffer cannot overflow because the peer is not allowed to send data beyond the advertised window. This is TCP's flow control, and if the peer ignores the advertised window and sends data beyond the window, the receiving TCP discards it.

With UDP, however, when a datagram arrives that will not fit in the socket receive buffer, that datagram is discarded. Recall that UDP has no flow control: It is easy for a fast sender to overwhelm a slower receiver, causing datagrams to be discarded by the receiver's UDP. In fact, a fast sender can overwhelm its own network interface, causing datagrams to be discarded by the sender itself.

These two socket options let us change the default sizes. The default values differ widely between implementations. Older Berkeley-derived implementations would default the TCP send and receive buffers to 4,096 bytes, but newer systems use larger values, anywhere from 8,192 to 61,440 bytes.

The UDP send buffer size often defaults to a value around 9,000 bytes if the host supports NFS, and the UDP receive buffer size often defaults to a value around 40,000 bytes.

When setting the size of the TCP socket receive buffer, the ordering of the function calls is important. This is because of TCP's window scale option, which is exchanged with the peer on the SYN segments when the connection is established. For a client, this means the SO_RCVBUF socket option must be set before calling connect. For a server, this means the socket option must be set for the listening socket before calling listen. Setting this option for the connected socket will have no effect whatsoever on the possible window scale option because accept does not return with the connected socket until TCP's three-way handshake is complete.

That is why this option must be set for the listening socket. (The sizes of the socket buffers are always inherited from the listening socket by the newly created connected socket: pp. 462–463 of TCPv2.)

The TCP socket buffer sizes should be at least four times the MSS for the connection. If are dealing with unidirectional data transfer, such as a file transfer in one direction, when say "socket buffer sizes," mean the socket send buffer size on the sending host and the socket receive buffer size on the receiving host. For bidirectional data transfer, mean both socket buffer sizes on the sender and both socket buffer sizes on the receiver. With typical default buffer sizes of 8,192 bytes or larger, and a typical MSS of 512 or 1,460, this requirement is normally met.

The minimum MSS multiple of four is a result of the way that TCP's fast recovery algorithm works. The TCP sender uses three duplicate acknowledgments to detect that a packet was lost (RFC 2581 [Allman, Paxson, and

Stevens 1999]). The receiver sends a duplicate acknowledgment for each segment it receives after a lost segment. If the window size is smaller than four segments, there cannot be three duplicate acknowledgments, so the fast recovery algorithm cannot be invoked.

To avoid wasting potential buffer space, the TCP socket buffer sizes should also be an even multiple of the MSS for the connection. Some implementations handle this detail for the application, rounding up the socket buffer size after the connection is established (p. 902 of TCPv2). This is another reason to set these two socket options before establishing a connection. For example, using the default 4.4BSD size of 8,192 and assuming an Ethernet with an MSS of 1,460, both socket buffers are rounded up to 8,760 (6 x 1,460) when the connection is established. This is not a crucial requirement; the additional space in the socket buffer above the multiple of the MSS is simply unused.

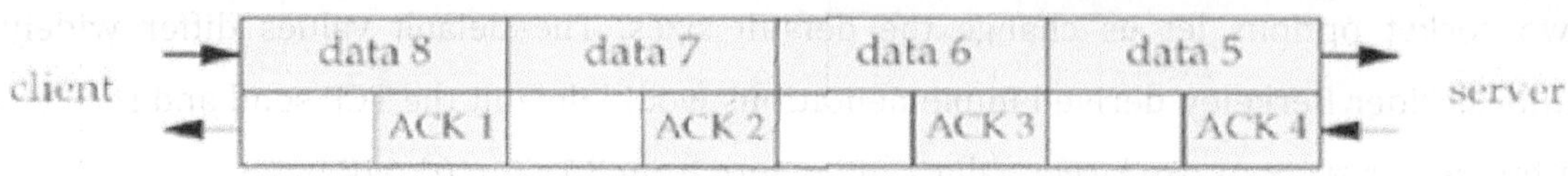

TCP connection (pipe) with a capacity of eight segments

The four data segments on the top and four ACKs on the bottom. Even though there are only four segments of data in the pipe, the client must have a send buffer capacity of at least eight segments, because the client TCP must keep a copy of each segment until the ACK is received from the server.

We are ignoring some details here. First, TCP's slow-start algorithm limits the rate at which segments are initially sent on an idle connection. Next, TCP often acknowledges every other segment, not every segment as show. All these details are covered in Chapters 20 and 24 of TCPv1.

What is important to understand is the concept of the full-duplex pipe, its capacity, and how that relates to the socket buffer sizes on both ends of the connection. The capacity of the pipe is called the bandwidth-delay product and calculate this by multiplying the bandwidth (in bits/sec) times the RTT (in seconds), converting the result from bits to bytes. The RTT is easily measured with the ping program.

The bandwidth is the value corresponding to the slowest link between two endpoints and must somehow be known. For example, a T1 line (1,536,000 bits/sec) with an RTT of 60 ms gives a bandwidth-delay product of 11,520 bytes. If the socket buffer sizes are less than this, the pipe will not stay full, and the performance will be less than expected. Large socket buffers are required when the bandwidth gets larger (e.g., T3 lines at 45 Mbits/sec) or when the RTT gets large (e.g., satellite links with an RTT around 500 ms). When the bandwidth-delay product exceeds TCP's maximum normal window size (65,535 bytes), both endpoints also need the TCP long fat pipe options.

Most implementations have an upper limit for the sizes of the socket send and receive buffers, and sometimes this limit can be modified by the administrator. Older Berkeley-derived implementations had a hard upper limit of around 52,000 bytes, but newer implementations have a default limit of 256,000 bytes or more, and this can usually be increased by the administrator. Unfortunately, there is no simple way for an application to determine this limit.

POSIX defines the fpathconf function, which most implementations support, and using the _PC_SOCK_MAXBUF constant as the second argument, can retrieve the maximum size of the socket buffers. Alternately, an application can try setting the socket buffers to the desired value, and if that fails, cut the value in half and try again until it succeeds. Finally, an application should make sure that it's not actually making the socket buffer smaller when it sets it to a preconfigured "large" value; calling getsockopt first to retrieve the system's default and seeing if that's large enough is often a good start.

SO_RCVLOWAT and SO_SNDLOWAT Socket Options

Every socket also has a receive low-water mark and a send low-water mark. These are used by the select function. These two socket options, SO_RCVLOWAT and SO_SNDLOWAT, let us change these two low-water marks.

The receive low-water mark is the amount of data that must be in the socket receive buffer or select to return "readable." It defaults to 1 for TCP, UDP, and SCTP sockets. The send low-water mark is the amount of available space that must exist in the socket send buffer for select to return "writable." This low-water mark normally defaults to 2,048 for TCP sockets. With UDP, the lowwater mark is used, but since the number of bytes of available space in the send buffer for a UDP socket never changes (since UDP does not keep a copy of the datagrams sent by the application), as long as the UDP socket send buffer size is greater than the socket's low-water mark, the UDP socket is always writable. The UDP does not have a send buffer; it has only a send buffer size.

SO_RCVTIMEO and SO_SNDTIMEO Socket Options

These two socket options allow us to place a timeout on socket receives and sends. Notice that the argument to the two sockopt functions is a pointer to a timeval structure, the same one used with select. This lets us specify the timeouts in seconds and microseconds. disable a timeout by setting its value to 0 seconds and 0 microseconds. Both timeouts are disabled by default.

The receive timeout affects the five input functions: read, readv, recdv, recvfrom, and recvmsg.

The send timeout affects the five output functions: write, writev, send, sendto, and sendmsg.

These two socket options and the concept of inherent timeouts on socket receives and ends were added with 4.3BSD Reno.

In Berkeley-derived implementations, these two values really implement an inactivity timer and not an absolute timer on the read or write system call. Pages 496 and 516 of TCPv2 talk about this in more detail.

SO_REUSEADDR and SO_REUSEPORT Socket Options

The SO_REUSEADDR socket option serves four different purposes:

1. SO_REUSEADDR allows a listening server to start and bind its well-known port, even if previously established connections exist that use this port as their local port. This condition is typically encountered as follows:
   - A listening server is started.
   - A connection request arrives and a child process is spawned to handle that client. The listening server terminates, but the child continues to service the client on the existing connection.
   - The listening server is restarted. By default, when the listening server is restarted in (d) by calling socket, bind, and listen, the call to bind fails because the listening server is trying to bind a port that is part of an existing connection (the one being handled by the previously spawned child). But if the server sets the SO_REUSEADDR socket option between the calls to socket and bind, the latter function will succeed. All TCP servers should specify this socket option to allow the server to be restarted in this situation.
   - This scenario is one of the most frequently asked questions on USENET.
2. SO_REUSEADDR allows a new server to be started on the same port as an existing server that is bound to the wildcard address, as long as each instance binds a different local IP address.

This is common for a site hosting multiple HTTP servers using the IP alias technique. Assume the local host's primary IP address is 198.69.10.2 but it has two aliases: 198.69.10.128 and 198.69.10.129. Three HTTP servers are started. The first HTTP server would call bind with the wildcard as the local IP address and a local port of 80 (the wellknown port for HTTP). The second server would call bind with a local IP address of 198.69.10.128 and a local port of 80. But, this second call to bind fails unless SO_REUSEADDR is set before the call. The third server would bind 198.69.10.129 and port 80. Again, SO_REUSEADDR is required for this final call to succeed. Assuming SO_REUSEADDR is set and the three servers are started, incoming TCP connection requests with a destination IP address of 198.69.10.128 and a destination port of 80 are delivered to the second server, incoming requests with a destination IP address of 198.69.10.129 and a destination port of 80 are delivered to the third server, and all other TCP connection requests with a destination port of 80 are delivered to the first server. This "default" server handles requests destined for 198.69.10.2 in addition to any other IP aliases that the host may have configured. The wildcard means "everything that doesn't have a better (more specific) match." Note that this scenario of allowing multiple servers for a given service is handled automatically if the server always sets the SO_REUSEADDR socket option (as recommend).

With TCP, are never able to start multiple servers that bind the same IP address and the same port: a completely duplicate binding. That is, cannot start one server that binds 198.69.10.2 port 80 and start another that also binds 198.69.10.2 port 80, even if set the SO_REUSEADDR socket option for the second server.

For security reasons, some operating systems prevent any "more specific" bind to a port that is already bound to the wildcard address, that is, the series of binds described here would not work with or without SO_REUSEADDR. On such a system, the server that performs the wildcard bind must be started last. This is to avoid the problem of a rogue server binding to an IP address and port that are being served already by a system service and intercepting legitimate requests. This is a particular problem for NFS, which generally does not use a privileged port.

3. SO_REUSEADDR allows a single process to bind the same port to multiple sockets, as long as each bind specifies a different local IP address. This is common for UDP servers that need to know the destination IP address of client requests on systems that do not provide the IP_RECVDSTADDR socket option. This technique is normally not used with TCP servers since a TCP server can always determine the destination IP address by calling getsockname after the connection is established. However, a TCP server wishing to serve connections to some, but not all, addresses belonging to a multihomed host should use this technique.
4. SO_REUSEADDR allows completely duplicate bindings: a bind of an IP address and port, when that same IP address and port are already bound to another socket, if the transport protocol supports it. Normally this feature is supported only for UDP sockets.

This feature is used with multicasting to allow the same application to be run multiple times on the same host. When a UDP datagram is received for one of these multiply bound sockets, the rule is that if the datagram is destined for either a broadcast address or a multicast address, one copy of the datagram is delivered to each matching socket. But if the datagram is destined for a unicast address, the datagram is delivered to only one socket. If, in the case of a unicast datagram, there are multiple sockets that match the datagram, the choice of which socket receives the datagram is implementation-dependent.

4.4BSD introduced the SO_REUSEPORT socket option when support for multicasting was added. Instead of overloading SO_REUSEADDR with the desired multicast semantics that allow completely duplicate bindings, this new socket option was introduced with the following semantics: This option allows completely duplicate bindings, but only if each socket that wants to bind the same IP address and port specify this socket option.

SO_REUSEADDR is considered equivalent to SO_REUSEPORT if the IP address being bound is a multicast address.

The problem with this socket option is that not all systems support it, and on those that do not support the option but do support multicasting, SO_REUSEADDR is used instead of SO_REUSEPORT to allow completely duplicate bindings when it makes sense (i.e., a UDP server that can be run multiple times on the same host at the same time and that expects to receive either broadcast or multicast datagrams).

The socket options with the following recommendations:

1. Set the SO_REUSEADDR socket option before calling bind in all TCP servers.
2. When writing a multicast application that can be run multiple times on the same host at the same time, set the SO_REUSEADDR socket option and bind the group's multicast address as the local IP address.

If a socket exists that is bound to, say, the wildcard address and port 5555, if specify SO_REUSEADDR, can bind that same port to a different IP address, say the primary IP address of the host. Any future datagrams that arrive destined to port 5555 and the IP address that bound to our socket are delivered to our socket, not to the other socket bound to the wildcard address. These could be TCP SYN segments, SCTP INIT chunks, or UDP datagrams. For most wellknown services, HTTP, FTP, and Telnet, for example, this is not a problem because these servers all bind a reserved port. Hence, any process that comes along later and tries to bind a more specific instance of that port (i.e., steal the port) requires superuser privileges. NFS, however, can be a problem since its normal port (2049) is not reserved.

One underlying problem with the sockets API is that the setting of the socket pair is done with two function calls (bind and connect) instead of one. [Torek 1994] proposes a single function that solves this problem.

```
int bind_connect_listen(int sockfd, const struct sockaddr *laddr, int
laddrlen, const struct sockaddr *faddr, int faddrlen, int listen);
```

laddr specifies the local IP address and local port, faddr specifies the foreign IP address and foreign port, and listen specifies a client (zero) or a server (nonzero; same as the backlog argument to listen). Then, bind would be a library function that calls this function with faddr a null pointer and faddrlen 0, and connect would be a library function that calls this function with laddr a null pointer and laddrlen 0. There are a few applications, notably TFTP, that need to specify both the local pair and the foreign pair, and they could call bind_connect_listen directly. With such a function, the need for SO_REUSEADDR disappears, other than for multicast UDP servers that explicitly need to allow completely duplicate bindings of the same IP address and port. Another benefit of this new function is that a TCP server could restrict itself to servicing connection requests that arrive from one specific IP address and port, something which RFC 793 [Postel 1981c] specifies but is impossible to implement with the existing sockets API.

SO_TYPE Socket Option

This option returns the socket type. The integer value returned is a value such as SOCK_STREAM or SOCK_DGRAM. This option is typically used by a process that inherits a socket when it is started.

SO_USELOOPBACK Socket Option

This option applies only to sockets in the routing domain (AF_ROUTE). This option defaults to ON for these sockets (the only one of the SO_xxx socket options that defaults to ON instead of OFF). When this option is enabled, the socket receives a copy of everything sent on the socket.

Another way to disable these loopback copies is to call shutdown with a second argument of SHUT_RD.

IPv4 Socket Options

These socket options are processed by IPv4 and have a level of IPPROTO_IP.

IP_HDRINCL Socket Option

If this option is set for a raw IP socket, must build our own IP header for all the datagrams send on the raw socket. Normally, the kernel builds the IP header for datagrams sent on a raw socket, but there are some applications (notably traceroute) that build their own IP header to override values that IP would place into certain header fields.

When this option is set, build a complete IP header, with the following exceptions:

IP always calculates and stores the IP header checksum. If set the IP identification field to 0, the kernel will set the field.

If the source IP address is INADDR_ANY, IP sets it to the primary IP address of the outgoing interface.

Setting IP options is implementation-dependent. Some implementations take any IP options that were set using the IP_OPTIONS socket option and append these to the header that build, while others require our header to also contain any desired IP options.

IP_OPTIONS Socket Option

Setting this option allows us to set IP options in the IPv4 header. This requires intimate knowledge of the format of the IP options in the IP header.

IP_RECVDSTADDR Socket Option

This socket option causes the destination IP address of a received UDP datagram to be returned as ancillary data by recvmsg.

IP_RECVIF Socket Option

This socket option causes the index of the interface on which a UDP datagram is received to be returned as ancillary data by recvmsg.

IP_TOS Socket Option

This option lets us set the type-of-service (TOS) field (which contains the DSCP and ECN fields) in the IP header for a TCP, UDP, or SCTP socket. If call getsockopt for this option, the current value that would be placed into the DSCP and ECN fields in the IP header (which defaults to 0) is returned. There is no way to fetch the value from a received IP datagram.

An application can set the DSCP to a value negotiated with the network service provider to receive prearranged services, e.g., low delay for IP telephony or higher throughput for bulk data transfer.

The diffserv architecture, defined in RFC 2474, provides for only limited backward compatibility with the historical TOS field definition

Application that set IP_TOS to one of the contents from <netinet/ip.h>, for instance, IPTOS_LOWDELAY or IPTOS_THROUGHPUT, should instead use a user-specified DSCP value. The only TOS values that diffserv retains are precedence levels 6 ("internetwork control") and 7 ("network control"); this means that applications that set IP_TOS to IPTOS_PREC_NETCONTROL or IPTOS_PREC_INTERNETCONTROL will work in a diffserv network.

Applications should generally leave the setting of the ECN field to the kernel, and should specify zero values in the low two bits of the value set with IP_TOS.

IP_TTL Socket Option

With this option, can set and fetch the default TTL that the system will use for unicast packets sent on a given socket. (The multicast TTL is set using the IP_MULTICAST_TTL socket option) 4.4BSD, for example, uses the default of 64 for both TCP and UDP sockets (specified in the IANA's "IP Option Numbers" registry [IANA]) and 255 for raw sockets. As with the TOS field, calling getsockopt returns the default value of the field that the system will use in outgoing datagrams—there is no way to obtain the value from a received datagram.

ICMPv6 Socket Option

This socket option is processed by ICMPv6 and has a level of IPPROTO_ICMPV6.

ICMP6_FILTER Socket Option

This option lets us fetch and set an icmp6_filter structure that specifies which of the 256 possible ICMPv6 message types will be passed to the process on a raw socket.

TCP Socket Options

There are two socket options for TCP. specify the level as IPPROTO_TCP.

TCP_MAXSEG Socket Option

This socket option allows us to fetch or set the MSS for a TCP connection. The value returned is the maximum amount of data that our TCP will send to the other end; often, it is the MSS announced by the other end with its SYN, unless our TCP chooses to use a smaller value than the peer's announced MSS. If this value is fetched before the socket is connected, the value returned is the default value that will be used if an MSS option is not received from the other end. Also be aware that a value smaller than the returned value can actually be used for the connection if the timestamp option, for example, is in use, because this option occupies 12 bytes of TCP options in each segment.

The maximum amount of data that our TCP will send per segment can also change during the life of a connection if TCP supports path MTU discovery. If the route to the peer changes, this value can go up or down.

The socket option can also be set by the application. This is not possible on all systems; it was originally a read-only option. 4.4BSD limits the application to decreasing the value: cannot increase the value (p. 1023 of TCPv2). Since this option controls the amount of data that TCP sends per segment, it makes sense to forbid the application from increasing the value. Once the connection is established, this value is the MSS option announced by the peer, and cannot exceed that value. Our TCP, however, can always send less than the peer's announced MSS.

TCP_NODELAY Socket Option

If set, this option disables TCP's Nagle algorithm. By default, this algorithm is enabled.

The purpose of the Nagle algorithm is to reduce the number of small packets on a WAN. The algorithm states that if a given connection has outstanding data (i.e., data that our TCP has sent, and for which it is currently awaiting an acknowledgment), then no small packets will be sent on the connection in response to a user write operation until the existing data is acknowledged. The definition of a "small" packet is any packet smaller than the MSS. TCP will always send a full-sized packet if possible; the purpose of the Nagle algorithm is to prevent a connection from having multiple small packets outstanding at any time.

The two common generators of small packets are the Rlogin and Telnet clients, since they normally send each keystroke as a separate packet. On a fast LAN, normally do not notice the Nagle algorithm with these clients, because the time required for a small packet to be acknowledged is typically a few milliseconds—far less than the time between two successive characters that type.

But on a WAN, where it can take a second for a small packet to be acknowledged, can notice a delay in the character echoing, and this delay is often exaggerated by the Nagle algorithm. Consider the following example: type the six-character string "hello!" to either an Rlogin or Telnet client, with exactly 250 ms between each character. The RTT to the server is 600 ms and the server immediately sends back the echo of each character.

assume the ACK of the client's character is sent back to the client along with the character echo and ignore the ACKs that the client sends for the server's echo.

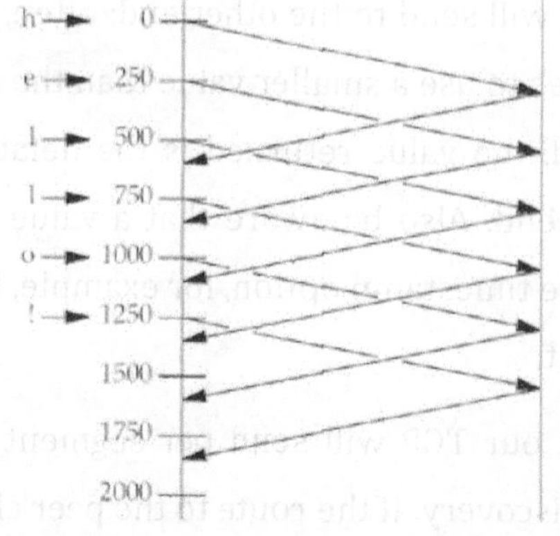

Six characters echoed by server with Nagle algorithm disabled

Each character is sent in a packet by itself: the data segments from left to right, and the ACKs from right to left.

The first character is sent as a packet by itself, but the next two characters are not sent, since the connection has a small packet outstanding. At time 600, when the ACK of the first packet is received, along with the echo of the first character, these two characters are sent. Until this packet is ACKed at time 1200, no more small packets are sent.

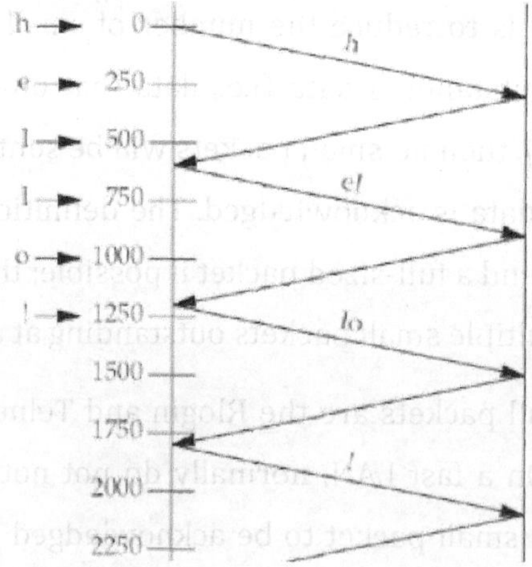

Six characters echoed by server with Nagle algorithm enabled

The Nagle algorithm often interacts with another TCP algorithm: the delayed ACK algorithm. This algorithm causes TCP to not send an ACK immediately when it receives data; instead, TCP will wait some small amount of time (typically 50–200 ms) and only then send the ACK. The hope is that in this small amount of time, there will be data to send back to the peer, and the ACK can piggyback with the data, saving one TCP segment. This is normally the case with the Rlogin and Telnet clients, because the servers typically echo each character sent by the client, so the ACK of the client's character piggybacks with the server's echo of that character.

The problem is with other clients whose servers do not generate traffic in the reverse direction on which ACKs can piggyback. These clients can detect noticeable delays because the client TCP will not send any data to the server until the server's delayed ACK timer expires. These clients need a way to disable the Nagle algorithm, hence the TCP_NODELAY option.

Another type of client that interacts badly with the Nagle algorithm and TCP's delayed ACKs is a client that sends a single logical request to its server in small pieces. For example, assume a client sends a 400-byte request to its server, but this is a 4-byte request type followed by 396 bytes of request data. If the client performs a 4-byte write followed by a 396-byte write, the second write will not be sent by the client TCP until the server TCP acknowledges the 4-byte write. Also, since the server application cannot operate on the 4 bytes of data until it receives the remaining 396 bytes of data, the server TCP will delay the ACK of the 4 bytes of data (i.e., there will not be any data from the server to the client on which to piggyback the ACK). There are three ways to fix this type of client: Use writev instead of two calls to write. A single call to writev ends up with one call to TCP output instead of two calls, resulting in one TCP segment for our example.

This is the preferred solution. Copy the 4 bytes of data and the 396 bytes of data into a single buffer and call write once for this buffer.

Set the TCP_NODELAY socket option and continue to call write two times. This is the least desirable solution, and is harmful to the network, so it generally should not even be

considered.

Elementary UDP Sockets

Introduction

There are some fundamental differences between applications written using TCP versus those that use UDP. These are because of the differences in the two transport layers: UDP is a connectionless, unreliable, datagram protocol, quite unlike the connection-oriented, reliable byte stream provided by TCP. Nevertheless, there are instances when it makes sense to use UDP instead of TCP. Some popular applications are built using UDP: DNS, NFS, and SNMP, for example.

The client does not stablish a connection with the server. Instead, the client just sends a datagram to the server using the sendto function (described in the next section), which requires the address of the destination (the server) as a parameter. Similarly, the server does not accept a connection from a client. Instead, the server just calls the recvfrom function, which waits until data arrives from some client. recvfrom returns the protocol address of the client, along with the datagram, so the server can send a response to the correct client.

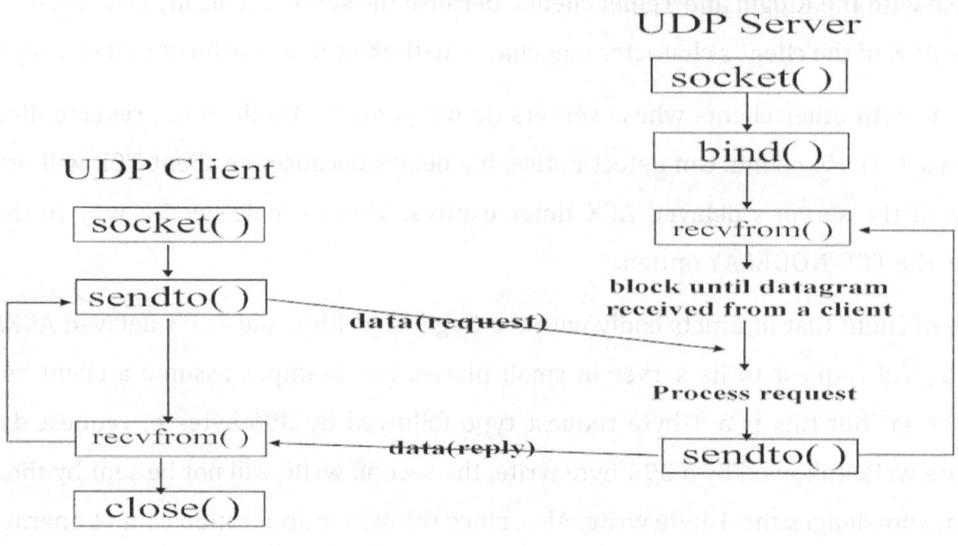

Socket functions for UDP client-server

Socket functions for UDP client/server

A timeline of the typical scenario that takes place for a UDP client/server exchange.

In this chapter, will describe the new functions that use with UDP sockets, recvfrom and sendto, and redo our echo client/server to use UDP. will also describe the use of the connect function with a UDP socket, and the concept of asynchronous errors.

UDP Echo Server: main Function

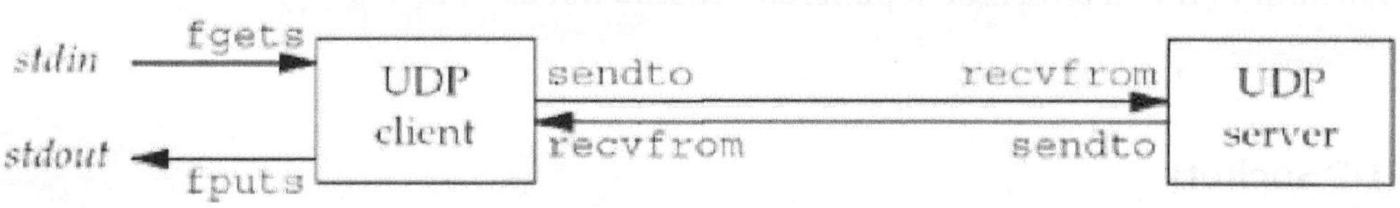

Simple echo client/server using UDP

UDP echo server

udpcliserv/udpserv01.c

```
#include "unp.h"
int
main(int argc, char **argv)
{
int sockfd;
struct sockaddr_in servaddr, cliaddr;
sockfd = Socket(AF_INET, SOCK_DGRAM, 0);
bzero(&servaddr, sizeof(servaddr));
```

```
9 servaddr.sin_family = AF_INET;
10 servaddr.sin_addr.s_addr = htonl(INADDR_ANY);
11 servaddr.sin_port = htons(SERV_PORT);
12 Bind(sockfd, (SA *) &servaddr, sizeof(servaddr));
13 dg_echo(sockfd, (SA *) &cliaddr, sizeof(cliaddr));
14 }
```

Create UDP socket, bind server's well-known port

7-12 create a UDP socket by specifying the second argument to socket as SOCK_DGRAM (a datagram socket in the IPv4 protocol). As with the TCP server example, the IPv4 address for the bind is specified as INADDR_ANY and the server's well-known port is the constant SERV_PORT from the unp.h header.

13 The function dg_echo is called to perform server processing.

UDP Echo Server: dg_echo Function

dg_echo function: echo lines on a datagram socket

lib/dg_echo.c

```
1 #include "unp.h"
2 void
3 dg_echo(int sockfd, SA *pcliaddr, socklen_t clilen)
4 {
5 int n;
6 socklen_t len;
7 char mesg[MAXLINE];
8 for ( ; ; ) {
9 len = clilen;
10 n = Recvfrom(sockfd, mesg, MAXLINE, 0, pcliaddr, &len);
11 Sendto(sockfd, mesg, n, 0, pcliaddr, len);
12 }
13 }
```

Read datagram, echo back to sender

8-12 This function is a simple loop that reads the next datagram arriving at the server's port using recvfrom and sends it back using sendto.

This function never terminates. Since UDP is a connectionless protocol, there is nothing like an EOF as have with TCP.

This function provides an iterative server, not a concurrent server as had with TCP. There is no call to fork, so a single server process handles any and all clients. In general, most TCP servers are concurrent and most UDP servers are iterative.

There is implied queuing taking place in the UDP layer for this socket. Indeed, each UDP socket has a receive buffer and each datagram that arrives for this socket is placed in that socket receive buffer. When the process calls recvfrom, the next datagram from the buffer is returned to the process in a first-in, first-out (FIFO) order. This way, if multiple datagrams arrive for the socket before the process can read what's already queued for the socket, the arriving datagrams are just added to the socket receive buffer. But, this buffer has a limited size.

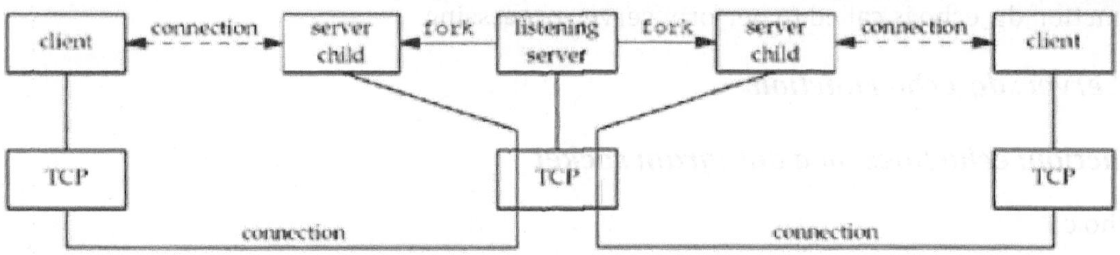

Summary of TCP client/server with two clients

There are two connected sockets and each of the two connected sockets on the server host has its own socket receive buffer.

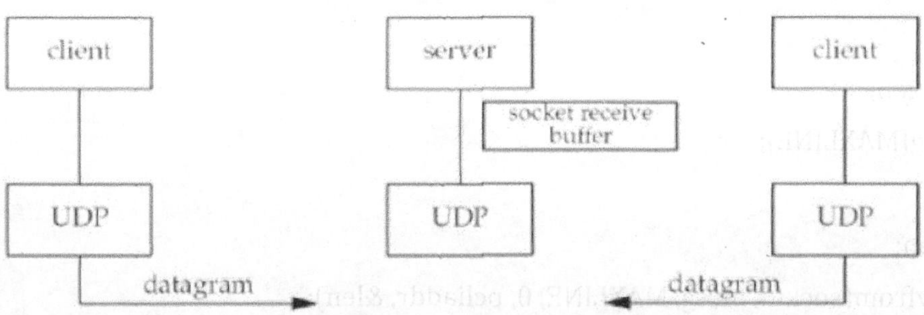

Summary of UDP client/server with two clients

There is only one server process and it has a single socket on which it receives all arriving datagrams and sends all responses. That socket has a receive buffer into which all arriving datagrams are placed.

The main function is protocol-dependent (it creates a socket of protocol AF_INET and allocates and initializes an IPv4 socket address structure), but the dg_echo function is protocolindependent.

The reason dg_echo is protocol-independent is because the caller (the main function in our case) must allocate a socket address structure of the correct size, and a pointer to this structure, along with its size, are passed as arguments to dg_echo. The function dg_echo never looks inside this protocol-dependent structure: It simply passes a pointer to the structure to recvfrom and sendto. recvfrom fills this structure with the IP address and port number of the client, and since the same pointer (pcliaddr) is then passed to sendto as the destination address, this is how the datagram is echoed back to the client that sent the datagram.

UDP Echo Client: main Function

UDP echo client.

udpcliserv/udpcli01.c

```
1 #include "unp.h"
2 int
3 main(int argc, char **argv)
4 {
5 int sockfd;
6 struct sockaddr_in servaddr;
7 if(argc != 2)
8 err_quit("usage: udpcli <IPaddress>");
9 bzero(&servaddr, sizeof(servaddr));
10 servaddr.sin_family = AF_INET;
11 servaddr.sin_port = htons(SERV_PORT);
12 Inet_pton(AF_INET, argv[1], &servaddr.sin_addr);
13 sockfd = Socket(AF_INET, SOCK_DGRAM, 0);
14 dg_cli(stdin, sockfd, (SA *) &servaddr, sizeof(servaddr));
15 exit(0);
16 }
```

Fill in socket address structure with server's address

9–12 An IPv4 socket address structure is filled in with the IP address and port number of the server. This structure will be passed to dg_cli, specifying where to send datagrams.

13–14 A UDP socket is created and the function dg_cli is called.

UDP Echo Client: dg_cli Function

The function dg_cli, which performs most of the client processing.

dg_cli function: client processing loop.

lib/dg_cli.c

```
1 #include "unp.h"
2 void
3 dg_cli(FILE *fp, int sockfd, const SA *pservaddr, socklen_t servlen)
4 {
5 int n;
6 char sendline[MAXLINE], recvline[MAXLINE + 1];
7 while (Fgets(sendline, MAXLINE, fp) != NULL) {
8 Sendto(sockfd, sendline, strlen(sendline), 0, pservaddr, servlen);
9 n = Recvfrom(sockfd, recvline, MAXLINE, 0, NULL, NULL);
10 recvline[n] = 0; /* null terminate */
11 Fputs(recvline, stdout);
12 }
13 }
```

7–12 There are four steps in the client processing loop: read a line from standard input using fgets, send the line to the server using sendto, read back the server's echo using recvfrom, and print the echoed line to standard output using fputs.

Our client has not asked the kernel to assign an ephemeral port to its socket. (With a TCP client, said the call to connect is where this takes place.) With a UDP socket, the first time the process calls sendto, if the socket has not yet had a local port bound to it, that is when an ephemeral port is chosen by the kernel for the socket. As with TCP, the client can call bind explicitly, but this is rarely done.

Notice that the call to recvfrom specifies a null pointer as the fifth and sixth arguments. This tells the kernel that are not interested in knowing who sent the reply. There is a risk that any process, on either the same host or some other host, can send a datagram to the client's IP address and port, and that datagram will be read by the client.

As with the server function dg_echo, the client function dg_cli is protocol-independent, but the client main function is protocol-dependent. The main function allocates and initializes a socket address structure of some protocol type and then passes a pointer to this structure, along with its size, to dg_cli.

TCP and UDP Echo Server Using select

Create listening TCP socket

14–22 A listening TCP socket is created that is bound to the server's well-known port. set the SO_REUSEADDR socket option in case connections exist on this port.

Create UDP socket

23–29 A UDP socket is also created and bound to the same port. Even though the same port is used for TCP and UDP sockets, there is no need to set the SO_REUSEADDR socket option before this call to bind, because TCP ports are independent of UDP ports.

Establish signal handler for SIGCHLD

30 A signal handler is established for SIGCHLD because TCP connections will be handled by a child process.

Prepare for select

31–32 initialize a descriptor set for select and calculate the maximum of the two descriptors for which will wait.

First half of echo server that handles TCP and UDP using select

udpcliserv/udpservselect01.c

```
1 #include "unp.h"
2 int
3 main(int argc, char **argv)
4 {
5 int listenfd, connfd, udpfd, nready, maxfdp1;
6 char mesg[MAXLINE];
7 pid_t childpid;
8 fd_set rset;
9 ssize_t n;
10 socklen_t len;
11 const int on = 1;
12 struct sockaddr_in cliaddr, servaddr;
13 void sig_chld(int);
14 /* create listening TCP socket */
15 listenfd = Socket(AF_INET, SOCK_STREAM, 0);
16 bzero(&servaddr, sizeof(servaddr));
17 servaddr.sin_family = AF_INET;
18 servaddr.sin_addr.s_addr = htonl(INADDR_ANY);
19 servaddr.sin_port = htons(SERV_PORT);
20 Setsockopt(listenfd, SOL_SOCKET, SO_REUSEADDR, &on, sizeof(on));
21 Bind(listenfd, (SA *) &servaddr, sizeof(servaddr));
```

```
22 Listen(listenfd, LISTENQ);
23 /* create UDP socket */
24 udpfd = Socket(AF_INET, SOCK_DGRAM, 0);
25 bzero(&servaddr, sizeof(servaddr));
26 servaddr.sin_family = AF_INET;
27 servaddr.sin_addr.s_addr = htonl(INADDR_ANY);
28 servaddr.sin_port = htons(SERV_PORT);
29 Bind(udpfd, (SA *) &servaddr, sizeof(servaddr));
```

Call select

34–41 call select, waiting only for readability on the listening TCP socket or readability on the UDP socket. Since our sig_chld handler can interrupt our call to select, handle an error of EINTR.

Handle new client connection

42–51 accept a new client connection when the listening TCP socket is readable, fork a child, and call our str_echo function in the child.

Second half of echo server that handles TCP and UDP using select.

udpcliserv/udpservselect01.c

```
30 Signal(SIGCHLD, sig_chld); /* must call waitpid() */
31 FD_ZERO(&rset);
32 maxfdp1 = max(listenfd, udpfd) + 1;
33 for ( ; ; ) {
34 FD_SET(listenfd, &rset);
35 FD_SET(udpfd, &rset);
36 if ( (nready = select(maxfdp1, &rset, NULL, NULL, NULL)) < 0) {
37 if (errno == EINTR)
38 continue; /* back to for() */
39 else
40 err_sys("select error");
41 }
42 if (FD_ISSET(listenfd, &rset)) {
43 len = sizeof(cliaddr);
44 connfd = Accept(listenfd, (SA *) &cliaddr, &len);
45 if ( (childpid = Fork()) == 0) { /* child process */
```

```
46 Close(listenfd); /* close listening socket */
47 str_echo(connfd); /* process the request */
48 exit(0);
49 }
50 Close(connfd); /* parent closes connected socket */
51 }
52 if (FD_ISSET(udpfd, &rset)) {
53 len = sizeof(cliaddr);
54 n = Recvfrom(udpfd, mesg, MAXLINE, 0, (SA *) &cliaddr, &len);
55 Sendto(udpfd, mesg, n, 0, (SA *) &cliaddr, len);
56 }
57 }
58 }
```

Handle arrival of datagram

52–57 If the UDP socket is readable, a datagram has arrived. read it with recvfrom and send it back to the client with sendto.

Name and Address Conversions

Domain Name System (DNS)

The DNS is used primarily to map between hostnames and IP addresses. A hostname can be either a simple name, such as solaris or freebsd, or a fully qualified domain name '(FQDN), such as solaris.unpbook.com.

Technically, an FQDN is also called an absolute name and must end with a period, but users often omit the ending period. The trailing period tells the resolver that this name is fully qualified and it doesn't need to search its list of possible domains.

Resource Records

Entries in the DNS are known as resource records (RRs). There are only a few types of RRs that are interested in.

A An A record maps a hostname into a 32-bit IPv4 address. For example, here are the four DNS records for the host freebsd in the unpbook.com domain, the first of which is an A record:

```
freebsd IN A 12.106.32.254
IN AAAA 3ffe:b80:1f8d:1:a00:20ff
:fea7:686b
IN MX 5 freebsd.unpbook.com.
```

IN MX 10 mailhost.unpbook.com.

AAAA A AAAA record, called a "quad A" record, maps a hostname into a 128-bit IPv6 address. The term "quad A" was chosen because a 128-bit address is four times larger than a 32- bit address.

PTR PTR records (called "pointer records") map IP addresses into hostnames. For an IPv4 address, then 4 bytes of the 32-bit address are reversed, each byte is converted to its

decimal ASCII value (0–255), and in-addr.arpa is the appended. The resulting string is used in the PTR query.

For an IPv6 address, the 32 4-bit nibbles of the 128-bit address are reversed, each nibble is converted to its corresponding hexadecimal ASCII value (0–9a–f), and ip6.arpa is appended.

For example, the two PTR records for our host freebsd would be 254.32.106.12.inaddr. arpa and b.6.8.6.7.a.e.f.f.f.0.2.0.0.a.0.1.0.0.0.d.8.f.1.0.8.b.0.e.f.f.3.ip6.arpa.

Earlier standards specified that IPv6 addresses were looked up in the ip6.int domain. This was changed to ip6.arpa for consistency with IPv4. There will be a transition period during which both zones will be populated.

MX An MX record specifies a host to act as a "mail exchanger" for the specified host. In the example for the host freebsd above, two MX records are provided: The first has a preference value of 5 and the second has a preference value of 10. When multiple MX records exist, they are used in order of preference, starting with the smallest value.

We do not use MX records in this text, but mention them because they are used

extensively in the real world.

CNAME CNAME stands for "canonical name." A common use is to assign CNAME records for common services, such as ftp and www. If people use these service names instead of the actual hostnames, it is transparent when a service is moved to another host.

For example, the following could be CNAMEs for our host linux:

ftp IN CNAME linux.unpbook.com.

www IN CNAME linux.unpbook.com.

It is too early in the deployment of IPv6 to know what conventions administrators will use for hosts that support both IPv4 and IPv6. In our example earlier in this section, specified both an A record and a AAAA record for our host freebsd. One possibility is to place both the A record and the AAAA record under the host's normal name (as shown earlier) and create another RR whose name ends in -4 containing the A record, another RR whose name ends in -6 containing the AAAA record, and another RR whose name ends in -611 containing a AAAA record with the host's linklocal address (which is sometimes handy for debugging purposes). All the records for another of our hosts are then

aix IN A 192.168.42.2

IN AAAA 3ffe:b80:1f8d:2:204:acff:fe17:bf38

IN MX 5 aix.unpbook.com.

IN MX 10 mailhost.unpbook.com.

aix-4 IN A 192.168.42.2

aix-6 IN AAAA 3ffe:b80:1f8d:2:204:acff:fe17:bf38

aix-611 IN AAAA fe80::204:acff:fe17:bf38

This gives us additional control over the protocol chosen by some applications, as will see in the next chapter.

Resolvers and Name Servers

Organizations run one or more name servers, often the program known as BIND (Berkeley Internet Name Domain). Applications such as the clients and servers that are writing in this text contact a DNS server by calling functions in a library known as the resolver. The common resolver functions are gethostbyname and gethostbyaddr, both of which are described in this chapter. The former maps a hostname into its IPv4 addresses, and the latter does the reverse mapping.

A typical arrangement of applications, resolvers, and name servers. now write the application code. On some systems, the resolver code is contained in a system library and is link-edited into the application when the application is built. On others, there is a centralized resolver daemon that all applications share, and the system library code performs RPCs to this daemon. In either case, application code calls the resolver code using normal function calls, typically calling the functions gethostbyname and gethostbyaddr.

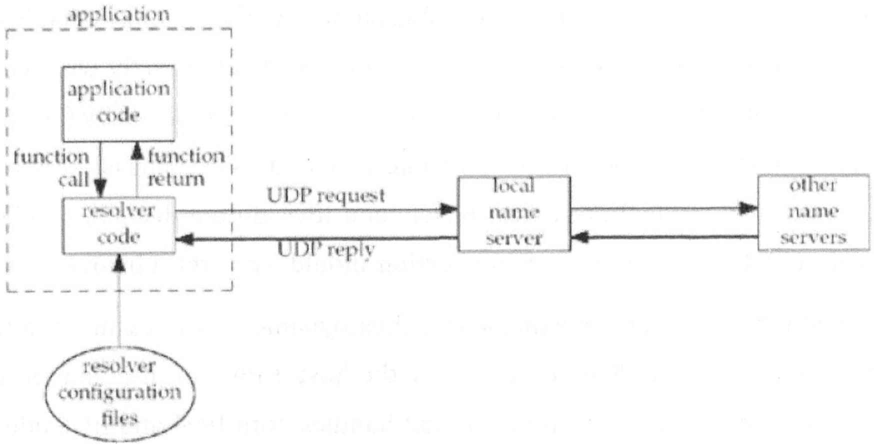

Typical arrangement of clients, resolvers, and name servers

The resolver code reads its system-dependent configuration files to determine the location of the organization's name servers. (We use the plural "name servers" because most organizations run multiple name servers, even though show only one local server in the figure. Multiple name servers are absolutely required for reliability and redundancy.) The file /etc/resolv.conf normally contains the IP addresses of the local name servers.

It might be nice to use the names of the name servers in the /etc/resolv.conf file, since the names are easier to remember and configure, but this introduces a chicken-and-egg problem of where to go to do the name-to-address conversion for the server that will do the name and address conversion!

The resolver sends the query to the local name server using UDP. If the local name server does not know the answer, it will normally query other name servers across the Internet, also using UDP. If the answers are too large to fit in a UDP packet, the resolver will automatically switch to TCP.

DNS Alternatives

It is possible to obtain name and address information without using the DNS. Common alternatives are static host files, the Network Information System (NIS) or Lightweight Directory Access Protocol (LDAP). Unfortunately, it is implementation-dependent how an administrator configures a host to use the different types of name services. Solaris 2.x, HP-UX 10 and later, and FreeBSD 5.x and later use the file /etc/nsswitch.conf, and AIX uses the file /etc/netsvc.conf. BIND 9.2.2 supplies its own version named the Information Retrieval Service (IRS), which uses the file /etc/irs.conf. If a name server is to be used for hostname lookups, then all these systems use the file /etc/resolv.conf to specify the IP addresses of the name servers. Fortunately, these differences are normally hidden to the application programmer, so just call the resolver functions such as gethostbyname and gethostbyaddr.

gethostbyname Function

Host computers are normally known by human-readable names. All the examples that have shown so far in this book have intentionally used IP addresses instead of names, so know exactly what goes into the socket address structures for functions such as connect and sendto , and what is returned by functions such as accept and recvfrom . But, most applications should deal with names, not addresses. This is especially true as move to IPv6, since IPv6 addresses (hex strings) are much longer than IPv4 dotted-decimal numbers. (The example AAAA record and ip6.arpa PTR record in the previous section should make this obvious.)

The most basic function that looks up a hostname is gethostbyname . If successful, it returns a pointer to a hostent structure that contains all the IPv4 addresses for the host. However, it is limited in that it can only return IPv4 addresses. See Section 11.6 for a function that handles both IPv4 and IPv6 addresses. The POSIX specification cautions that gethostbyname may be withdrawn in a future version of the spec.

It is unlikely that gethostbyname implementations will actually disappear until the whole Internet is using IPv6, which will be far in the future. However, withdrawing the function from the POSIX specification is a way to assert that it should not be used in new code. encourage the use of getaddrinfo (Section 11.6) in new programs.

```
#include <netdb.h>
struct hostent *gethostbyname (const char * hostname );
Returns: non-null pointer if OK,NULL on error with h_errno set
```

The non-null pointer returned by this function points to the following hostent structure:

```
struct hostent {
char *h_name; /* official (canonical) name of host */
char **h_aliases; /* pointer to array of pointers to alias names */
int h_addrtype; /* host address type: AF_INET */
int h_length; /* length of address: 4 */
char **h_addr_list; /* ptr to array of ptrs with IPv4 addrs */
};
```

In terms of the DNS, gethostbyname performs a query for an A record. This function can return only IPv4 addresses.

The arrangement of the hostent structure and the information that it points to assuming the hostname that is looked up has two alias names and three IPv4 addresses. Of these fields, the official hostname and all the aliases are null-terminated C strings.

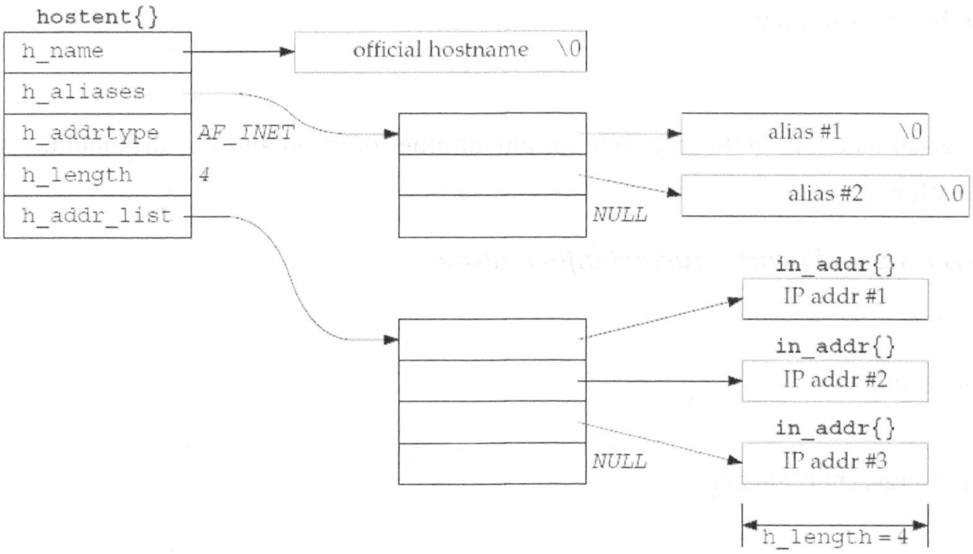

hostent structure and the information it contains

The returned h_name is called the canonical name of the host. For example, given the CNAME records shown in the previous section, the canonical name of the host ftp.unpbook.com would be linux.unpbook.com. Also, if call gethostbyname from the host aix with an unqualified hostname, say solaris , the FQDN (solaris.unpbook.com) is returned as the canonical name.

Some versions of gethostbyname allow the hostname argument to be a dotted-decimal string. That is, a call of the form hptr = gethostbyname ("192.168.42.2"); will work. This code was added because the Rlogin client accepts only a hostname, calling gethostbyname , and will not accept a dotted-decimal string [Vixie 1996]. The POSIX specification permits, but does not require, this behavior, so a portable application cannot depend on it.

gethostbyname differs from the other socket functions that have described in that it does not set errno when an error occurs. Instead, it sets the global integer h_errno to one of the following constants defined by including <netdb.h>:

HOST_NOT_FOUND

TRY_AGAIN

NO_RECOVERY

NO_DATA (identical to NO_ADDRESS)

The NO_DATA error means the specified name is valid, but it does not have an A record. An example of this is a hostname with only an MX record.

Most modern resolvers provide the function hstrerror , which takes an h_errno value as its only argument and returns a const char * pointer to a description of the error. show some examples of the strings returned by this function in the next example.

Example

A simple program that calls gethostbyname for any number of command-line arguments and prints all the returned information.

Call gethostbyname and print returned information.

names/hostent.c

```
#include "unp.h"
int
main(int argc, char **argv)
{
char *ptr, **pptr;
char str [INET_ADDRSTRLEN];
```

```
7 struct hostent *hptr;
8 while (--argc > 0) {
9 ptr = *++argv;
10 if ( (hptr = gethostbyname (ptr) ) == NULL) {
11 err_msg ("gethostbyname error for host: %s: %s",
12 ptr, hstrerror (h_errno) );
13 continue;
14 }
15 printf ("official hostname: %s\n", hptr->h_name);
16 for (pptr = hptr->h_aliases; *pptr ! = NULL; pptr++)
17 printf ("\talias: %s\n", *pptr);
18 switch (hptr->h_addrtype) {
19 case AF_INET:
20 pptr = hptr->h_addr_list;
21 for ( ; *pptr != NULL; pptr++)
22 printf ("\taddress: %s\n",
23 Inet_ntop (hptr->h_addrtype, *pptr, str, sizeof (str)));
24 break;
25 default:
26 err_ret ("unknown address type");
27 break;
28 }
29 }
30 exit(0);
31 }
```

8–14 gethostbyname is called for each command-line argument.

15–17 The official hostname is output followed by a list of alias names.

18–24 pptr points to the array of pointers to the individual addresses. For each address, call inet_ntop and print the returned string.

To execute the program with the name of our host aix , which has just one IPv4 address.

```
freebsd % hostent aix
official hostname: aix.unpbook.com
address: 192.168.42.2
```

address, only the IPv4 address is returned. Next is a Web server with multiple IPv4 addresses.

```
freebsd % hostent cnn.com
official hostname: cnn.com
address: 64.236.16.20
address: 64.236.16.52
address: 64.236.16.84
address: 64.236.16.116
address: 64.236.24.4
address: 64.236.24.12
address: 64.236.24.20
address: 64.236.24.28
```

Next is a name that showed in Section 11.2 as having a CNAME record.

```
freebsd % hostent www
official hostname: linux. unpbook. com
alias: www.unpbook.com
address: 206.168.112.219
```

As expected, the official hostname differs from our command-line argument. To see the error strings returned by the hstrerror function, first specify a non-existent hostname, and then a name that has only an MX record.

```
freebsd % hostent nosuchname.invalid
gethostbyname error for host: nosuchname.invalid: Unknown host
freebsd % hostent uunet.uu.net
gethostbyname error for host: uunet.uu.net: No address associated with name
```

gethostbyaddr Function

The function gethostbyaddr takes a binary IPv4 address and tries to find the hostname corresponding to that address. This is the reverse of gethostbyname.

```
#include <netdb.h>
struct hostent *gethostbyaddr (const char *addr, socklen_t len, int family);
Returns: non-null pointer if OK, NULL on error with h_errno set
```

This function returns a pointer to the same hostent structure that described with gethostbyname. The field of interest in this structure is normally h_name, the canonical hostname.

The addr argument is not a char*, but is really a pointer to an in_addr structure containing the IPv4 address. len is the size of this structure: 4 for an IPv4 address. The family argument is AF_INET.

In terms of the DNS, gethostbyaddr queries a name server for a PTR record in the in-addr.arpa domain.

getservbyname and getservbyport Functions

Services, like hosts, are often known by names. If refer to a service by its name in our code, instead of by its port number, and if the mapping from the name to port number is contained in a file (normally /etc/services), then if the port number changes, all need to modify is one line in the /etc/services file instead of having to recompile the applications. The next function, getservbyname , looks up a service given its name.

The canonical list of port numbers assigned to services is maintained by the IANA at http://www.iana.org/assignments/port-numbers (Section 2.9). A given /etc/services file is likely to contain a subset of the IANA assignments.

```
#include <netdb.h>
struct servent *getservbyname (const char * servname , const char * protoname );
Returns: non-null pointer if OK, NULL on error
```

This function returns a pointer to the following structure:

```
struct servent {
char *s_name; /* official service name */
char **s_aliases; /* alias list */
int s-port; /* port number, network-byte order */
char *s_proto; /* protocol to use */
};
```

The service name servname must be specified. If a protocol is also specified (protoname is a non-null pointer), then the entry must also have a matching protocol. Some Internet services are provided using either TCP or UDP, while others support only a single protocol (e.g., FTP requires TCP). If protoname is not specified and the service supports multiple protocols, it is implementation-dependent as to which port number is returned. Normally this does not matter, because services that support multiple protocols often use the same TCP and UDP port number, but this is not guaranteed.

The main field of interest in the servent structure is the port number. Since the port number is returned in network byte order, must not call htons when storing this into a socket address structure.

Typical calls to this function could be as follows:

```
struct servent *sptr;
sptr = getservbyname("domain", "udp"); /* DNS using UDP */
sptr = getservbyname("ftp", "tcp"); /* FTP using TCP */
sptr = getservbyname("ftp", NULL); /* FTP using TCP */
sptr = getservbyname("ftp", "udp"); /* this call will fail */
```

Since FTP supports only TCP, the second and third calls are the same, and the fourth call will fail. Typical lines from the /etc/services file are

```
freebsd % grep -e ^ftp -e ^domain /etc/services
ftp-data 20/tcp #File Transfer [Default Data]
ftp 21/tcp #File Transfer [Control]
domain 53/tcp #Domain Name Server
domain 53/udp #Domain Name Server
ftp-agent 574/tcp #FTP Software Agent System
ftp-agent 574/udp #FTP Software Agent System
ftps-data 989/tcp # ftp protocol, data, over TLS/SSL
ftps 990/tcp # ftp protocol, control, over TLS/SSL
```

The next function, getservbyport, looks up a service given its port number and an optional protocol.

```
#include <netdb.h>
struct servent *getservbyport (int port , const char *protoname );
Returns: non-null pointer if OK, NULL on error
```

The port value must be network byte ordered. Typical calls to this function could be as follows:

```
struct servent *sptr;
sptr = getservbyport (htons (53), "udp"); /* DNS using UDP */
sptr = getservbyport (htons (21), "tcp"); /* FTP using TCP */
sptr = getservbyport (htons (21), NULL); /* FTP using TCP */
sptr = getservbyport (htons (21), "udp"); /* this call will fail */
```

The last call fails because there is no service that uses port 21 with UDP. Be aware that a few port numbers are used with TCP for one service, but the same port number is used with UDP for a totally different service. For example, the following:

```
freebsd % grep 514 /etc/services
shell 514/tcp cmd #like exec, but automatic
syslog 514/udp
```

The port 514 is used by the rsh command with TCP, but with the syslog daemon with UDP. Ports 512–514 have this property.

Example: Using gethostbyname and getservbyname

TCP daytime client to use gethostbyname and getservbyname and take two command-line arguments: a hostname and a service name. Figure 11.4 shows our program. This program also shows the desired behavior of attempting to connect to all the IP addresses for a multihomed server, until one succeeds or all the addresses have been tried.

Our daytime client that uses gethostbyname and getservbyname .

names/daytimetcpcli1.c

```
#include "unp.h"
int
main (int argc, char **argv)
{
int sockfd, n;
char recvline [MAXLINE + 1];
struct sockaddr_in servaddr;
struct in_addr **pptr;
struct in_addr *inetaddrp [2];
struct in_addr inetaddr;
struct hostent *hp;
struct servent *sp;
if (argc ! = 3)
err_quit ("usage: daytimetcpclil <hostname> <service>");
if ( (hp = gethostbyname (argv [1]) ) == NULL) {
if (inet_aton (argv [1], &inetaddr) == 0) {
err_quit ("hostname error for %s: %s", argv [1],
hstrerror (h_errno) );
} else {
inetaddrp [0] = &inetaddr;
inetaddrp [1] = NULL;
pptr = inetaddrp;
}
} else {
pptr = (struct in_addr **) hp->h_addr_list;
}
if ( (sp = getservbyname (argv [2], "tcp") ) == NULL)
err_quit ("getservbyname error for %s", argv [2] );
for ( ; *pptr != NULL; pptr++) {
sockfd = Socket (AF_INET, SOCK_STREAM, 0) ;
```

```
31 bzero (&servaddr, sizeof (servaddr) ) ;
32 servaddr.sin_family = AF_INET;
33 servaddr.sin_port = sp->s_port;
34 memcpy (&servaddr.sin_addr, *pptr, sizeof (struct in_addr) ) ;
35 printf ("trying %s\n", Sock_ntop ( (SA *) &servaddr, sizeof (servaddr)));
36 if (connect (sockfd, (SA *) &servaddr, sizeof (servaddr) ) == 0)
37 break; /* success */
38 err_ret ("connect error");
39 close (sockfd) ;
40 }
41 if (*pptr == NULL)
42 err_quit ("unable to connect");
43 while ( (n = Read (sockfd, recvline, MAXLINE) ) > 0) {
44 recvline [n] = 0; /* null terminate */
45 Fputs (recvline, stdout);
46 }
47 exit (0);
48 }
```

Call gethostbyname and getservbyname

13–28 The first command-line argument is a hostname, which pass as an argument to gethostbyname , and the second is a service name, which pass as an argument to getservbyname .

Our code assumes TCP, and that is what use as the second argument to getservbyname . If gethostbyname fails to look up the name, try using the inet_aton function (Section 3.6) to see if the argument was an ASCII-format address. If it was, construct a single-element list consisting of the corresponding address.

Try each server address

29–35 now code the calls to socket and connect in a loop that is executed for every server address until a connect succeeds or the list of IP addresses is exhausted. After calling socket , fill in an Internet socket address structure with the IP address and port of the server. While could move the call to bzero and the subsequent two assignments out of the loop, for efficiency, the code is easier to read as shown. Establishing the connection with the server is rarely a performance bottleneck for a network client.

Call connect

36–39 connect is called, and if it succeeds, break terminates the loop. If the connection establishment fails, print an error and close the socket. Recall that a descriptor that fails a call to connect must be closed and is no longer usable.

Check for failure

41–42 If the loop terminates because no call to connect succeeded, the program terminates.

Read server's reply

43–47 Otherwise, read the server's response, terminating when the server closes the connection.

If run this program specifying one of our hosts that is running the daytime server, get the expected output.

```
freebsd % daytimetcpcli1 aix daytime
trying 192.168.42.2:13
Sun Jul 27 22:44:19 2003
```

What is more interesting is to run the program to a multihomed system that is not running the daytime server.

```
freebsd % daytimetcpcli1 gateway.tuc.noao.edu daytime
trying 140.252.108.1:13
connect error: Operation timed out
trying 140.252.1.4:13
connect error: Operation timed out
trying 140.252.104.1:13
connect error: Connection refused
unable to connect
```

UNIT- IV

QUESTION BANK

PART-A

1. Differentiate TCP from UDP

- TCP is a sophisticated, reliable byte-stream protocol
- TCP is connection-oriented protocol
- UDP is a simple, unreliable datagram protocol
- UDP is connection-less protocol

Define IPV6

IPV6 was designed as a replacement for IPV4. This is due to a larger address comprising 128 bits. IPV6 provides packet delivery service for TCP, UDP, SCTP and ICMPv6

2. What is ICMP

Internet Control Message Protocol handles error and control information between routers and hosts. These messages are generated by and processed by the TCP/IP networking software.

3. What is ARP

Address Resolution Protocol maps an IPV4 address into a hardware address. ARP is used on broadcast networks such as Ethernet, token ring and FDDI and is not needed on point-to-point networks.

4. Give a brief note on TCP three-way handshake

- Server-Passive open (SYN J)
- Client- Active open (SYN K, ACK J+1)
- Acknowledgement (ACK K+1)

The minimum number of packets required for this exchange is three. Hence it is called TCP's three-way handshake.

5. Define MSS option in TCP

With this option, the TCP sending the SYN announces its maximum segment size, the maximum amount of data that it is willing to accept in each TCP segment, on this connection. The sending TCP uses the receiver's MSS value as the maximum size of a segment that it sends.

6. What are sockets

- A socket is an endpoint for communication
- Socket is an abstraction for an endpoint of communication that can be manipulated with a file descriptor.
- Scope of a socket is the communication domain in which it exists.

7. Differentiate Well-known ports from ephemeral ports

- Servers listen on well-known ports . Well-known ports are 0- 1023. In Unix these are reserved ports.
- Clients use ephemeral (ie, transient) ports. These ports are usually assigned by TCP or UDP to the client

8. Why should an application in a network call "shutdown" with an argument of SHUT_RDWR instead of just calling close?

If we use the close() to release the connection, the socket fd is no longer available in the kernel. It will immediately delete the socket fd.

But in shutdown() with has an argument of SHUT_RDWR, we can't read or write from the socket but the socket is still available in the kernel.

9. Mention the 5 I/O models available in Unix

- Blocking I/O
- Non blocking I/O
- I/O multiplexing
- Signal driven I/O
- Asynchronous I/O

10. Define polling

When an application sits in a loop calling recvfrom on a nonblocking descriptor, it is called polling. The application is continually polling the kernel to see if some operation is ready. The disadvantage is the waste of CPU time.

11. Differentiate Synchronous I/O from Asynchronous I/O

- A Synchronous I/O operation causes the requesting process to be blocked until that I/O operation completes
- An Asynchronous I/O operation does not cause the requesting process to be blocked.

12. When does the error EWOULDBLOCK occur.

It occurs in a non blocking I/O model. When we call recvfrom system call and if there is no data to return, the kernel immediately returns an error of EWOULDBLOCK. When a datagram is ready, recvfrom returns successfully.

13. What is the use of select function

The select function allows the process to instruct the kernel to wait for any one of multiple events to occur and to wake up the process only when one or more of these events occurs or when a specified amount of time has passed.

14. Define Signal-driven I/O

We can use signals, telling the kernel to notify us with the SIGIO signal when the descriptor is ready. This is called signal-driven I/O

15. Define TCP_KEEPALIVE Socket Option

It specifies the idle time in seconds for the connection before TCP starts sending keepalive probes. The default values must be atleast 7200 seconds, which is 2 hours. This option is enabled only if SO_KEEPALIVE socket option is enabled.

16. Give any two Socket options in IPv6 .

IPv6_ADDFORM – This option allows a socket to be converted from IPv4 to IPv6 or viceversa.

IPv6_CHECKSUM – This socket option specifies the byte offset into the user data of where the checksum fields is located.

17. Define Resource Records

Entries in the DNS are known as resource records(RR). The following are the types of Resource Records.

- A
- AAAA
- PTR
- MX
- CNAME

18. Define CNAME

CNAME stands for "canonical name". A common use is to assign CNAME records for common services such as ftp and www.

Eg: ftp IN CNAMElinux.unpbook.com

www IN CNAMElinux.unpbook.com

19. Give the syntax of gethostbyname function

```
#include <netdb.h>

struct hostent *gethostbyname( const char *hostname);
```

UNIT- IV

PART-B (16 MARKS)

1. Assume both a client and server set the SO_KEEPALIVE socket option and the connectivity is maintained between the peers but them is no exchange of data. When the keep alive timer expires every 2 hours, how many TCP segments are exchanged across the connection? Justify your answer with an illustration.
2. Write a program that checks all the socket option of a socket and sets the value for receiver buffer size to 520 bytes.
3. Write notes on RES_USE_INET6 resolver option in gethostbyname and gethostbyname2 functions.
4. Discuss any four TCP socket option in detail.
5. Discuss about IP socket option and ICMP socket options in detail with suitable example
6. Write the similarities between UDP socket, TCP socket and raw socket.
7. Explain the purpose and usage of UDP sockets and their different functions
8. Brief the way in which a TCP client server different from UDP client server
9. Briefly discuss about DNS with an example
10. Briefly discuss about TCP Echo server and client
11. Briefly discuss about UDP Echo server and client

UNIT- V

ADVANCED SOCKETS

IPv4 and IPv6 Interoperability

- IPv4 client, IPv6 server over dual-stack server host
- IPv6 client over dual-stack client host, IPv4 server
- IPv6 address macro, function and option
- Source code portability

IPv4 Client, IPv6 Server over Dual-Stack Server Host

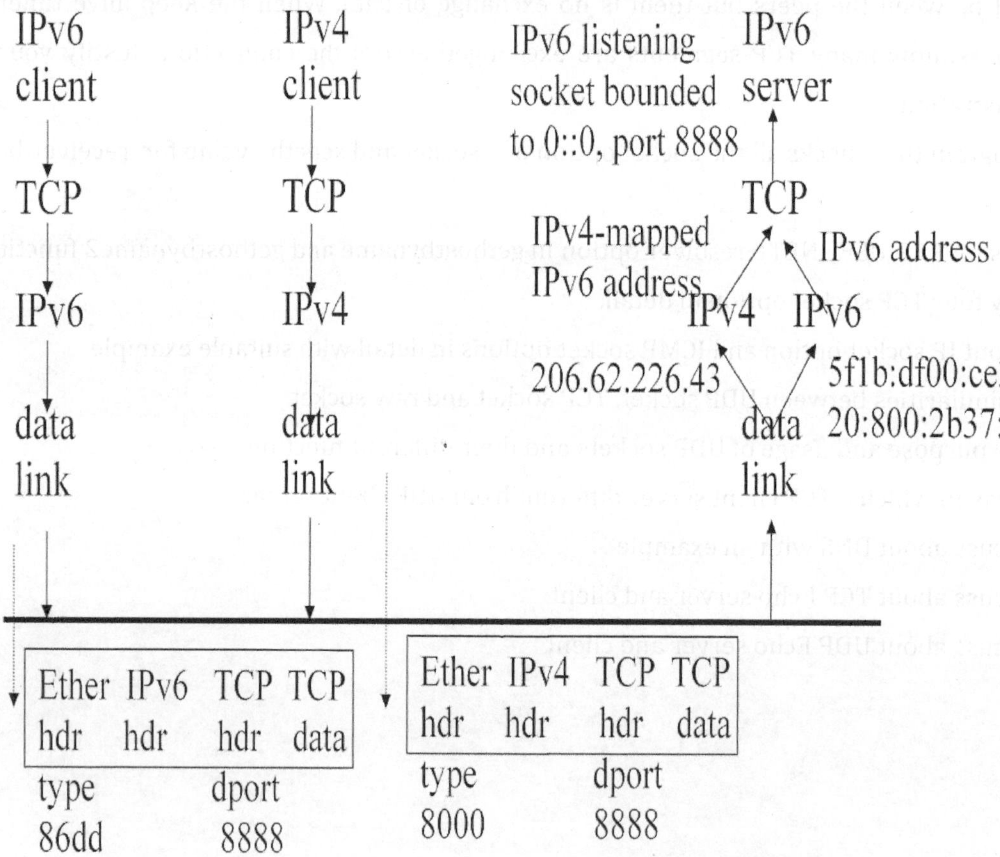

Dual-Stack Kernel at Server Side

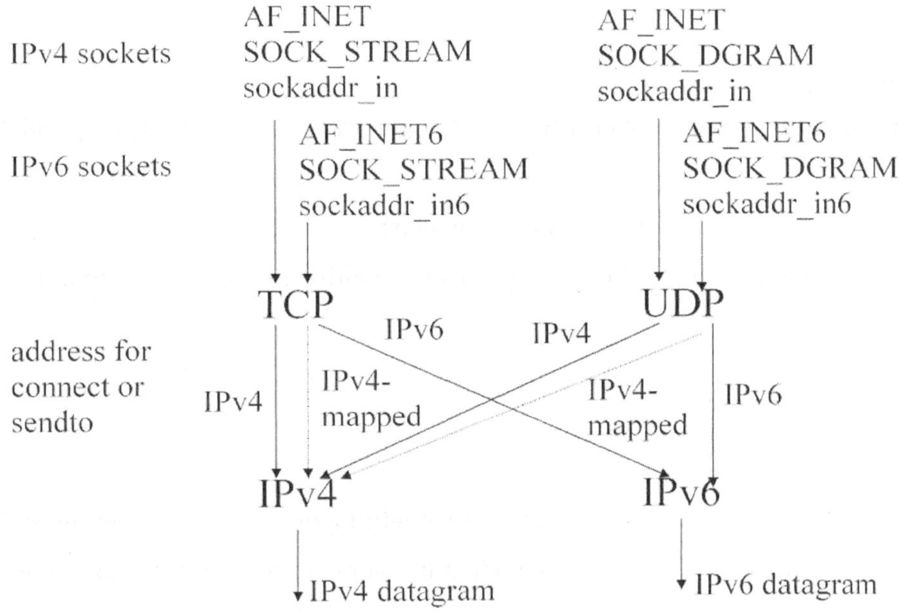

Interoperability between IPv4 and IPv6 Clients and Servers

	IPv4 server IPv4-only host (A only)	IPv6 server IPv6-only host (AAAA only)	IPv4 server dual-stack host (A and AAAA)	IPv6 server dual-stack host (A and AAAA)
IPv4 client, IPv4-only host	IPv4	(no)	IPv4	IPv4
IPv6 client, IPv6-only host	(no)	IPv6	(no)	IPv6
IPv4 client, dual-stack host	IPv4	(no)	IPv4	IPv4
IPv6 client, dual-stack host	IPv4	IPv6	(no*)	IPv6

IPv4-mapped IPv6 address if client chooses A record; no if client chooses AAAA record Note that most implementations of IPv6 client/server will be on dual-stack hosts. (Second row and second column may disappear.)

IPv6 Address Macro, Function, Option

- IPv6 address testing macros:
  IN6_IS_ADDR_* (e.g. V4MAPPED)
- Protocol independent socket address functions:
  sock_* (e.g. cmp_addr) (section 3.8)

- IPv6_ADDRFORM socket option:

  change a socket type between IPv4 and IPv6, by setsockopt function with IPv6_ADDRFORM option

Source Code Portability

- Automatic program conversion from IPv4 to IPv6 (sockaddr_in, AF_INET, etc) and #ifdef to use IPv6 when possible
- Deal with socket address structures as opaque objects:

  remove gethostbyname and gethostbyaddr, use getaddrinfo and getnameinfo (which use #ifdef internally)

Threads

Introduction

In the traditional Unix model, when a process needs something performed by another entity, it forks a child process and lets the child perform the processing. Most network servers under Unix are written this way, as have seen in our concurrent server examples: The parent accepts the connection, forks a child, and the child handles the client.

While this paradigm has served well for many years, there are problems with fork:

fork is expensive. Memory is copied from the parent to the child, all descriptors are duplicated in the child, and so on. Current implementations use a technique called copy-onwrite, which avoids a copy of the parent's data space to the child until the child needs its own copy. But, regardless of this optimization, fork is expensive.

IPC is required to pass information between the parent and child after the fork. Passing information from the parent to the child before the fork is easy, since the child starts with a copy of the parent's data space and with a copy of all the parent's descriptors. But, returning information from the child to the parent takes more work.

Threads help with both problems. Threads are sometimes called lightweight processes since a thread is "lighter weight" than a process. That is, thread creation can be 10–100 times faster than process creation.

All threads within a process share the same global memory. This makes the sharing of information easy between the threads, but along with this simplicity comes the problem of synchronization.More than just the global variables are shared. All threads within a process share the following:

- Process instructions
- Most data
- Open files (e.g., descriptors)

- Signal handlers and signal dispositions
- Current working directory
- User and group IDs
- But each thread has its own
- Thread ID
- Set of registers, including program counter and stack pointer
- Stack (for local variables and return addresses)
- errno
- Signal mask
- Priority

The traditional Unix model, have the main flow of execution (one thread) and a signal handler (another thread). If the main flow is in the middle of updating a linked list when a signal occurs, and the signal handler also tries to update the linked list, havoc normally results. The main flow and signal handler share the same global variables, but each has its own stack.

The POSIX threads, also called Pthreads. These were standardized in 1995 as part of the POSIX.1c standard and most versions of Unix will support them in the future. will see that all the Pthread functions begin with pthread_.

Basic Thread Functions: Creation and Termination

The five basic thread functions and then use these in the next two sections to recode our TCP client/server using threads instead of fork.

pthread_create Function

When a program is started by exec, a single thread is created, called the initial thread or main thread. Additional threads are created by pthread_create.

```
#include <pthread.h>
int pthread_create(pthread_t *tid, const pthread_attr_t *attr, void *(*func) (void
*), void *arg);
Returns: 0 if OK, positive Exxx value on error
```

Each thread within a process is identified by a thread ID, whose datatype is pthread_t (often an unsigned int). On successful creation of a new thread, its ID is returned through the pointer tid.

Each thread has numerous attributes: its priority, its initial stack size, whether it should be a daemon thread or not, and so on. When a thread is created, can specify these attributes by initializing a pthread_attr_t variable that overrides the default. normally take the default, in which case, specify the attr argument as a null pointer.

Finally, when create a thread, specify a function for it to execute. The thread starts by calling this function and then terminates either explicitly (by calling pthread_exit) or implicitly (by letting the function return). The address of the function is specified as the func argument, and this function is called with a single pointer argument, arg. If need multiple arguments to the function, must package them into a structure and then pass the address of this structure as the single argument to the start function.

Notice the declarations of func and arg. The function takes one argument, a generic pointer (void *), and returns a generic pointer (void *). This lets us pass one pointer (to anything want) to the thread, and lets the thread return one pointer (again, to anything want).

The return value from the Pthread functions is normally 0 if successful or nonzero on an error. But unlike the socket functions, and most system calls, which return -1 on an error and set errno to a positive value, the Pthread functions return the positive error indication as the function's return value. For example, if pthread_create cannot create a new thread because of exceeding some system limit on the number of threads, the function return value is EAGAIN. The Pthread functions do not set errno. The convention of 0 for success or nonzero for an error is fine since all the Exxx values in <sys/errno.h> are positive. A value of 0 is never assigned to one of the Exxx names.

pthread_join Function

To wait for a given thread to terminate by calling pthread_join. Comparing threads to Unix processes, pthread_create is similar to fork, and pthread_join is similar to waitpid.

```
#include <pthread.h>
int pthread_join (pthread_t tid, void ** status);
Returns: 0 if OK, positive Exxx value on error
```

To specify the tid of the thread that want to wait for. Unfortunately, there is no way to wait for any of our threads (similar to waitpid with a process ID argument of -1).

If the status pointer is non-null, the return value from the thread (a pointer to some object) is stored in the location pointed to by status.

pthread_self Function

Each thread has an ID that identifies it within a given process. The thread ID is returned by pthread_create and saw it was used by pthread_join. A thread fetches this value for itself using pthread_self.

```
#include <pthread.h>
pthread_t pthread_self (void);
```

Returns: thread ID of calling thread

Comparing threads to Unix processes, pthread_self is similar to getpid.

pthread_detach Function

A thread is either joinable (the default) or detached. When a joinable thread terminates, its thread ID and exit status are retained until another thread calls pthread_join. But a detached thread is like a daemon process: When it terminates, all its resources are released and cannot wait for it to terminate. If one thread needs to know when another thread terminates, it is best to leave the thread as joinable.

The pthread_detach function changes the specified thread so that it is detached.

```
#include <pthread.h>
int pthread_detach (pthread_t tid);
```

Returns: 0 if OK, positive Exxx value on error

This function is commonly called by the thread that wants to detach itself, as in pthread_detach (pthread_self());

pthread_exit Function

One way for a thread to terminate is to call pthread_exit.

```
#include <pthread.h>
void pthread_exit (void *status);
```

Does not return to caller

If the thread is not detached, its thread ID and exit status are retained for a later pthread_join by some other thread in the calling process. The pointer status must not point to an object that is local to the calling thread since that object disappears when the thread terminates.

There are two other ways for a thread to terminate:

- The function that started the thread (the third argument to pthread_create) can return. Since this function must be declared as returning a void pointer, that return value is the exit status of the thread.
- If the main function of the process returns or if any thread calls exit, the process terminates, including any threads.

TCP Echo Server Using Threads

The TCP echo server using one thread per client instead of one child process per client. also make it protocol-independent, using our tcp_listen function.

Create thread

17–21 When accept returns, call pthread_create instead of fork. The single argument that pass to the doit function is the connected socket descriptor, connfd.

The integer descriptor connfd to be a void pointer. ANSI C does not guarantee that this works. It works only on systems on which the size of an integer is less than or equal to the size of a pointer. Fortunately, most Unix implementations have this property.

Thread function

23–30 doit is the function executed by the thread. The thread detaches itself since there is no reason for the main thread to wait for each thread it creates. When this function returns, must close the connected socket since the thread shares all descriptors with the main thread. With fork, the child did not need to close the connected socket because when the child terminated, all open descriptors were closed on process termination.

Also notice that the main thread does not close the connected socket, which always did with a concurrent server that calls fork. This is because all threads within a process share the descriptors, so if the main thread called close, it would terminate the connection. Creating a new thread does not affect the reference counts for open descriptors, which is different from fork.

TCP echo server using threads

threads/tcpserv01.c

```
1 #include "unpthread.h"
2 static void *doit(void *); /* each thread executes this function */
3 int
4 main(int argc, char **argv)
5 {
6 int listenfd, connfd;
7 pthread_t tid;
8 socklen_t addrlen, len;
9 struct sockaddr *cliaddr;
10 if (argc == 2)
11 listenfd = Tcp_listen(NULL, argv[1], &addrlen);
12 else if (argc == 3)
13 listenfd = Tcp_listen(argv[1], argv[2], &addrlen);
14 else
15 err_quit("usage: tcpserv01 [ <host> ] <service or port>");
```

```
cliaddr = Malloc(addrlen);
for (; ; ) {
len = addrlen;
connfd = Accept(listenfd, cliaddr, &len);
Pthread_create(&tid, NULL, &doit, (void *) connfd);
}
}
static void *
doit(void *arg)
{
Pthread_detach(pthread_self());
str_echo((int) arg); /* same function as before */
Close((int) arg); /* done with connected socket */
return (NULL);
}
```

Passing Arguments to New Threads

The cast the integer variable connfd to be a void pointer, but this is not guaranteed to work on all systems. To handle this correctly requires additional work.

First, notice that cannot just pass the address of connfd to the new thread. That is, the following does not work:

```
int
main(int argc, char **argv)
{
int listenfd, connfd;
...
for ( ; ; ) {
len = addrlen;
connfd = Accept(listenfd, cliaddr, &len);
Pthread_create(&tid, NULL, &doit, &connfd);
}
}
static void *
doit(void *arg)
```

```
{
int connfd;
connfd = * ((int *) arg);
pthread_detach (pthread_self());
str_echo (connfd); /* same function as before */
Close (connfd); /* done with connected socket */
return (NULL);
}
```

From an ANSI C perspective this is acceptable: are guaranteed that can cast the integer pointer to be a void * and then cast this pointer back to an integer pointer. The problem is what this pointer points to.

There is one integer variable, connfd in the main thread, and each call to accept overwrites this variable with a new value (the connected descriptor). The following scenario can occur: accept returns, connfd is stored into (say the new descriptor is 5), and the main thread calls pthread_create. The pointer to connfd (not its contents) is the final argument to pthread_create.

A thread is created and the doit function is scheduled to start executing. Another connection is ready and the main thread runs again (before the newly created thread). accept returns, connfd is stored into (say the new descriptor is now 6), and the main thread calls pthread_create.

Even though two threads are created, both will operate on the final value stored in connfd, which assume is 6. The problem is that multiple threads are accessing a shared variable (the integer value in connfd) with no synchronization. To solved this problem by passing the value of connfd to pthread_create instead of a pointer to the value. This is fine, given the way that C passes integer values to a called function (a copy of the value is pushed onto the stack for the called function).

TCP echo server using threads with more portable argument passing.

threads/tcpserv02.c

```
#include "unpthread.h"
static void *doit(void *); /* each thread executes this function */
int
main(int argc, char **argv)
{
int listenfd, *iptr;
thread_t tid;
socklen_t addrlen, len;
struct sockaddr *cliaddr;
```

```
10 if (argc == 2)
11 listenfd = Tcp_listen(NULL, argv[1], &addrlen);
12 else if (argc == 3)
13 listenfd = Tcp_listen(argv[1], argv[2], &addrlen);
14 else
15 err_quit("usage: tcpserv01 [ <host> ] <service or port>");
16 cliaddr = Malloc(addrlen);
17 for ( ; ; ) {
18 len = addrlen;
19 iptr = Malloc(sizeof(int));
20 *iptr = Accept(listenfd, cliaddr, &len);
21 Pthread_create(&tid, NULL, &doit, iptr);
22 }
23 }
24 static void *
25 doit(void *arg)
26 {
27 int connfd;
28 connfd = *((int *) arg);
29 free(arg);
30 Pthread_detach(pthread_self());
31 str_echo(confd); /* same function as before */
32 Close(confd); /* done with connected socket */
33 return (NULL);
34 }
```

17–22 Each time call accept, first call malloc and allocate space for an integer variable, the connected descriptor. This gives each thread its own copy of the connected descriptor.

28–29 The thread fetches the value of the connected descriptor and then calls free to release the memory.

Historically, the malloc and free functions have been nonre-entrant. That is, calling either function from a signal handler while the main thread is in the middle of one of these two functions has been a recipe for disaster, because of static data structures that are manipulated by these two functions.

The POSIX requires that these two functions, along with many others, be thread-safe. This is normally done by some form of synchronization performed within the library functions that is transparent to us.

Thread-Safe Functions

POSIX.1 requires that all the functions defined by POSIX.1 and by the ANSI C standard be thread safe, with the exceptions.

Need not be thread-safe	Must be thread-safe	
asctime	asctime_r	
	ctermid	thread-safe only if nonnull argument
ctime	ctime_r	
getc_unblocked		
getchar_unblocked		
getgrid	getgrid_r	
getgrnam	getgrnam_r	
getlogin	getlogin_r	
getpwnam	getpwnam_r	
getpwuid	getpwuid_r	
gmtime	gmtime_r	
localtime	localtime_r	
putc_unlocked		
putchar_unlocked		
rand	rand_r	
readdir	readdir_r	
strtok	strtok_r	
	tmpnam	thread-safe only if nonnull argument
ttyname	ttyname_r	
gethostXXX		
getnetXXX		
getprotoXXX		
getservXXX		
inet_ntoa		

Threads-safe functions.

The POSIX says nothing about thread safety with regard to the networking API functions. The last five lines in this table are from Unix 98. The nonre-entrant property of gethostbyname and gethostbyaddr. Some vendors have defined thread-safe versions whose names end in _r, there is no standard for these functions and they should be avoided.

The common technique for making a function thread-safe is to define a new function whose name ends in _r. Two of the functions are thread-safe only if the caller allocates space for the result and passes that pointer as the argument to the function.

Mutexes: Mutual Exclusion

When a thread terminates, the main loop decrements both nconn and nlefttoread. could have placed these two decrements in the function do_get_read, letting each thread decrement these two counters immediately before the thread terminates. But this would be a subtle, yet significant, concurrent programming error.

The problem with placing the code in the function that each thread executes is that these two variables are global, not thread-specific. If one thread is in the middle of decrementing a variable, that thread is suspended, and if another thread executes and decrements the same variable, an error can result. For example, assume that the C compiler turns the decrement operator into three instructions: load from memory into a register, decrement the register, and store from the register into memory.

Consider the following possible scenario:

1. Thread A is running and it loads the value of nconn (3) into a register. The system switches threads from A to B. A's registers are saved, and B's registers are restored.
2. Thread B executes the three instructions corresponding to the C expression nconn--, storing the new value of 2.
3. Sometime later, the system switches threads from B to A. A's registers are restored and A continues where it left off, at the second machine instruction in the three-instruction sequence. The value of the register is decremented from 3 to 2, and the value of 2 is stored in nconn.
4. The end result is that nconn is 2 when it should be 1. This is wrong.

These types of concurrent programming errors are hard to find for numerous reasons. First, they occur rarely. Nevertheless, it is an error and it will fail (Murphy's Law). Second, the error is hard to duplicate since it depends on the nondeterministic timing of many events. Lastly, on some systems, the hardware instructions might be atomic; that is, there might be a hardware instruction to decrement an integer in memory (instead of the three-instruction sequence assumed above) and the hardware cannot be interrupted during this instruction. But, this is not guaranteed by all systems, so the code works on one system but not on another.

To call threads programming concurrent programming, or parallel programming, since multiple threads can be running concurrently (in parallel), accessing the same variables. While the error scenario just discussed assumes a single-CPU system, the potential for error also exists if threads A and B are running at the same time on different CPUs on a multiprocessor system. With normal Unix programming, do not encounter these concurrent programming problems because with fork, nothing besides descriptors is shared between the parent and child. will, however, encounter this same type of problem when discuss shared memory between processes.

To demonstrate this problem with threads. A simple program that creates two threads and then has each thread increment a global variable 5,000 times. exacerbate the potential for a problem by fetching the current value of counter, printing the new value, and then storing the new value.

Two threads that increment a global variable incorrectly

threads/example01.c

```
#include "unpthread.h"
#define NLOOP 5000
int counter; /* incremented by threads */
```

```
void *doit(void *);
int
main(int argc, char **argv)
{
pthread_t tidA, tidB;
Pthread_create(&tidA, NULL, &doit, NULL);
Pthread_create(&tidB, NULL, &doit, NULL);
/* wait for both threads to terminate */
Pthread_join(tidA, NULL);
Pthread_join(tidB, NULL);
exit(0);
}
void *
doit(void *vptr)
{
int i, val;
/*
* Each thread fetches, prints, and increments the counter NLOOP times.
* The value of the counter should increase monotonically.
*/
for (i = 0; i < NLOOP; i++) {
val = counter;
printf("%d: %d\n", pthread_self(), val + 1);
counter = val + 1;
}
return (NULL);
}
```

Notice the error the first time the system switches from thread 4 to thread 5: The value 518 is stored by each thread. This happens numerous times through the 10,000 lines of output.

The nondeterministic nature of this type of problem is also evident if run the program a few times: Each time, the end result is different from the previous run of the program. Also, if redirect the output to a disk file, sometimes the error does not occur since the program runs faster, providing fewer opportunities to switch between the threads. The greatest number of errors occurs when run the program interactively, writing the output to the (slow) terminal, but saving the output in a file using the Unix script program (discussed in detail in Chapter 19 of APUE).

The problem just discussed, multiple threads updating a shared variable, is the simplest problem. The solution is to protect the shared variable with a mutex (which stands for "mutual exclusion") and access the variable only when hold the mutex. In terms of Pthreads, a mutex is a variable of type pthread_mutex_t. lock and unlock a mutex using the following two functions:

```
#include <pthread.h>
int pthread_mutex_lock(pthread_mutex_t * mptr);
int pthread_mutex_unlock(pthread_mutex_t * mptr);
Both return: 0 if OK, positive Exxx value on error
```

If try to lock a mutex that is already locked by some other thread, are blocked until the mutex is unlocked.

If a mutex variable is statically allocated, must initialize it to the constant PTHREAD_MUTEX_INITIALIZER. If allocate a mutex in shared memory, must initialize it at runtime by calling the pthread_mutex_init function.

Some systems (e.g., Solaris) define PTHREAD_MUTEX_INITIALIZER to be 0, so omitting this initialization is acceptable, since statically allocated variables are automatically initialized to 0.

But there is no guarantee that this is acceptable and other systems (e.g., Digital Unix) define the initializer to be nonzero.

Corrected version using a mutex to protect the shared variable

threads/example02.c

```
#include "unpthread.h"
#define NLOOP 5000
int counter; /* incremented by threads */
pthread_mutex_t counter_mutex = PTHREAD_MUTEX_INITIALIZER;
void *doit(void *);
int
main(int argc, char **argv)
{
pthread_t tidA, tidB;
Pthread_create(&tidA, NULL, &doit, NULL);
Pthread_create(&tidB, NULL, &doit, NULL);
/* wait for both threads to terminate */
Pthread_join(tidA, NULL);
```

```
Pthread_join(tidB, NULL);
exit(0);
}
void *
doit(void *vptr)
{
int i, val;
/*
* Each thread fetches, prints, and increments the counter NLOOP times.
* The value of the counter should increase monotonically.
*/
for (i = 0; i < NLOOP; i++) {
Pthread_mutex_lock(&counter_mutex);
val = counter;
printf("%d: %d\n", pthread_self(), val + 1);
counter = val + 1;
Pthread_mutex_unlock(&counter_mutex);
}
return (NULL);
}
```

To declare a mutex named counter_mutex and this mutex must be locked by the thread before the thread manipulates the counter variable. When run this program, the output is always correct: The value is incremented monotonically and the final value printed is always 10,000.

The difference in CPU time from the incorrect version with no mutex to the correct version that used a mutex was 10%. This tells us that mutex locking is not a large overhead.

Condition Variables

A mutex is fine to prevent simultaneous access to a shared variable, but need something else to let us go to sleep waiting for some condition to occur. Let's demonstrate this with an example. To replace the Solaris thr_join with pthread_join. But, cannot call the Pthread function until know that a thread has terminated. first declare a global variable that counts the number of terminated threads and protect it with a mutex.

```
int ndone; /* number of terminated threads */
pthread_mutex_t ndone_mutex = PTHREAD_MUTEX_INITIALIZER;
```

To require that each thread increment this counter when it terminates, being careful to use the associated mutex.

```
void *
do_get_read (void *vptr)
{
...
Pthread_mutex_lock(&ndone_mutex);
ndone++;
Pthread_mutex_unlock(&ndone_mutex);
return(fptr); /* terminate thread */
}
```

This is fine, but how do code the main loop? It needs to lock the mutex continually and check if any threads have terminated.

```
while (nlefttoread > 0) {
while (nconn < maxnconn && nlefttoconn > 0) {
/* find a file to read */
...
}
/* See if one of the threads is done */
Pthread_mutex_lock(&ndone_mutex);
if (ndone > 0) {
for (i = 0; i < nfiles; i++) {
if (file[i].f_flags & F_DONE) {
Pthread_join(file[i].f_tid, (void **) &fptr);
/* update file[i] for terminated thread */
...
}
}
}
Pthread_mutex_unlock(&ndone_mutex);
}
```

The main loop never goes to sleep; it just loops, checking ndone every time around the loop. This is called polling and is considered a waste of CPU time.

A method for the main loop to go to sleep until one of its threads notifies it that something is ready. A condition variable, in conjunction with a mutex, provides this facility. The mutex provides mutual exclusion and the condition variable provides a signaling mechanism.

In terms of Pthreads, a condition variable is a variable of type pthread_cond_t. They are used with the following two functions:

```
#include <pthread.h>
int pthread_cond_wait(pthread_cond_t *cptr, pthread_mutex_t *mptr);
int pthread_cond_signal(pthread_cond_t *cptr);
Both return: 0 if OK, positive Exxx value on error
```

The term "signal" in the second function's name does not refer to a Unix SIGxxx signal. An example is the easiest way to explain these functions. Returning to our Web client example, the counter ndone is now associated with both a condition variable and a mutex.

```
int ndone;
pthread_mutex_t ndone_mutex = PTHREAD_MUTEX_INITIALIZER;
pthread_cond_t ndone_cond = PTHREAD_COND_INITIALIZER;
```

A thread notifies the main loop that it is terminating by incrementing the counter while its mutex lock is held and by signaling the condition variable.

```
Pthread_mutex_lock(&ndone_mutex);
ndone++;
Pthread_cond_signal(&ndone_cond);
Pthread_mutex_unlock(&ndone_mutex);
```

The main loop then blocks in a call to pthread_cond_wait, waiting to be signaled by a terminating thread.

```
while (nlefttoread > 0) {
while (nconn < maxnconn && nlefttoconn > 0) {
/* find file to read */
...
}
/* Wait for thread to terminate */
Pthread_mutex_lock(&ndone_mutex);
while (ndone == 0)
Pthread_cond_wait (&ndone_cond, &ndone_mutex);
for (i = 0; i < nfiles; i++) {
if (file[i].f_flags & F_DONE) {
Pthread_join(file[i].f_tid, (void **) &fptr);
/* update file[i] for terminated thread */
```

```
...
}
}
Pthread_mutex_unlock (&ndone_mutex);
}
```

The variable ndone is still checked only while the mutex is held. Then, if there is nothing to do, pthread_cond_wait is called. This puts the calling thread to sleep and releases the mutex lock it holds. Furthermore, when the thread returns from pthread_cond_wait (after some other thread has signaled it), the thread again holds the mutex.

The "condition" is normally the value of some variable that is shared between the threads. The mutex is required to allow this variable to be set and tested by the different threads. For example, if did not have the mutex in the example code just shown, the main loop would test it as follows:

```
/* Wait for thread to terminate */
while (ndone == 0)
Pthread_cond_wait(&ndone_cond, &ndone_mutex);
```

But, there is a possibility that the last of the threads increments ndone after the test of ndone == 0, but before the call to pthread_cond_wait. If this happens, this last "signal" is lost and the main loop would block forever, waiting for something that will never occur again.

This is the same reason that pthread_cond_wait must be called with the associated mutex locked, and why this function unlocks the mutex and puts the calling thread to sleep as a single, atomic operation. If this function did not unlock the mutex and then lock it again when it returns, the thread would have to unlock and lock the mutex and the code would look like the following:

```
/* Wait for thread to terminate */
Pthread_mutex_lock(&ndone_mutex);
while (ndone == 0) {
Pthread_mutex_unlock(&ndone_mutex);
Pthread_cond_wait(&ndone_cond, &ndone_mutex);
Pthread_mutex_lock(&ndone_mutex);
}
```

But again, there is a possibility that the final thread could terminate and increment the value of ndone between the call to pthread_mutex_unlock and pthread_cond_wait.

The pthread_cond_signal awakens one thread that is waiting on the condition variable.

There are instances when a thread knows that multiple threads should be awakened, in which case, pthread_cond_broadcast will wake up all threads that are blocked on the condition variable.

```
#include <pthread.h>
int pthread_cond_broadcast (pthread_cond_t * cptr);
int pthread_cond_timedwait (pthread_cond_t * cptr, pthread_mutex_t *mptr, const
struct timespec *abstime);
```

Both return: 0 if OK, positive Exxx value on error

pthread_cond_timedwait lets a thread place a limit on how long it will block. abstime is a timespec structure that specifies the system time when the function must return, even if the condition variable has not been signaled yet. If this timeout occurs, ETIME is returned.

This time value is an absolute time; it is not a time delta. That is, abstime is the system time—the number of seconds and nanoseconds past January 1, 1970, UTC—when the function should return.

This differs from both select and pselect, which specify the number of seconds and microseconds (nanoseconds for pselect) until some time in the future when the function should return. The normal procedure is to call gettimeofday to obtain the current time (as a timeval structure!), and copy this into a timespec structure, adding in the desired time limit. For example,

```
struct timeval tv;
struct timespec ts;
if (gettimeofday(&tv, NULL) < 0)
err_sys("gettimeofday error");
ts.tv_sec = tv.tv_sec + 5; /* 5 seconds in future */
ts.tv_nsec = tv.tv_usec * 1000; /* microsec to nanosec */
pthread_cond_timedwait( ..., &ts);
```

The advantage in using an absolute time instead of a delta time is if the function prematurely returns (perhaps because of a caught signal), the function can be called again, without having to change the contents of the timespec structure. The disadvantage, however, is having to call gettimeofday before the function can be called the first time.

The POSIX specification defines a clock_gettime function that returns the current time as a timespec structure.

Raw Sockets

Introduction

Raw sockets provide three features not provided by normal TCP and UDP sockets: Raw sockets let us read and write ICMPv4, IGMPv4, and ICMPv6 packets. The ping program, for example, sends ICMP echo requests and receives ICMP echo replies. The multicast routing daemon, mrouted, sends and receives IGMPv4 packets.

This capability also allows applications that are built using ICMP or IGMP to be handled entirely as user processes, instead of putting more code into the kernel. The router discovery daemon (in. rdisc under Solaris 2.x; Appendix F of TCPv1 describes how to obtain the source code for a publicly available version), for example, is built this way. It processes two ICMP messages (router advertisement and router solicitation) that the kernel knows nothing about.

With a raw socket, a process can read and write IPv4 datagrams with an IPV4 protocol field that is not processed by the kernel. Most kernels only process datagrams containing values of 1 (ICMP), 2 (IGMP), 6 (TCP), and 17 (UDP). But many other values are defined for the protocol field: The IANA's "Protocol Numbers" registry lists all the values. For example, the OSPF routing protocol does not use TCP or UDP, but it uses IP directly, setting the protocol field of the IP datagram to 89. The gated program that implements OSPF must use a raw socket to read and write these IP datagrams since they contain a protocol field the kernel knows nothing about. This capability carries over to IPv6 also.

With a raw socket, a process can build its own IPv4 header using the IP_HDRINCL socket option. This chapter describes raw socket creation, input, and output. will also develop versions of the ping and traceroute programs that work with both IPv4 and IPv6.

Raw Socket Creation

The steps involved in creating a raw socket are as follows:

The socket function creates a raw socket when the second argument is SOCK_RAW. The third argument (the protocol) is normally nonzero. For example, to create an IPv4 raw socket would write

```
int sockfd;
sockfd = socket(AF_INET, SOCK_RAW, protocol);
```

where protocol is one of the constants, IPPROTO_xxx, defined by including the <netinet/in.h> header, such as IPPROTO_ICMP. Only the superuser can create a raw socket. This prevents normal users from writing their own IP datagrams to the network.

The IP_HDRINCL socket option can be set as follows:

```
const int on = 1;
```

```
if (setsockopt(sockfd, IPPROTO_IP, IP_HDRINCL, &on, sizeof(on)) < 0)
error
```

bind can be called on the raw socket, but this is rare. This function sets only the local address: There is no concept of a port number with a raw socket. With regard to output, calling bind sets the source IP address that will be used for datagrams sent on the raw socket (but only if the IP_HDRINCL socket option is not set). If bind is not called, the kernel sets the source IP address to the primary IP address of the outgoing interface.

connect can be called on the raw socket, but this is rare. This function sets only the foreign address: Again, there is no concept of a port number with a raw socket. With regard to output, calling connect lets us call write or send instead of sendto, since the destination IP address is already specified.

Raw Socket Output

Output on a raw socket is governed by the following rules:

Normal output is performed by calling sendto or sendmsg and specifying the destination IP address. write, writev, or send can also be called if the socket has been connected.

If the IP_HDRINCL option is not set, the starting address of the data for the kernel to send specifies the first byte following the IP header because the kernel will build the IP header and prepend it to the data from the process. The kernel sets the protocol field of the IPv4 header that it builds to the third argument from the call to socket.

If the IP_HDRINCL option is set, the starting address of the data for the kernel to send specifies the first byte of the IP header. The amount of data to write must include the size of the caller's IP header. The process builds the entire IP header, except: (i) the IPv4 identification field can be set to 0, which tells the kernel to set this value; (ii) the kernel always calculates and stores the IPv4 header checksum; and (iii) IP options may or may not be included;

The kernel fragments raw packets that exceed the outgoing interface MTU. Raw sockets are documented to provide an identical interface to the one a protocol would have if it was resident in the kernel [McKusick et al. 1996] Unfortunately, this means that certain pieces of the API are dependent on the OS kernel, specifically with regard to the byte ordering of the fields in the IP header. On many Berkeley-derived kernels, all fields are in network byte order except ip_len and ip_off, which are in host byte order (pp. 233 and 1057 of TCPv2). On Linux and OpenBSD, however, all the fields must be in network byte order.

The IP_HDRINCL socket option was introduced with 4.3BSD Reno. Before this, the only way for an application to specify its own IP header in packets sent on a raw IP socket was to apply a kernel patch that was introduced in 1988 by Van Jacobson to support traceroute. This patch required the application to create a raw

IP socket specifying a protocol of IPPROTO_RAW, which has a value of 255 (and is a reserved value and must never appear as the protocol field in an IP header).

The functions that perform input and output on raw sockets are some of the simplest in the kernel. For example, in TCPv2, each function requires about 40 lines of C code (pp. 1054–1057), compared to TCP input at about 2,000 lines and TCP output at about 700 lines.

Our description of the IP_HDRINCL socket option is for 4.4BSD. Earlier versions, such as Net/2, filled in more fields in the IP header when this option was set. With IPv4, it is the responsibility of the user process to calculate and set any header checksums contained in whatever follows the IPv4 header.

The ICMPv4 checksum and store it in the ICMPv4 header before calling sendto.

IPv6 Differences

There are a few differences with raw IPv6 sockets:

All fields in the protocol headers sent or received on a raw IPv6 socket are in network byte order. There is nothing similar to the IPv4 IP_HDRINCL socket option with IPv6. Complete IPv6 packets (including the IPv6 header or extension headers) cannot be read or written on an IPv6 raw socket. Almost all fields in an IPv6 header and all extension headers are available to the application through socket options or ancillary data. An application need to read or write complete IPv6 datagrams, datalink access must be used. Checksums on raw IPv6 sockets are handled differently.

IPV6_CHECKSUM Socket Option

For an ICMPv6 raw socket, the kernel always calculates and stores the checksum in the ICMPv6 header. This differs from an ICMPv4 raw socket, where the application must do this itself. While ICMPv4 and ICMPv6 both require the sender to calculate the checksum, ICMPv6 includes a pseudoheader in its checksum. One of the fields in this pseudoheader is the source IPv6 address, and normally the application lets the kernel choose this value. To prevent the application from having to try to choose this address just to calculate the checksum, it is easier to let the kernel calculate the checksum.

For other raw IPv6 sockets (i.e., those created with a third argument to socket other than IPPROTO_ICMPV6), a socket option tells the kernel whether to calculate and store a checksum in outgoing packets and verify the checksum in received packets. By default, this option is disabled, and it is enabled by setting the option value to a nonnegative value, as in

```
int offset = 2;
if (setsockopt(sockfd, IPPROTO_IPV6, IPV6_CHECKSUM,
&offset, sizeof(offset)) < 0)
Error
```

This not only enables checksums on this socket, it also tells the kernel the byte offset of the 16-bit checksum: 2 bytes from the start of the application data in this example. To disable the option, it must be set to -1. When enabled, the kernel will calculate and store the checksum for outgoing packets sent on the socket and also verify the checksums for packets received on the socket.

Raw Socket Input

The first question that must answer regarding raw socket input is: Which received IP datagrams does the kernel pass to raw sockets? The following rules apply: Received UDP packets and received TCP packets are never passed to a raw socket. If a process wants to read IP datagrams containing UDP or TCP packets, the packets must be read at the datalink layer.

Most ICMP packets are passed to a raw socket after the kernel has finished processing the ICMP message. Berkeley-derived implementations pass all received ICMP packets to a raw socket other than echo request, timestamp request, and address mask request (pp. 302–303 of TCPv2). These three ICMP messages are processed entirely by the kernel.

All IGMP packets are passed to a raw socket after the kernel has finished processing the IGMP message.

All IP datagrams with a protocol field that the kernel does not understand are passed to a raw socket. The only kernel processing done on these packets is the minimal verification of some IP header fields: the IP version, IPv4 header checksum, header length, and destination IP address (pp. 213–220 of TCPv2).

If the datagram arrives in fragments, nothing is passed to a raw socket until all fragments have arrived and have been reassembled.

When the kernel has an IP datagram to pass to the raw sockets, all raw sockets for all processes are examined, looking for all matching sockets. A copy of the IP datagram is delivered to each matching socket. The following tests are performed for each raw socket and only if all three tests are true is the datagram delivered to the socket: If a nonzero protocol is specified when the raw socket is created (the third argument to socket), then the received datagram's protocol field must match this value or the datagram is not delivered to this socket.

If a local IP address is bound to the raw socket by bind, then the destination IP address of the received datagram must match this bound address or the datagram is not delivered to this socket.

If a foreign IP address was specified for the raw socket by connect, then the source IP address of the received datagram must match this connected address or the datagram is not delivered to this socket.

Notice that if a raw socket is created with a protocol of 0, and neither bind nor connect is called, then that socket receives a copy of every raw datagram the kernel passes to raw sockets.

Whenever a received datagram is passed to a raw IPv4 socket, the entire datagram, including the IP header, is passed to the process. For a raw IPv6 socket, only the payload (i.e., no IPv6 header or any extension headers) is passed to the socket.

In the IPv4 header passed to the application, ip_len, ip_off, and ip_id are host byte ordered, and ip_len contains only the IP payload length (with the IP header length subtracted), but the remaining fields are network byte ordered. Under Linux, all fields are left in network byte order.

The raw socket interface is defined to provide an identical interface to the one a protocol would have if it was resident in the kernel, so the contents of the fields are dependent on the OS kernel.

ICMPv6 Type Filtering

A raw ICMPv4 socket receives most ICMPv4 messages received by the kernel. But ICMPv6 is a superset of ICMPv4, including the functionality of ARP and IGMP (Section 2.2). Therefore, a raw ICMPv6 socket can potentially receive many more packets compared to a raw ICMPv4 socket. But most applications using a raw socket are interested in only a small subset of all ICMP messages.

To reduce the number of packets passed from the kernel to the application across a raw ICMPv6 socket, an application-specified filter is provided. A filter is declared with a datatype of struct icmp6_filter, which is defined by including <netinet/icmp6.h>. The current filter for a raw ICMPv6 socket is set and fetched using setsockopt and getsockopt with a level of IPPROTO_ICMPv6 and an optname of ICMP6_FILTER. Six macros operate on the icmp6_filter structure.

```
#include <netinet/icmp6.h>
void ICMP6_FILTER_SETPASSALL (struct icmp6_filter *filt);
void ICMP6_FILTER_SETBLOCKALL (struct icmp6_filter *filt);
void ICMP6_FILTER_SETPASS (int msgtype, struct icmp6_filter *filt);
void ICMP6_FILTER_SETBLOCK (int msgtype, struct icmp6_filter *filt);
int ICMP6_FILTER_WILLPASS (int msgtype, const struct icmp6_filter *filt);
int ICMP6_FILTER_WILLBLOCK (int msgtype, const struct icmp6_filter *filt);
Both return: 1 if filter will pass (block) message type, 0 otherwise
```

The filt argument to all the macros is a pointer to an icmp6_filter variable that is modified by the first four macros and examined by the final two macros. The msgtype argument is a value between 0 and 255 and specifies the ICMP message type.

The SETPASSALL macro specifies that all message types are to be passed to the application, while the SETBLOCKALL macros specifies that no message types are to be passed. By default, when an ICMPv6 raw socket is created, all ICMPv6 message types are passed to the application.

The SETPASS macro enables one specific message type to be passed to the application while the SETBLOCK macro blocks one specific message type. The WILLPASS macro returns 1 if the specified message type is passed by the filter, or 0 otherwise; the WILLBLOCK macro returns 1 if the specified message type is blocked by the filter, or 0 otherwise.

As an example, consider the following application, which wants to receive only ICMPv6 router advertisements:

```
struct icmp6_filter myfilt;
fd = socket (AF_INET6, SOCK_RAW, IPPROTO_ICMPV6);
ICMP6_FILTER_SETBLOCKALL (&myfilt);
ICMP6_FILTER_SETPASS (ND_ROUTER_ADVERT, &myfilt);
Setsockopt (fd, IPPROTO_ICMPV6, ICMP6_FILTER. &myfilt, sizeof (myfilt));
```

To block all message types (since the default is to pass all message types) and then pass only router advertisements. Despite our use of the filter, the application must be prepared to receive all types of ICMPv6 packets since any ICMPv6 packets that arrive between the socket and the setsockopt will be added to the receive queue. The ICMP6_FILTER option is simply an optimization.

ping Program

To develop and present a version of the ping program that works with both IPv4 and IPv6. will develop our own program instead of presenting the publicly available source code for two reasons. First, the publicly available ping program suffers from a common programming disease known as creeping featurism: It supports a dozen different options. Our goal in examining a ping program is to understand the network programming concepts and techniques without being distracted by all these options. Our version of ping supports only one option and is about five times smaller than the public version. Second, the public version works only with IPv4 and want to show a version that also supports IPv6.

The operation of ping is extremely simple: An ICMP echo request is sent to some IP address and that node responds with an ICMP echo reply. These two ICMP messages are supported under both IPv4 and IPv6.

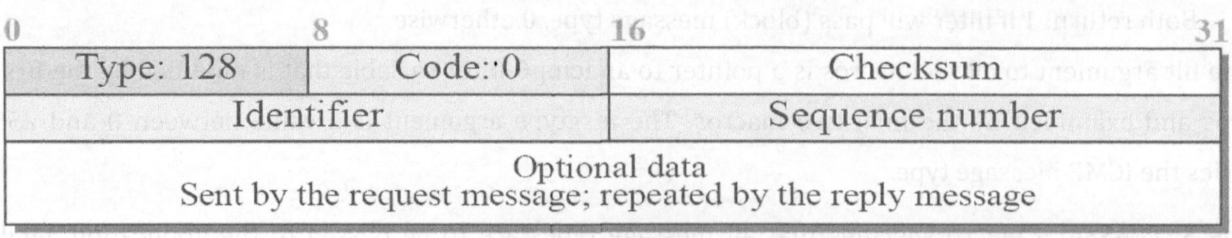

Format of ICMPv4 and ICMPv6 echo request and echo reply messages

The identifier to the PID of the ping process and increment the sequence number by one for each packet send. store the 8-byte timestamp of when the packet is sent as the optional data. The rules of ICMP require that the identifier, sequence number, and any optional data be returned in the echo reply. Storing the timestamp in the packet lets us calculate the RTT when the reply is received.

Sample output from our ping program.

```
freebsd % ping www.google.com
PING www.google.com (216.239.57.99): 56 data bytes
64 bytes from 216.239.57.99: seq=0, ttl=53, rtt=5.611 ms
64 bytes from 216.239.57.99: seq=1, ttl=53, rtt=5.562 ms
64 bytes from 216.239.57.99: seq=2, ttl=53, rtt=5.589 ms
64 bytes from 216.239.57.99: seq=3, ttl=53, rtt=5.910 ms
freebsd % ping www.kame.net
PING orange.kame.net (2001:200:0:4819:203:47ff:fea5:3085): 56 data bytes
64 bytes from 2001:200:0:4819:203:47ff:fea5:3085: seq=0, hlim=52, rtt=422.066 ms
64 bytes from 2001:200:0:4819:203:47ff:fea5:3085: seq=1, hlim=52, rtt=417.398 ms
64 bytes from 2001:200:0:4819:203:47ff:fea5:3085: seq=2, hlim=52, rtt=416.528 ms
64 bytes from 2001:200:0:4819:203:47ff:fea5:3085: seq=3, hlim=52, rtt=429.192 ms
```

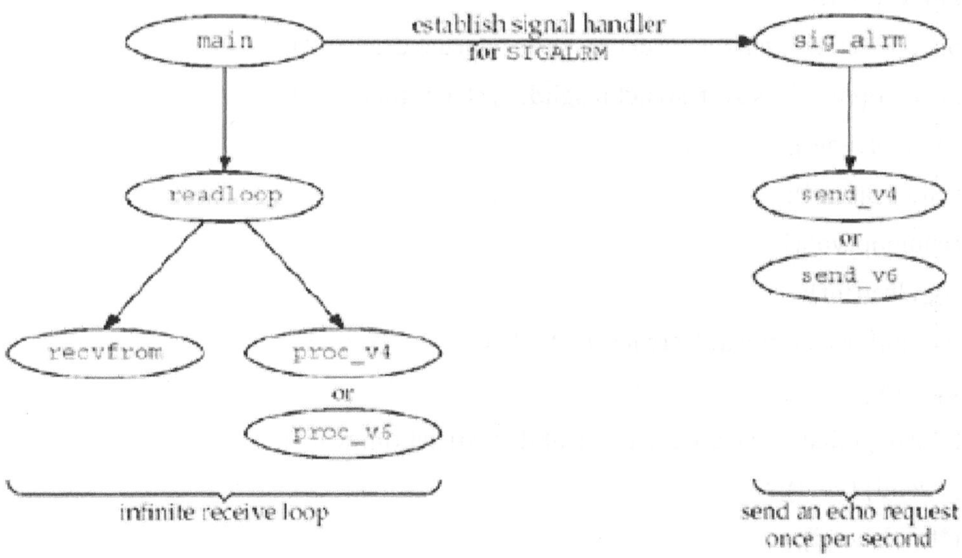

Overview of the functions in our ping program

The program operates in two parts: One half reads everything received on a raw socket, printing the ICMP echo replies, and the other half sends an ICMP echo request once per second. The second half is driven by a SIGALRM signal once per second.

ping.h header.

ping/ping.h

```
#include "unp.h"
#include <netinet/in_systm.h>
#include <netinet/ip.h>
#include <netinet/ip_icmp.h>
#define BUFSIZE 1500
/* globals */
char sendbuf[BUFSIZE];
int datalen; /* #bytes of data following ICMP header */
char *host;
int nsent; /* add 1 for each sendto() */
pid_t pid; /* our PID */
int sockfd;
int verbose;
/* function prototypes */
void init_v6(void);
void proc_v4(char *, ssize_t, struct msghdr *, struct timeval *);
void proc_v6(char *, ssize_t, struct msghdr *, struct timeval *);
void send_v4(void);
void send_v6(void);
void readloop(void);
void sig_alrm(int);
void tv_sub(struct timeval *, struct timeval *);
struct proto {
void (*fproc) (char *, ssize_t, struct msghdr *, struct timeval *);
void (*fsend) (void);
void (*finit) (void);
struct sockaddr *sasend; /* sockaddr{} for send, from getaddrinfo */
struct sockaddr *sarecv; /* sockaddr{} for receiving */
socklen_t salen; /* length of sockaddr {}s */
int icmpproto; /* IPPROTO_xxx value for ICMP */
} *pr;
#ifdef IPV6
```

```
33 #include <netinet/ip6.h>
34 #include <netinet/icmp6.h>
35 #endif
```

Include IPv4 and ICMPv4 headers

1–22 include the basic IPv4 and ICMPv4 headers, define some global variables, and our function prototypes.

Define proto structure

23–31 use the proto structure to handle the difference between IPv4 and IPv6. This structure contains two function pointers, two pointers to socket address structures, the size of the socket address structures, and the protocol value for ICMP. The global pointer pr will point to one of the structures that will initialize for either IPv4 or IPv6.

Include IPv6 and ICMPv6 headers

32–35 include two headers that define the IPv6 and ICMPv6 structures and constants.

main function

ping/main.c

```
#include "ping.h"
struct proto proto_v4 =
{ proc_v4, send_v4, NULL, NULL, NULL, 0, IPPROTO_ICMP };
#ifdef IPV6
struct proto proto_v6 =
{ proc_v6, send_v6, NULL, NULL, 0, IPPROTO_ICMPV6 };
#endif
int datalen = 56; /* data that goes with ICMP echo request */
int
main(int argc, char **argv)
{
int c;
struct addrinfo *ai;
char *h;
opterr = 0; /* don't want getopt() writing to stderr */
while ( (c = getopt (argc, argv, "v") ) != -1) {
switch (c) {
```

```
case 'v':
verbose++;
break;
case '?':
err_quit ("unrecognized option: %c", c);
}
}
if (optind != argc - 1)
err_quit ("usage: ping [ -v ] <hostname>");
host = argv [optind];
pid = getpid() & Oxffff; /* ICMP ID field is 16 bits */
Signal(SIGALRM, sig_alrm);
ai = Host_serv (host, NULL, 0, 0);
h = Sock_ntop_host(ai->ai_addr, ai->ai_addrlen);
printf ("PING %s (%s): %d data bytes\n",
ai->ai_canonname ? ai->ai_canonname : h, h, datalen);
/* initialize according to protocol */
if (ai->ai_family == AF_INET) {
pr = &proto_v4;
#ifdef IPV6
} else if (ai->ai_family == AF_INET6) {
pr = &proto_v6;
if (IN6_IS_ADDR_V4MAPPED (&(((struct sockaddr_in6 *)
ai->ai_addr)->sin6_addr)))
err_quit ("cannot ping IPv4-mapped IPv6 address");
#endif
} else
err_quit ("unknown address family %d", ai->ai_family);
pr->sasend = ai->ai_addr;
pr->sacrecv = Calloc (1, ai->ai_addrlen);
pr->salen = ai->ai_addrlen);
readloop();
exit(0);
}
```

Define proto structures for IPv4 and IPv6

2–7 define a proto structure for IPv4 and IPv6. The socket address structure pointers are initialized to null pointers, as do not yet know whether will use IPv4 or IPv6.

Length of optional data

8 set the amount of optional data that gets sent with the ICMP echo request to 56 bytes. This will yield an 84-byte IPv4 datagram (20-byte IPv4 header and 8-byte ICMP header) or a 104-byte IPv6 datagram. Any data that accompanies an echo request must be sent back in the echo reply.

To store the time at which send an echo request in the first 8 bytes of this data area and then use this to calculate and print the RTT when the echo reply is received.

Handle command-line options

15–24 The only comman-line option support is -v, which will cause us to print most received ICMP messages. A signal handler is established for SIGALRM, and will see that this signal is generated once per second and causes an ICMP echo request to be sent.

Process hostname argument

31–48 A hostname or IP address string is a required argument and it is processed by our host_serv function. The returned addrinfo structure contains the protocol family, either AF_INET or AF_INET6. initialize the pr global to the correct proto structure. also make certain that an IPv6 address is not really an IPv4-mapped IPv6 address by calling IN6_IS_ADDR_V4MAPPED, because even though the returned address is an IPv6 address, IPv4 packets will be sent to the host. (We could switch and use IPv4 when this happens.) The socket address structure that has already been allocated by the getaddrinfo function is used as the one for sending, and another socket address structure of the same size is allocated for receiving.

49 The function readloop is where the processing takes place.

Create socket

12–13 A raw socket of the appropriate protocol is created. The call to setuid sets our effective user ID to our real user ID, in case the program was set-user-ID instead of being run by root. The program must have superuser privileges to create the raw socket, but now that the socket is created, can give up the extra privileges. It is always best to give up an extra privilege when it is no longer needed, just in case the program has a latent bug that someone could exploit.

readloop function

ping/readloop.c

```
1 #include "ping.h"
```

```
void
readloop(void)
{
int size;
char recvbuf[BUFSIZE];
char controlbuf[BUFSIZE];
struct msghdr msg;
struct iovec iov;
ssize_t n;
struct timeval tval;
sockfd = Socket(pr->sasend->sa_family, SOCK_RAW, pr->icmpproto);
setuid(getuid()); /* don't need special permissions any more */
if (pr->finit)
(*pr->finit) ();
size = 60 * 1024; /* OK if setsockopt fails */
setsockopt (sockfd, SOL_SOCKET, SO_RCVBUF, &size, sizeof (size));
sig_alrm (SIGALRM); /* send first packet */
iov.iov_base = recvbuf;
iov.iov_len = sizeof (recvbuf);
msg.msg_name = pr->sarecv;
msg.msg_iov = &iov;
msg.msg_iovlen = 1;
msg.msg_control = controlbuf;
for ( ; ; ) {
msg.msg_namelen = pr->salen;
msg.msg_controllen = sizeof (controlbuf);
n = recvmsg (sockfd, &msg, 0);
if (n < o) {
if (errno == EINTR)
continue;
else
err_sys("recvmsg error");
}
Gettimeofday (&tval, NULL);
```

```
36 (*pr->fproc) (recvbuf, n, &msg, &tval);
37 }
38 }
```

Perform protocol-specific initialization

14–15 If the protocol specified an initialization function, call it.

Set socket receive buffer size

16–17 try to set the socket receive buffer size to 61,440 bytes (60 x 1024), which should be larger than the default. do this in case the user pings either the IPv4 broadcast address or a multicast address, either of which can generate lots of replies. By making the buffer larger, there is a smaller chance that the socket receive buffer will overflow.

Send first packet

18 call our signal handler, which will see sends a packet and schedules a SIGALRM for one second in the future. It is not common to see a signal handler called directly, as do here, but it is acceptable. A signal handler is just a C function, even though it is normally called asynchronously.

Set up msghdr for recvmsg

19–24 set up the unchanging fields in the msghdr and iovec structs that will pass to recvmsg.

Infinite loop reading all ICMP messages

25–37 The main loop of the program is an infinite loop that reads all packets returned on the raw ICMP socket. call gettimeofday to record the time that the packet was received and then call the appropriate protocol function (proc_v4 or proc_v6) to process the ICMP message.

tv_sub function: subtracts two timeval structures.

lib/tv_sub.c

```
#include "unp.h"
void
tv_sub (struct timeval *out, struct timeval *in)
{
if ((out->tv_usec -= in->tv_usec) < 0) { /* out -= in */
--out->tv_sec;
out->tv_usec += 1000000;
}
out->tv_sec -= in->tv_sec;
```

```
}
```

proc_v4 function: processes ICMPv4 message

ping/proc_v4.c

```
#include "ping.h"
void
proc_v4 (char *ptr, ssize_t len, struct msghdr *msg, struct timeval *tvrecv)
{
int hlenl, icmplen;
double rtt;
struct ip *ip;
struct icmp *icmp;
struct timeval *tvsend;
ip = (struct ip *) ptr; /* start of IP header */
hlenl = ip->ip_hl << 2; /* length of IP header */
if (ip->ip_p != IPPROTO_ICMP)
return; /* not ICMP */
icmp = (struct icmp *) (ptr + hlenl); /* start of ICMP header */
if ( (icmplen = len - hlenl) < 8)
return; /* malformed packet */
if (icmp->icmp_type == ICMP_ECHOREPLY) {
if (icmp->icmp_id != pid)
return; /* not a response to our ECHO_REQUEST */
if (icmplen < 16)
return; /* not enough data to use */
tvsend = (struct timeval *) icmp->icmp_data;
tv_sub (tvrecv, tvsend);
rtt = tvrecv->tv_sec * 1000.0 + tvrecv->tv_usec / 1000.0;
printf ("%d bytes from %s: seq=%u, ttl=%d, rtt=%.3f ms\n",
icmplen, Sock_ntop_host (pr->sarecv, pr->salen),
icmp->icmp_seq, ip->ip_ttl, rtt);
} else if (verbose) {
printf (" %d bytes from %s: type = %d, code = %d\n",
icmplen, Sock_ntop_host (pr->sarecv, pr->salen),
icmp->icmp_type, icmp->icmp_code);
```

```
32 }
33 }
```

Get pointer to ICMP header

10–16 The IPv4 header length field is multiplied by 4, giving the size of the IPv4 header in bytes. (Remember that an IPv4 header can contain options.) This lets us set icmp to point to the beginning of the ICMP header. make sure that the IP protocol is ICMP and that there is enough data echoed to look at the timestamp included in the echo request.

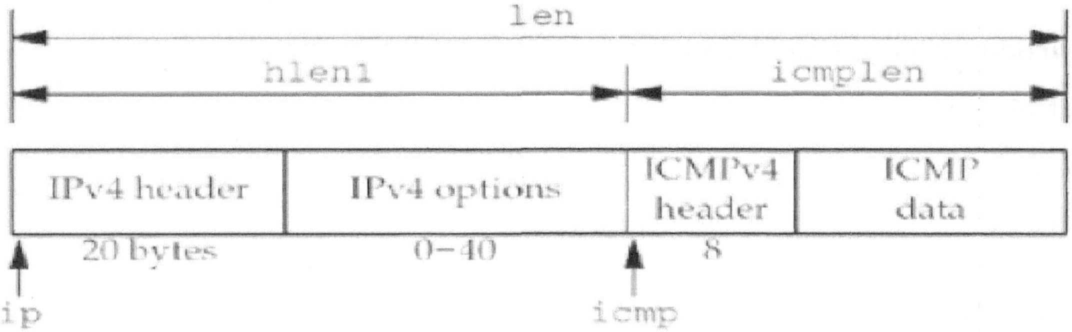

Headers, pointers, and lengths in processing ICMPv4 reply

Check for ICMP echo reply

17–21 If the message is an ICMP echo reply, then must check the identifier field to see if this reply is in response to a request our process sent. If the ping program is running multiple times on this host, each process gets a copy of all received ICMP messages.

22–27 calculate the RTT by subtracting the time the message was sent (contained in the optional data portion of the ICMP reply) from the current time (pointed to by the tvrecv function argument). The RTT is converted from microseconds to milliseconds and printed, along with the sequence number field and the received TTL. The sequence number field lets the user see if packets were dropped, reordered, or duplicated, and the TTL gives an indication of the number of hops between the two hosts.

Print all received ICMP messages if verbose option specified

28–32 If the user specified the -v command-line option, print the type and code fields from all other received ICMP messages.

The processing of ICMPv6 messages is handled by the proc_v6 function. It is similar to the proc_v4 function; however, since IPv6 raw sockets do not return the IPv6 header, it receives the hop limit as ancillary data.

Set ICMPv6 receive filter

6–14 If the -v command-line option was not specified, install a filter that blocks all ICMP message types except for the expected echo reply. This reduces the number of packets received on the socket.

Request IPV6_HOPLIMIT ancillary data

15–22 The API to request reception of the hop limit with incoming packets has changed over time. prefer the newer API: setting the IPV6_RECVHOPLIMIT socket option. However, if the constant for this option is not defined, can try the older API: setting IPV6_HOPLIMIT as an option. don't check the return value from setsockopt, since the program can still do useful work without receiving the hop limit.

init_v6 function: initializes ICMPv6 socket

ping/init_v6.c

```
1 void
2 init_v6()
3 {
4 #ifdef IPV6
5 int on = 1;
6 if (verbose == 0) {
7 /* install a filter that only passes ICMP6_ECHO_REPLY unless verbose */
8 struct icmp6_filter myfilt;
9 ICMP6_FILTER_SETBLOCKALL (&myfilt);
10 ICMP6_FILTER_SETPASS (ICMP6_ECHO_REPLY, &myfilt);
11 setsockopt (sockfd, IPPROTO_IPV6, ICMP6_FILTER, &myfilt,
12 sizeof (myfilt));
13 /* ignore error return; the filter is an optimization */
14 }
15 /* ignore error returned below; just won't receive the hop limit */
16 #ifdef IPV6_RECVHOPLIMIT
17 /* RFC 3542 */
18 setsockopt (sockfd, IPPROTO_IPV6, IPV6_RECVHOPLIMIT, &on, sizeof(on));
19 #else
20 /* RFC 2292 */
21 setsockopt (sockfd, IPPROTO_IPV6, IPV6_HOPLIMIT, &on, sizeof(on));
22 #endif
23 #endif
```

```
24 }
```

The proc_v6 function processes incoming packets.

Get pointer to ICMPv6 header

11–13 The ICMPv6 header is the data returned by the receive operation. (Recall that the IPv6 header and extension headers, if any, are never returned as normal data, but as ancillary data.)

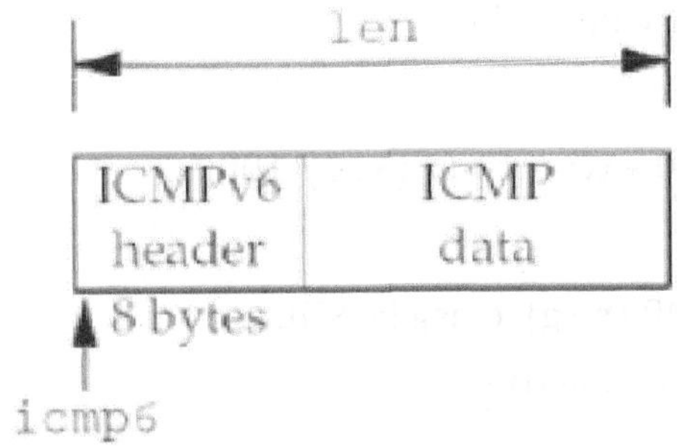

Headers, pointers, and lengths in processing ICMPv6 reply

Check for ICMP echo reply

14–37 If the ICMP message type is an echo reply, check the identifier field to see if the reply is for us. If so, calculate the RTT and then print it along with the sequence number and IPv6 hop limit. obtain the hop limit from the IPV6_HOPLIMIT ancillary data.

proc_v6 function: processes received ICMPv6 message.

ping/proc_v6.c

```
1 #include "ping.h"
2 void
3 proc_v6 (char *ptr, ssize_t len, struct msghdr *msg, struct timeval *tvrecv)
4 {
5 #ifdef IPV6
6 double rtt;
7 struct icmp6_hdr *icmp6;
8 struct timeval *tvsend;
9 struct cmsghdr *cmsg;
10 int hlim;
11 icmp6 = (struct icmp6_hdr *) ptr;
12 if (len < 8)
```

```
return; /* malformed packet */
if (icmp6->icmp6_type == ICMP6_ECHO_REPLY) {
if (icmp6->icmp6_id != pid)
return; /* not a response to our ECHO_REQUEST */
if (len < 16)
return; /* not enough data to use */
tvsend = (struct timeval *) (icmp6 + 1);
tv_sub (tvrecv, tvsend);
rtt = tvrecv->tv_sec * 1000.0 + tvrecv->tv_usec / 1000.0;
hlim = -1;
for (cmsg = CMSG_FIRSTHDR (msg); cmsg != NULL;
cmsg = CMSG_NXTHDR (msg, cmsg)) {
if (cmsg->cmsg_level == IPPROTO_IPV6
&& cmsg->cmsg_type == IPV6_HOPLIMIT) {
hlim = * (u_int32_t *) CMSG_DATA (cmsg);
break;
}
}
printf("%d bytes from %s: seq=%u, hlim=",
len, Sock_ntop_host (pr->sarecv, pr->salen), icmp6->icmp6_seq);
if (hlim == -1)
printf("???"); /* ancillary data missing */
else
printf("%d", hlim);
printf(", rtt=%.3f ms\n", rtt);
} else if (verbose) {
printf(" %d bytes from %s: type = %d, code = %d\n",
len, Sock_ntop_host (pr->sarecv, pr->salen),
icmp6->icmp6_type, icmp6->icmp6_code);
}
#endif /* IPV6 */
}
```

Print all received ICMP messages if verbose option specified

38–41 If the user specified the -v command-line option, print the type and code fields from all other received ICMP messages. Our signal handler for the SIGALRM signal is the sig_alrm function, the readloop function calls this signal handler once at the beginning to send the first packet. This function just calls the protocol-dependent function to send an ICMP echo request (send_v4 or send_v6) and then schedules another SIGALRM for one second in the future.

sig_alrm function: SIGALRM signal handler

ping/sig_alrm.c

```
#include "ping.h"
void
sig_alrm (int signo)
{
(*pr->fsend) ();
alarm(1);
return;
}
```

The function send_v4, builds an ICMPv4 echo request message and writes it to the raw socket.

send_v4 function: builds an ICMPv4 echo request message and sends it

ping/send_v4.c

```
#include "ping.h"
void
send_v4 (void)
{
int len;
struct icmp *icmp;
icmp = (struct icmp *) sendbuf;
icmp->icmp_type = ICMP_ECHO;
icmp->icmp_code = 0;
icmp->icmp_id = pid;
icmp->icmp-seq = nsent++;
memset (icmp->icmp_data, 0xa5, datalen); /* fill with pattern */
Gettimeofday ((struct timeval *) icmp->icmp_data, NULL);
len = 8 + datalen; /* checksum ICMP header and data */
```

```
15 icmp->icmp_cksum = 0;
16 icmp->icmp_cksum = in_cksum ((u_short *) icmp, len);
17 Sendto (sockfd, sendbuf, len, 0, pr->sasend, pr->salen);
18 }
```

Build ICMPv4 message

7–13 The ICMPv4 message is built. The identifier field is set to our PID and the sequence number field is set to the global nsent, which is then incremented for the next packet. store a pattern of 0xa5 in the data portion of the ICMP message. The current time-of-day is then stored in the beginning of the data portion.

Calculate ICMP checksum

14–16 To calculate the ICMP checksum, set the checksum field to 0 and call the function in_cksum, storing the result in the checksum field. The ICMPv4 checksum is calculated from the ICMPv4 header and any data that follows.

Send datagram

17 The ICMP message is sent on the raw socket. Since have not set the IP_HDRINCL socket option, the kernel builds the IPv4 header and prepends it to our buffer.

The Internet checksum is the one's complement of the one's complement sum of the 16-bit values to be checksummed. If the data length is an odd number, then 1 byte of 0 is logically appended to the end of the data, just for the checksum computation. Before computing the checksum, the checksum field itself is set to 0. This algorithm is used for the IPv4, ICMPv4, IGMPv4, ICMPv6, UDP, and TCP checksums. RFC 1071 contains additional information and some numeric examples. Section 8.7 of TCPv2 talks about this algorithm in more detail and shows a more efficient implementation. Our in_cksum function, calculates the checksum.

in_cksum function: calculate the Internet checksum.

libfree/in_cksum.c

```
uint16_t
in_cksum (uint16_t * addr, int len)
{
int nleft = len;
uint32_t sum = 0;
uint16_t *w = addr;
uint16_t answer = 0;
/*
* Our algorithm is simple, using a 32 bit accumulator (sum), add
```

```
10 * sequential 16 bit words to it, and at the end, fold back all the
11 * carry bits from the top 16 bits into the lower 16 bits.
12 */
13 while (nleft > 1) {
14 sum += *w++;
15 nleft -= 2;
16 }
17 /* mop up an odd byte, if necessary */
18 if (nleft == 1) {
19 * (unsigned char *) (&answer) = * (unsigned char *) w;
20 sum += answer;
21 }
22 /* add back carry outs from top 16 bits to low 16 bits */
23 sum = (sum >> 16) + (sum & 0xffff); /* add hi 16 to low 16 */
24 sum += (sum >> 16); /* add carry */
25 answer = ~sum; /* truncate to 16 bits */
26 return (answer);
27 }
```

Internet checksum algorithm

1–27 The first while loop calculates the sum of all the 16-bit values. If the length is odd, then the final byte is added in with the sum. The kernel often has a specially optimized checksum algorithm due to the high volume of checksum computations performed by the kernel. This function is taken from the public domain version of ping by Mike Muuss. The final function for our ping program is send_v6, which builds and sends an ICMPv6 echo request.

send_v6 function: builds and sends an ICMPv6 echo request message

ping/send_v6.c

```
#include "ping.h"
void
send_v6 ()
{
#ifdef IPV6
int len;
struct icmp6_hdr *icmp6;
```

```
icmp6 = (struct icmp6_hdr *) sendbuf;
icmp6->icmp6_type = ICMP6_ECHO_REQUEST;
icmp6->icmp6_code = 0;
icmp6->icmp6_id = pid;
icmp6->icmp6_seq = nsent++;
memset ((icmp6 + 1), 0xa5, datalen); /* fill with pattern */
Gettimeofday ((struct timeval *) (icmp6 + 1), NULL);
len = 8 + datalen; /* 8-byte ICMPv6 header */
Sendto (sockfd, sendbuf, len, 0, pr->sasend, pr->salen);
/* kernel calculates and stores checksum for us */
#endif /* IPV6 */
}
```

The send_v6 function is similar to send_v4, but notice that it does not compute the ICMPv6 checksum. As mentioned earlier in the chapter, since the ICMPv6 checksum uses the source address from the IPv6 header in its computation, this checksum is calculated by the kernel for us, after the kernel chooses the source address.

traceroute Program

In the traceroute lets us determine the path that IP datagrams follow from our host to some other destination. Its operation is simple and Chapter 8 of TCPv1 covers it in detail with numerous examples of its usage. traceroute uses the IPv4 TTL field or the IPv6 hop limit field and two ICMP messages. It starts by sending a UDP datagram to the destination with a TTL (or hop limit) of 1. This datagram causes the first-hop router to return an ICMP "time exceeded in transit" error. The TTL is then increased by one and another UDP datagram is sent, which locates the next router in the path.

When the UDP datagram reaches the final destination, the goal is to have that host return an ICMP "port unreachable" error. This is done by sending the UDP datagram to a random port that is (hopefully) not in use on that host.

Early versions of traceroute were able to set the TTL field in the IPv4 header only by setting the IP_HDRINCL socket option and then building their own IPv4 header. Current systems, however, provide an IP_TTL socket option that lets us specify the TTL to use for outgoing datagrams. (This socket option was introduced with the 4.3BSD Reno release.) It is easier to set this socket option than to build a complete IPv4 header (although will show how to build IPv4 and UDP headers in Section 29.7). The IPv6 IPV6_UNICAST_HOPS socket option lets us control the hop limit field for IPv6 datagrams. Figure 28.17 shows our trace.h header, which all our program files include.

1–11 include the standard IPv4 headers that define the IPv4, ICMPv4, and UDP structures and constants. The rec structure defines the data portion of the UDP datagram that send, but will see that never need to examine this data. It is sent mainly for debugging purposes.

Define proto structure

32–43 As with our ping program in the previous section, handle the protocol differences between IPv4 and IPv6 by defining a proto structure that contains function pointers, pointers to socket address structures, and other constants that differ between the two IP versions. The global pr will be set to point to one of these structures that is initialized for either IPv4 or IPv6, after the destination address is processed by the main function (since the destination address is what specifies whether use IPv4 or IPv6).

Include IPv6 headers

44–47 include the headers that define the IPv6 and ICMPv6 structures and constants.

trace.h header

traceroute/trace.h

```
1 #include "unp.h"
2 #include <netinet/in_systm.h>
3 #include <netinet/ip.h>
4 #include <netinet/ip_icmp.h>
5 #include <netinet/udp.h>
6 #define BUFSIZE 1500
7 struct rec { /* of outgoing UDP data */
8 u_short rec_seq; /* sequence number */
9 u_short rec_ttl; /* TTL packet left with */
10 struct timeval rec_tv; /* time packet left */
11 };
12 /* globals */
13 char recvbuf [BUFSIZE];
14 char sendbuf [BUFSIZE];
15 int datalen; /* # bytes of data following ICMP header */
16 char *host;
17 u_short sport, dport;
18 int nsent; /* add 1 for each sendto () */
19 pid_t pid; /* our PID */
```

```
20 int probe, nprobes;
21 int sendfd, recvfd; /* send on UDP sock, read on raw ICMP sock */
22 int ttl, max_ttl;
23 int verbose;
24 /* function prototypes */
25 const char *icmpcode_v4 (int);
26 const char *icmpcode_v6 (int);
27 int recv_v4 (int, struct timeval *);
28 int recv_v6 (int, struct timeval *);
29 void sig_alrm (int);
30 void traceloop (void);
31 void tv_sub (struct timeval *, struct timeval *);
32 struct proto {
33 const char *(*icmpcode) (int);
34 int (*recv) (int, struct timeval *);
35 struct sockaddr *sasend; /* sockaddr{} for send, from getaddrinfo */
36 struct sockaddr *sarecv; /* sockaddr{} for receiving */
37 struct sockaddr *salast; /* last sockaddr{} for receiving */
38 struct sockaddr *sabind; /* sockaddr{} for binding source port */
39 socklen_t salen; /* length of sockaddr{}s */
40 int icmpproto; /* IPPROTO_xxx value for ICMP */
41 int ttllevel; /* setsockopt () level to set TTL */
42 int ttloptname; /* setsockopt () name to set TTL */
43 } *pr;
44 #ifdef IPV6
45 #include <netinet/ip6.h>
46 #include <netinet/icmp6.h>
47 #endif
```

The main function is shown in Figure 28.18 (p. 759). It processes the command-line arguments, initializes the pr pointer for either IPv4 or IPv6, and calls our traceloop function.

Define proto structures

2–9 define the two proto structures, one for IPv4 and one for IPv6, although the pointers to the socket address structures are not allocated until the end of this function.

Set defaults

10–13 The maximum TTL or hop limit that the program uses defaults to 30, although provide the -m command-line option to let the user change this. For each TTL, send three probe packets, but this could be changed with another command-line option. The initial destination port is 32768+666, which will be incremented by one each time send a UDP datagram. hope that these ports are not in use on the destination host when the datagrams finally reach the destination, but there is no guarantee.

Process command-line arguments

19–37 The -v command-line option causes most received ICMP messages to be printed.

Process hostname or IP address argument and finish initialization

38–58 The destination hostname or IP address is processed by our host_serv function, returning a pointer to an addrinfo structure. Depending on the type of returned address, IPv4 or IPv6, finish initializing the proto structure, store the pointer in the pr global, and allocate additional socket address structures of the correct size.

59 The function traceloop , shown in Figure 28.19 , sends the datagrams and reads the returned ICMP messages. This is the main loop of the program.

main function for traceroute program

traceroute/main.c

```
1 #include "trace.h"
2 struct proto proto_v4 = { icmpcode_v4, recv_v4, NULL, NULL, NULL, NULL, 0,
3 IPPROTO_ICMP, IPPROTO_IP, IP_TTL
4 };
5 #ifdef IPV6
6 struct proto proto_v6 = { icmpcode_v6, recv_v6, NULL, NULL, NULL, NULL, 0,
7 IPPROTO_ICMPV6, IPPROTO_IPV6, IPV6_UNICAST_HOPS
8 };
9 #endif
10 int datalen = sizeof (struct rec); /* defaults */
11 int max_ttl = 30;
12 int nprobes = 3;
13 u_short dport = 32768 + 666;
14 int
15 main(int argc, char **argv)
```

```
{
int c;
struct addrinfo *ai;
char *h;
opterr = 0; /* don't want getopt () writing to stderr */
while ( (c = getopt (argc, argv, "m:v")) != -1) {
switch (c) {
case 'm':
if ( (max_ttl = atoi (optarg)) <= 1)
err_quit ("invalid -m value");
break;
case 'v':
verbose++;
break;
case '?':
err_quit ("unrecognized option: %c", c);
}
}
if (optind != argc - 1)
err_quit ("usage: traceroute [ -m <maxttl> -v ] <hostname>");
host = argv [optind];
pid = getpid();
Signal (SIGALRM, sig_alrm);
ai = Host_serv (host, NULL, 0, 0);
h = Sock_ntop_host (ai->ai_addr, ai->ai_addrlen);
printf ("traceroute to %s (%s) : %d hops max, %d data bytes\n",
ai->ai_canonname ? ai->ai_canonname : h, h, max_ttl, datalen);
/* initialize according to protocol */
if (ai->ai_family == AF_INET) {
pr = &proto_v4;
#ifdef IPV6
} else if (ai->ai_family == AF_INET6) {
pr = &proto_v6;
if (IN6_IS_ADDR_V4MAPPED
```

```
50 (&(((struct sockaddr_in6 *) ai->ai_addr)->sin6_addr)))
51 err_quit ("cannot traceroute IPv4-mapped IPv6 address");
52 #endif
53 } else
54 err_quit ("unknown address family %d", ai->ai_family);
55 pr->sasend = ai->ai_addr; /* contains destination address */
56 pr->sarecv = Calloc (1, ai->ai_addrlen);
57 pr->salast = Calloc (1, ai->ai_addrlen);
58 pr->sabind = Calloc (1, ai->ai_addrlen);
59 pr->salen = ai->ai_addrlen;
60 traceloop();
61 exit (0);
62 }
```

Create raw socket

9–10 need two sockets: a raw socket on which read all returned ICMP messages and a UDP socket on which send the probe packets with the increasing TTLs. After creating the raw socket, reset our effective user ID to our real user ID since no longer require superuser privileges.

Set ICMPv6 receive filter

11–20 If are tracing the route to an IPv6 address and the -v command-line option was not specified, install a filter that blocks all ICMP message types except for the ones expect: "time exceeded" or "destination unreachable." This reduces the number of packets received on the socket.

Create UDP socket and bind source port

21–25 bind a source port to the UDP socket that is used for sending, using the low-order 16 bits of our PID with the high-order bit set to 1. Since it is possible for multiple copies of the traceroute program to be running at any given time, need a way to determine if a received ICMP message was generated in response to one of our datagrams, or in response to a datagram sent by another copy of the program. use the source port in the UDP header to identify the sending process because the returned ICMP message is required to include the UDP header from the datagram that caused the ICMP error.

Establish signal handler for SIGALRM

26 establish our function sig_alrm as the signal handler for SIGALRM because each time send a UDP datagram, wait three seconds for an ICMP message before sending the next probe.

traceloop function: main processing loop.

traceroute/traceloop.c

```
#include "trace.h"
void
traceloop(void)
{
int seq, code, done;
double rtt;
struct rec *rec;
struct timeval tvrecv;
recvfd = Socket (pr->sasend->sa_family, SOCK_RAW, pr->icmpproto);
setuid (getuid()); /* don't need special permissions anymore */
#ifdef IPV6
if (pr->sasend->sa_family == AF_INET6 && verbose == 0) {
struct icmp6_filter myfilt;
ICMP6_FILTER_SETBLOCKALL (&myfilt);
ICMP6_FILTER_SETPASS (ICMP6_TIME_EXCEEDED, &myfilt);
ICMP6_FILTER_SETPASS (ICMP6_DST_UNREACH, &myfilt);
setsockopt (recvfd, IPPROTO_IPV6, ICMP6_FILTER,
&myfilt, sizeof (myfilt));
}
#endif
sendfd = Socket (pr->sasend->sa_family, SOCK_DGRAM, 0);
pr->sabind->sa_family = pr->sasend->sa_family;
sport = (getpid() & 0xffff) | 0x8000; /* our source UDP port # */
sock_set_port (pr->sabind, pr->salen; htons (sport));
Bind (sendfd, pr->sabind, pr->salen);
sig_alrm (SIGALRM);
seq = 0;
done = 0;
for (ttl = 1; ttl <= max_ttl && done == 0; ttl++) {
Setsockopt (sendfd, pr->ttllevel, pr->ttloptname, &ttl, sizeof (int));
bzero (pr->salast, pr->salen);
printf ("%2d ", ttl);
```

```
fflush (stdout);
for (probe = 0; probe < nprobes; probe++) {
rec = (struct rec *) sendbuf;
rec->rec_seq = ++seq;
rec->rec_ttl = ttl;
Gettimeofday (&rec->rec_tv, NULL);
sock_set_port (pr->sasend, pr->salen, htons (dport + seq));
Sendto (sendfd, sendbuf, datalen, 0, pr->sasend, pr->salen),
if ( (code = (*pr->recv) (seq, &tvrecv)) == -3)
printf (" *"); /* timeout, no reply */
else {
char str [NI_MAXHOST];
if (sock_cmp_addr (pr->sarecv, pr->salast, pr->salen) != 0) {
if (getnameinfo (pr->sarecv, pr->salen, str, sizeof (str),
NULL, 0, 0) == 0)
printf (" %s (%s)", str,
Sock_ntop_host (pr->sarecv, pr->salen));
else
printf (" %s", Sock_ntop_host (pr->sarecv, pr->salen));
memcpy (pr->salast, pr->sarecv, pr->salen);
}
tv_sub (&tvrecv, &rec->rec_tv);
rtt = tvrecv.tv_sec * 1000.0 + tvrecv.tv_usec / 1000.0;
printf (" %.3f ms", rtt);
if (code == -1) /* port unreachable; at destination */
done++;
else if (code >= 0)
printf (" (ICMP %s)", (*pr->icmpcode) (code));
}
fflush (stdout);
}
printf ("\n");
}
}
```

Main loop; set TTL or hop limit and send three probes

27–38 The main loop of the function is a double nested for loop. The outer loop starts the TTL or hop limit at 1, and increases it by 1, while the inner loop sends three probes (UDP datagrams) to the destination. Each time the TTL changes, call setsockopt to set the new value using either the IP_TTL or IPV6_UNICAST_HOPS socket option.

Each time around the outer loop, initialize the socket address structure pointed to by salast to 0. This structure will be compared to the socket address structure returned by recvfrom when the ICMP message is read, and if the two structures are different, the IP address from the new structure will be printed. Using this technique, the IP address corresponding to the first probe for each TTL is printed, and should the IP address change for a given value of the TTL (say a route changes while are running the program), the new IP address will then be printed.

Set destination port and send UDP datagram

39–40 Each time a probe packet is sent, the destination port in the sasend socket address structure is changed by calling our sock_set_port function. The reason for changing the port for each probe is that when reach the final destination, all three probes are sent to a different port, and hopefully at least one of the ports is not in use. sendto sends the UDP datagram.

Read ICMP message

41–42 One of our functions, recv_v4 or recv_v6 , calls recvfrom to read and process the returned ICMP messages. These two functions return -3 if a timeout occurs (telling us to send another probe if haven't sent three for this TTL), -2 if an ICMP "time exceeded in transit" error is received, -1 if an ICMP "port unreachable" error is received (which means have reached the final destination), or the non-negative ICMP code if some other ICMP destination unreachable error is received.

Print reply

43–63 As mentioned earlier, if this is the first reply for a given TTL, or if the IP address of the node sending the ICMP message has changed for this TTL, print the hostname and IP address, or just the IP address (if the call to getnameinfo doesn't return the hostname). The RTT is calculated as the time difference from when sent the probe to the time when the ICMP message was returned and printed. Our recv_v4 function is showin in Figure 28.20 .

recv_v4 function: reads and processes ICMPv4 messages

traceroute/recv_v4.c

```
1 #include "trace.h"
```

```
extern int gotalarm;
/*
* Return: -3 on timeout
* -2 on ICMP time exceeded in transit (caller keeps going)
* -1 on ICMP port unreachable (caller is done)
* >= 0 return value is some other ICMP unreachable code
*/
int
recv_v4(int seq, struct timeval *tv)
{
int hlen1, hlen2, icmplen, ret;
socklen_t len;
ssize_t n;
struct ip *ip, *hip;
struct icmp *icmp;
struct udphdr *udp;
gotalarm = 0;
alarm(3);
for ( ; ; ) {
if (gotalarm)
return (-3); /* alarm expried */
len = pr->salen;
n = recvfrom (recvfd, recvbuf, sizeof (recvbuf), 0, pr->sarecv, &len);
if (n < 0) {
if (errno == EINTR)
continue;
else
err_sys ("recvfrom error");
}
ip = (struct ip *) recvbuf; /* start of IP header */
hlen1 = ip->ip_hl << 2; /* length of IP header */
icmp = (struct icmp *) (recvbuf + hlen1); /* start of ICMP header */
if ( (icmplen = n - hlen1) < 8)
continue; /* not enough to look at ICMP header */
```

```
if (icmp->icmp_type == ICMP_TIMXCEED &&
icmp->icmp_code == ICMP_TIMXCEED_INTRANS) {
if (icmplen < 8 + sizeof (struct ip))
continue; /* not enough data to look at inner IP */
hip = (struct ip *) (recvbuf + hlen1 + 8);
hlen2 = hip->ip_hl << 2;
if (icmplen < 8 + hlen2 + 4)
continue; /* not enough data to look at UDP ports */
udp = (struct udphdr *) (recvbuf + hlen1 + 8 + hlen2);
if (hip->ip_p == IPPROTO_UDP &&
udp->uh_sport == htons (sport) &&
udp->uh_dport == htons (dport + seq)) {
ret = -2; /* hit an intermediate router */
break;
}
} else if (icmp->icmp_type == ICMP_UNREACH) {
if (icmplen <8 + sizeof (struct ip))
continue; /* not enough data to look at inner IP */
hip = (struct ip *) (recvbuf + hlen1 + 8);
hlen2 = hip->ip_hl << 2;
if (icmplen < 8 + hlen2 + 4)
continue; /* not enough data to look at UDP ports */
udp = (struct udphdr *) (recvbuf + hlen1 + 8 + hlen2);
if (hip->ip_p == IPPROTO_UDP &&
udp->uh_sport == htons (sport) &&
udp->uh_dport == htons (dport + seq)) {
if (icmp->icmp_code == ICMP_UNREACH_PORT)
ret = -1; /* have reached destination */
else
ret = icmp->icmp_code; /* 0, 1, 2, ... */
break;
}
}
if (verbose) {
```

```
70 printf (" (from %s: type = %d, code = %d)\n",
71 Sock_ntop_host (pr->sarecv, pr->salen),
72 icmp->icmp_type, icmp->icmp_code);
73 }
74 /* Some other ICMP error, recvfrom() again */
75 }
76 alarm(0); /* don't leave alarm running */
77 Gettimeofday (tv, NULL); /* get time of packet arrival */
78 return (ret);
79 }
```

Set alarm and read each ICMP message

19–30 An alarm is set for three seconds in the future and the function enters a loop that calls recvfrom , reading each ICMPv4 message returned on the raw socket. This function avoids the race condition described in Section 20.5 by using a global flag.

Get pointer to ICMP header

31–35 ip points to the beginning of the IPv4 header (recall that a read on a raw socket always returns the IP header), and icmp points to the beginning of the ICMP header. Figure 28.21 shows the various headers, pointers, and lengths used by the code.

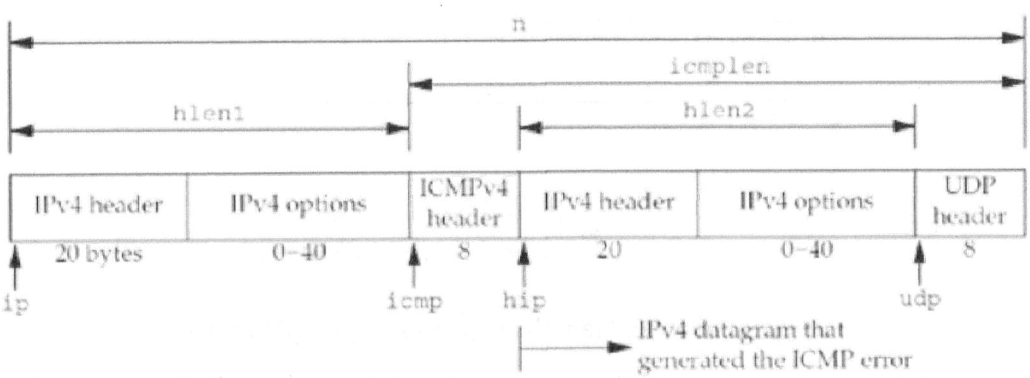

Headers, pointers, and lengths in processing ICMPv4 error

Process ICMP "time exceeded in transit" message

36–50 If the ICMP message is a "time exceeded in transit" message, it is possibly a reply to one of our probes. hip points to the IPv4 header that is returned in the ICMP message following the 8-byte ICMP header. udp points to the UDP header that follows. If the ICMP message was generated by a UDP datagram and if the source and destination ports of that datagram are the values sent, then this is a reply to our probe from an intermediate router.

Process ICMP "port unreachable" message

51–68 If the ICMP message is "destination unreachable," then look at the UDP header returned in the ICMP message to see if the message is a response to our probe. If so, and if the ICMP code is "port unreachable," return -1 as have reached the final destination. If the ICMP message is from one of our probes but it is not a "port unreachable," then that ICMP code value is returned. A common example of this is a firewall returning some other unreachable code for the destination host are probing.

Handle other ICMP messages

69–73 All other ICMP messages are printed if the -v flag was specified. The next function, recv_v6 , is shown in Figure 28.24 (p.767) and is the IPv6 equivalent to the previously described function. This function is nearly identical to recv_v4 except for the different constant names and the different structure member names. Also, the IPv6 header is not part of the data received on an IPv6 raw socket; the data starts with the ICMPv6 header. Figure 28.22 shows the various headers, pointers, and lengths used by the code.

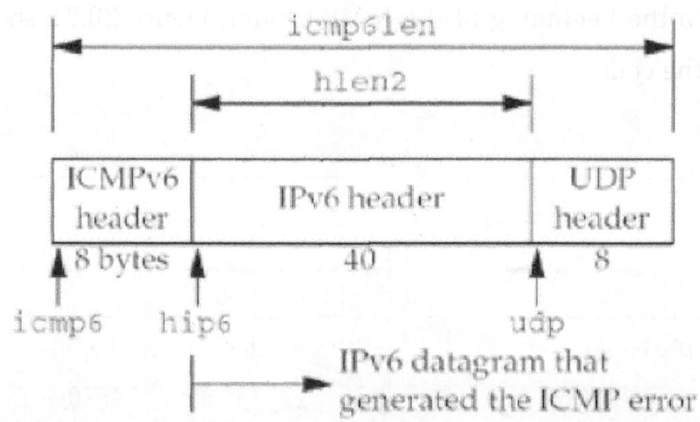

Headers, pointers, and lengths in processing ICMPv6 error

To define two functions, icmpcode_v4 and icmpcode_v6 , that can be called from the bottom of the traceloop function to print a description string corresponding to an ICMP "destination unreachable" error. Figure 28.25 (p.767) shows just the IPv6 function. The IPv4 function is similar, albeit longer, as there are more ICMPv4 "destination unreachable" codes (Figure A.15).

The final function in our traceroute program is our SIGALRM handler, the sig_alrm function shown in Figure 28.23 . All this function does is return, causing an error return of EINTR from the recvfrom in either recv_v4 or recv_v6 .

sig_alrm function

traceroute/sig_alrm.c

```
#include "trace.h"
int gotalarm;
void
sig_alrm(int signo)
{
gotalarm = 1: /* set flag to note that alarm occurred */
return; /* and interrupt the recvfrom() */
}
```

recv_v6 function: reads and processes ICMPv6 messages

traceroute/recv_v6.c

```
#include "trace.h"
extern int gotalarm;
/*
* Return: -3 on timeout
* -2 on ICMP time exceeded in transit (caller keeps going)
* -1 on ICMP port unreachable (caller is done)
* >= 0 return value is some other ICMP unreachable code
*/
int
recv_v6 (int seq, struct timeval *tv)
{
#ifdef IPV6
int hlen2, icmp6len, ret;
ssize_t n;
socklen_t len;
struct ip6_hdr *hip6;
struct icmp6_hdr *icmp6;
struct udphdr *udp;
gotalarm = 0;
alarm(3);
for ( ; ; ) {
```

```
if (gotalarm)
return (-3); /* alarm expired */
len = pr->salen;
n = recvfrom (recvfd, recvbuf, sizeof (recvbuf), 0, pr->sarecv, &len);
if (n < 0) {
if (errno == EINTR)
continue;
else
err_sys ("recvfrom error");
}
icmp6 = (struct icmp6_hdr *) recvbuf; /* ICMP header */
if ( (icmp6len = n) < 8)
continue; /* not enough to look at ICMP header */
if (icmp6->icmp6_type == ICMP6_TIME_EXCEEDED &&
icmp6->icmp6_code == ICMP6_TIME_EXCEED_TRANSIT) {
if (icmp6len < 8 + sizeof (struct ip6_hdr) + 4)
continue; /* not enough data to look at inner header */
hip6 = (struct ip6_hdr *) (recvbuf + 8);
hlen2 = sizeof (struct ip6_hdr);
udp = (struct udphdr *) (recvbuf + 8 + hlen2);
if (hip6->ip6_nxt == IPPROTO_UDP &&
udp->uh_sport == htons (sport) &&
udp->uh_dport == htons (dport + seq))
ret = -2; /* hit an intermediate router */
break;
} else if (icmp6->icmp6_type == ICMP6_DST_UNREACH) {
if (icmp6len <8 + sizeof (struct ip6_hdr) + 4)
continue; /* not enough data to look at inner header */
hip6 = (struct ip6_hdr *) (recvbuf + 8);
hlen2 = sizeof (struct ip6_hdr);
udp = (struct udphdr *) (recvbuf + 8 + hlen2);
if (hip6->ip6_nxt == IPPROTO_UDP &&
udp->uh_sport == htons (sport) &&
udp->uh_dport == htons (dport + seq)) {
```

```
if (icmp6->icmp6_code == ICMP6_DST_UNREACH_NOPORT)
ret = -1; /* have reached destination */
else
ret = icmp6->icmp6_code; /* 0, 1, 2, ... */
break;
}
} else if (verbose) {
printf (" (from %s: type = %d, code = %d)\n",
Sock_ntop_host (pr->sarecv, pr->salen),
icmp6->icmp6_type, icmp6->icmp6_code);
}
/* Some other ICMP error, recvfrom () again */
}
alarm (0); /* don't leave alarm running */
Gettimeofday (tv, NULL); /* get time of packet arrival */
return (ret);
#endif
}
```

Return the string corresponding to an ICMPv6 unreachable code

traceroute/icmpcode_v6.c

```
#include "trace.h"
const char *
icmpcode_v6 (int code)
{
#ifdef IPV6
static char errbuf [100];
switch (code) {
case ICMP6_DST_UNREACH_NOROUTE:
return ("no route to host");
case ICMP6_DST_UNREACH_ADMIN:
return ("administratively prohibited");
case ICMP6_DST_UNREACH_NOTNEIGHBOR:
return ("not a neighbor");
case ICMP6_DST_UNREACH_ADDR:
```

```
return ("address unreachable");
case ICMP6_DST_UNREACH_NOPORT:
return ("port unreachable");
default:
sprintf (errbuf, "[unknown code %d]", code);
return errbuf;
}
#endif
}
```

Example

An example using IPv4.

```
freebsd % traceroute www.unpbook.com
traceroute to www.unpbook.com (206.168.112.219): 30 hops max, 24 data bytes
1 12.106.32.1 (12.106.32.1) 0.799 ms 0.719 ms 0.540 ms
2 12.124.47.113 (12.124.47.113) 1.758 ms 1.760 ms 1.839 ms
3 gbr2-p27.sffca.ip.att.net (12.123.195.38) 2.744 ms 2.575 ms 2.648 ms
4 tbr2-p012701.sffca.ip.att.net (12.122.11.85) 3.770 ms 3.689 ms 3.848 ms
5 gbr3-p50.dvmco.ip.att.net (12.122.2.66) 26.202 ms 26.242 ms 26.102 ms
6 gbr2-p20.dvmco.ip.att.net (12.122.5.26) 26.255 ms 26.194 ms 26.470 ms
7 gar2-p370.dvmco.ip.att.net (12.123.36.141) 26.443 ms 26.310 ms 26.427 ms
8 att-46.den.internap.ip.att.net (12.124.158.58) 26.962 ms 27.130 ms
27.279 ms
9 border10.ge3-0-bbnet2.den.pnap.net (216.52.40.79) 27.285 ms 27.293 ms
26.860 ms
10 coop-2.border10.den.pnap.net (216.52.42.118) 28.721 ms 28.991 ms
30.077 ms
11 199.45.130.33 (199.45.130.33) 29.095 ms 29.055 ms 29.378 ms
12 border-to-141-netrack.boulder.co.coop.net (207.174.144.178) 30.875 ms
29.747 ms 30.142 ms
13 linux.unpbook.com (206.168.112.219) 31.713 ms 31.573 ms 33.952 ms
```

To wrapped the long lines for a more readable output. Here is an example using IPv6.

```
freebsd % traceroute www.kame.net
traceroute to orange.kame.net (2001:200:0:4819:203:47ff:fea5:3085):
30 hops max, 24 data bytes
```

1 3ffe:b80:3:9adl::1 (3ffe:b80:3:9adl::1) 107.437 ms 99.341 ms 103.477 ms

2 Viagenie-gw.int.ipv6.ascc.net (2001:288:3b0::55)

105.129 ms 89.418 ms 90.016 ms

3 gw-Viagenie.int.ipv6.ascc.net (2001:288:3b0::54)

302.300 ms 291.580 ms 289.839 ms

4 c7513-gw.int.ipv6.ascc.net (2001:288:3b0::c)

296.088 ms 298.600 ms 292.196 ms

5 m160-c7513.int.ipv6.ascc.net (2001:288:3b0::1e)

296.266 ms 314.878 ms 302.429 ms

6 m20jp-m160tw.int.ipv6.ascc.net (2001:288:3b0::1b)

327.637 ms 326.897 ms 347.062 ms

7 hitachil.otemachi.wide.ad.jp (2001:200:0:1800::9c4:2)

420.140 ms 426.592 ms 422.756 ms

8 pc3.yagami.wide.ad.jp (2001:200:0:1c04::1000:2000)

415.471 ms 418.308 ms 461.654 ms

9 gr2000.k2c.wide.ad.jp (2001:200:0:8002::2000:1)

416.581 ms 422.430 ms 427.692 ms

10 2001:200:0:4819:203:47ff:fea5:3085 (2001:200:0:4819:203:47ff:fea5:3085)

417.169 ms 434.674 ms 424.037 ms

Wrapped the long lines for a more readable output.

UNIT-V

QUESTION BANK

PART-A

1. Give the syntax of connect( ) in TCP

int connect(int sockfd, const struct sockaddr *servaddr, socklen_t addrlen);

connect to server

sockfd is socket descriptor from socket( )

servaddr is a pointer to a structure and addrlen is the length of structure.

2. Give the syntax of listen( ) in TCP

listen(int sockfd, int backlog)

sockfd => socket descriptor from socket( )

backlog => number of connection requests queued by system while waiting for server to accept( ) an incoming connection.

3. Give the syntax of sendto( ) systemcall in UDP

sendto(int sockfd, char *buffer, int nbytes, int flags, struct sockaddr *toaddr, int toaddr_len);

sockfd => socket on which to send datagram

buffer => address of the buffer to send

nbytes => number of bytes to send

flags => special send options

toaddr => internet address and port to use

toaddr_len => length in bytes of toaddr structure

4. What is the processing function of an Echo Client

It reads a line of text from standard input, writes it to the server, reads back the server's echo of the line and outputs the echoed line to standard output.

5. Give an example of an Echo Server

- The client reads a line of text from its standard input and writes the line to the server
- The server reads the line from its network input and echoes the line back to the client
- The client reads the echoed line and prints it on its standard output

6. Differentiate system call and a function

- The system call is an entry point into the kernel
- Function is used to describe what appears to the user to the functions, even though on some implementations they may be system calls.

7. Define Source client

The program performs a fixed number of writes to a network of some specified size.

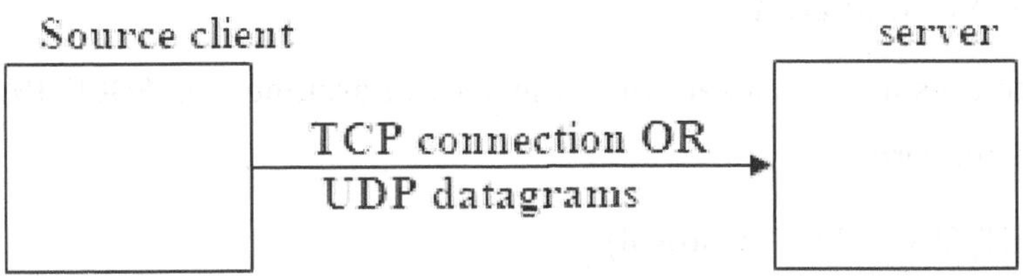

8. Define Sink Server

The program performs a fixed number of reads from a network.

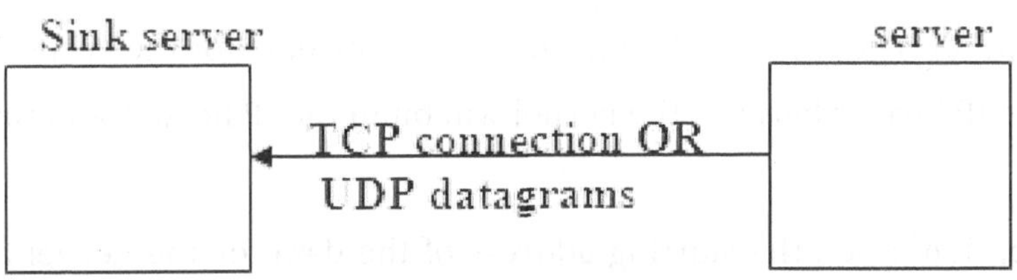

9. Define tcpdump program

This program reads packets from a network and prints lots of information about the packets. It also has the capability of printing only packets that match some criteria that we specify.

Eg: tcpdump '(udp and port daytime) or icmp'

Prints only the UDP datagrams with a source or destination port of 13(the daytime server) or ICMP packets.

10. Mention the uses of netstat program

- It shows the status of networking endpoints
- It shows the multicast groups that a host belongs to on each interface
- It shows the per-protocol statistics
- It displays the routing table and the interface information.

11. What are the capabilities provided by raw socket?

Capabilities of Raw Sockets

- Raw sockets let us read and write ICMPv4, TGMPv4 and ICMPv6 packets.
- With a raw socket a process can read and write IPv4 datagrams with an IPv4 protocol field that is not processed by the kernel.
- We can build our own UDP or TCP packets.

12. How do you create a raw socket

The socket function creates a raw socket when the second argument is SOCK_RAW. The third argument (the protocol)is normally nonzero.

sockfd= socket(AF_INET, SOCK_RAW, protocol);

where protocol is one of the constants, IPPROTO_xxx defined by including the <netinet/in.h> header such as IPPROTO_ICMP. Only the superuser can create a raw socket.

13. Mention the use of IP_HDRINCL option in a raw socket.

- If IP_HDRINCL option is not set, the starting address of the data for the kernel to send specifies the first byte following the IP header because the kernel will build the IP header and prepend it to the data from the process.
- If IP_HDRINCL option is set, the starting address of the data for the kernel to send specifies the first byte of the IP header. The amount of data to write must include the size of the caller's IP header.

14. What are the inputs passed to a raw socket.

- Most ICMP packets are passed to a raw socket after the kernel has finished processing the ICMP messages.
- All IGMP packets are passed to a raw socket after the kernel has finished processing the IGMP messages.
- All IP datagram with a protocol field that the kernel doesnot understand are passed to a raw socket.

15. Differentiate fgets and fputs function

- The function fgets reads a line of text from the standard input
- The function fputs prints the line on the standard output.

16. What is the goal of ping program

The goal of Ping program is to understand the network programming concepts and techniques without being distracted from some common programming disease known as creeping featurism. (supporting a dozen different options)

17. What are the 2 parts in operating a ping program

- The first part reads everything received on a raw socket, printing the ICMP echo replies
- The second half sends an ICMP echo request once per second. The second part is driven by a SIGALRM signal once per second.

18. Mention the advantage of traceroute

Trace route lets us determine the path that IP datagrams follow from our host to some other destination.

19. What are the two proto structures defined in trace route

- IPv4
- IPv6

20. What are the 2 sockets needed in a trace route program

- A raw socket on which we read all returned ICMP messages
- An UDP socket on which we send the probe packets with the increasing TTLs.

UNIT- V

PART-B (16 MARKS)

1. Explain Fork and Thread with example
2. Compare Wait and Waitpid with suitable example
3. Write a 'C' program that can generate an ICMPv4 echo request packet and process the received ICMPv4 echo reply.
4. Write notes on i) raw socket creation (4) ii) raw socket output iii) raw socket input
5. Explain how a TCP echo server using thread created and also give their advantages.
6. Write short notes on mutexes and condition variables.
7. Compare IPv4 and IPv6
8. Explain about thread creation and thread termination with suitable example. (8)
9. Explain the trace route program with sample code and example (16)
10. Explain in detail IPv4 and IPv6 interoperability

I. SNS COLLEGE OF ENGINEERING

Department of MCA

Model Question Paper With Answer Key SET – 1

SUBJECT: NETWORK PROGRAMMING MAX MARKS :100

SUB.CODE:MC9241 TIME : 3HRS

Part-A (10 X 2=20)

1. What are the ways for Normal Termination?

a. Return from main

b. Calling exit

c. Calling _exit or _Exit

d. Return of the last thread from its start routine

e. Calling pthread_exit

2. Give the syntax of sendto( ) systemcall in UDP

sendto(int sockfd, char *buffer, int nbytes, int flags,struct sockaddr *toaddr, int toaddr_len);

3. What are the functions of getty( )?

getty calls open for the terminal device. The terminal is opened for reading and writing. If the device is a modem, the open may delay inside the device driver until the modem is dialed and the call is answered. Once the device is open, file descriptors 0, 1, and 2 are set to the device. Then getty outputs something like login: and waits for us to enter our user name.

4. Define readset

Specifies the descriptors that we want the kernel to test for reading operation.

5. What does an error EWOULDBLOCK represent?

EWOULDBLOCK represents that no datagram is ready in Non.Blocking I/O mode.

6. Differentiate SHUT_RD and SHUT_WR

SHUT-RD The read half of the connection is closed. ie, The process can no longer issue any of the read functions on the socket.

SHUT-WR The write half of the connection is closed. ie, The process can no longer issue any of the write functions on the socket.

7. **List ICMP socket option**

ICMP6_FILTER

8. **Write the advantages of thread.**

Threads are lightweight processes since a thread is lighter weight than a process. It determines the flow of a program.

9. **What is Mutex?**

Mutex is used to protect the shared variable (which stands for "mutual exclusion"). The variable can be accessed only when we hold the mutex

10. **Write the operation of ping command.**

- An ICMP echo request is sent to some IP address and that node responds with an ICMP echo reply.
- These two ICMP messages are supported under both IPv4 and IPv6

Part-B (5 X16=80)

11.a) Explain the functions which are used to control the process with an example.

- Process creation – fork( ), vfork( )
- Process Execution – 6 forms of exec( )
- Process suspension – wait( ) , waitpid( )
- wait3( ) , wait4( )

(Or)

b) i) Explain the following i) Terminal Login ii) Network Login iii) Job Control (8)

Terminal Login

In early UNIX systems, such as Version 7, users logged in using dumb terminals that were connected to the host with hard-wired connections. The terminals were either local (directly connected) or remote (connected through a modem). In either case, these logins came through a terminal device driver in the kernel.

- init process
- exec function
- getty program
- getpass( ), crypt( ) functions

Network Login

A user on another host (that is connected to the server's host through a network of some form) or on the same host initiates the login by starting the TELNET client:

telnet hostname

The client opens a TCP connection to hostname, and the program that's started on hostname is called the TELNET server. The client and the server then exchange data across the TCP connection using the TELNET application protocol.

- init process
- inetd
- telnetd
- login shell

Job Control

Job control is a feature added to BSD around 1980. This feature allows us to start multiple jobs (groups of processes) from a single terminal and to control which jobs can access the terminal and which jobs are to run in the background. Job control requires three forms of support:

1. A shell that supports job control
2. The terminal driver in the kernel must support job control
3. The kernel must support certain job-control signals

ii) Differentiate fork() and vfork() with an example. (8)

fork( )

- fork() is the ONLY way to create a process in Unix kernel by user
  #include <unistd.h>
  pid_t fork(void);
  Called once but returns twice
- Returns: 0 in child process //only one parent
- Returns the child PID in parent process
- Returns -1 on error
- Example program

Vfork( )

- Creates a new process when the purpose of the new process is to 'exec' a new program
- Vfork creates the new process just like fork, without fully copying parent's address space into the child since the child won't reference that address space.
- Until the child calls either exec (or) exit, the child runs in "address space of parent"
- vfork guarantees that the Child always runs first until the child calls either exec (or) exit
- When the child calls either of these functions, the parent resumes.

- Example Program

12.a i) What is socket address structure? Explain general socket address structure (10)

Explain the following type of socket address structure

a) General address structure

```
struct sockaddr
{
        uint8_t sa_len;
        sa_family_t sa_family;
        char sa_data[14];
};
```

sa_family specifies the address type.

sa_data specifies the address value

b) IPv4 socket address structure

Defined by including the <netinet/in.h> header.

```
struct in_addr {
 in_addr_t s_addr;        /* 32-bit IPv4 address */
 };
struct sockaddr_in {
uint8_t      sin_len;    /* length of structure */
sa_family_t  sin_family; /* AF_INET */
in_port_t    sin_port;   /* 16-bit TCP or UDP port num */
struct in_addr sin_addr; /* 32-bit IPv4 address */
char         sin_zero[8]; /* unused (padding) */
};
```

c) IPv6 socket address structure

```
struct in6_addr
 {
uint8_t  s6addr[16];        /* 128-bit IPv6 address */
};
struct sockaddr_in6
{
uint8_t        sin6_len;   /* length of structure */
```

```
sa_family_t    sin6_family; /* AF_INET6 */
in_port_t      sin6_port;   /* port num */
uint32_t       sin6_flowinfo; /*flow information */
struct in6_addr sin6_addr;   /* IPv6 address */
uint32_t       sin6_scope_id; /* set of interfaces for a scope */
};
```

ii) Explain byte ordering functions with suitable example(6)

Consider a 16-bit integer that is made up of 2 bytes. There are two ways to store the two bytes in memory: with the low-order byte at the starting address, known as little-endian byte order, or with the high-order byte at the starting address, known as big-endian byte order.

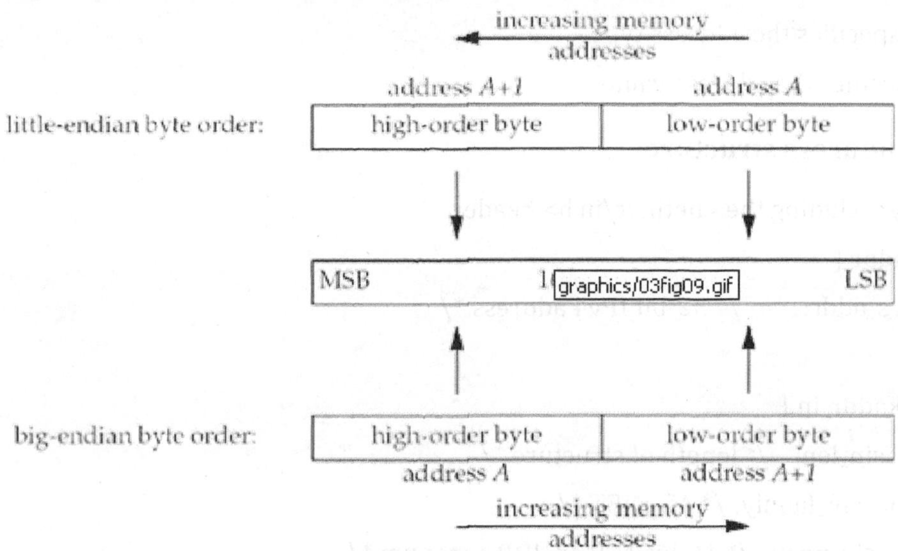

In this figure, we show increasing memory addresses going from right to left in the top, and from left to right in the bottom. We also show the most significant bit (MSB) as the leftmost bit of the 16-bit value and the least significant bit (LSB) as the rightmost bit.The terms "little-endian" and "big-endian" indicate which end of the multibyte value, the little end or the big end, is stored at the starting address of the value.
Converts between host byte order and network byte order

- 'h' = host byte order
- 'n' = network byte order
- 'l' = long (4 bytes), converts IP addresses
- 's' = short (2 bytes), converts port numbers

```
#include <netinet/in.h>
unsigned long int htonl(unsigned long int hostlong);
```

unsigned short int htons(unsigned short int hostshort);

unsigned long int ntohl(unsigned long int netlong);

unsigned short int ntohs(unsigned short int netshort);

(Or)

b) Explain about elementary TCP and UDP socket options with the suitable example

TCP Client

- sockfd = socket(int family, int type, int protocol)
- int connect(int sockfd,const struct sockaddr *servaddr, socklen_t addrlen);
- send(int sockfd, char *buffer, int buflen, int flags)
- recv(int sockfd, char *buffer, int nbytes, int flags)
- int close(int sockfd);

TCP Server

- socket – same as TCP client
- int bind(int sockfd,const struct sockaddr*myaddr,socklen_t addrlen);
- listen(int sockfd, int backlog)
- newsockfd = accept(int sockfd, struct sockaddr_in *peername, int peername_len)
- send, recv – same as TCP client
- close – same as TCP client

UDP Client

- socket
- bind (optional) if not specified, connect/sendto/recvfrom will bind
- connect (optional) - allows use send/recv
- sendto/recvfrom (send/recv if connected) retransmit if necessary
- close

UDP Server

- socket
- bind
- sendto/recvfrom
- close

13.a) Describe the various I/O Models with working diagram

Five I/O models are available under Unix :

- blocking I/O
- nonblocking I/O
- I/O multiplexing (select and poll)
- signal driven I/O (SIGIO)
- asynchronous I/O (aio_functions)

(Or)

b) What is multiplexing? Write a TCP echo client program with multiplexing.

TCP Echo Client: main Function Steps

- Create socket, fill in Internet socket address structure
- Connect to server

1. connect establishes the connection with the server.
2. The function str-cli handles the rest of the client processing.

TCP Echo Client: str_cli Function Steps

- Read a line, write to server
    - * fgets reads a line of text
    - * Writen sends the line to the server
- Read echoed line from server, write to standard output
    - * Readline reads the line echoed back from the server
    - * Fputs writes it to standard output
- Return to main

14.a) Write a DNS program to map hostname with its IP address

CLIENT

```
#include<stdio.h>
#include<sys/socket.h>
#include<sys/types.h>
#include<arpa/inet.h>
#include<netinet/in.h>
#include<unistd.h>
#define SER_PORT 8013
```

```
int main(int count,char *argv[])
{
int a;
int clisock,x,b,c;
char str[25],host[25];
char str2[25];
struct sockaddr_in cliaddr;
cliaddr.sin_port=htons(SER_PORT);
cliaddr.sin_family=AF_INET;
cliaddr.sin_addr.s_addr=inet_addr(argv[1]);
clisock=socket(AF_INET,SOCK_STREAM,0);
if(clisock<0)
{
perror("\n no socket");
exit(0);
}
if((x=connect(clisock,(struct sockaddr*)&cliaddr,sizeof(cliaddr)))<0)
{
perror("\n no connect");
exit(0);
}
printf("enter domain name");
scanf("%s",host);
write(clisock,host,strlen(host)+1);
read(clisock,str2,sizeof(str2));
printf("%s\n",str2);
close(clisock);
return 0;
}
```

SERVER

```
#include<stdio.h>
#include<sys/socket.h>
#include<sys/types.h>
#include<stdlib.h>
```

```
#include<arpa/inet.h>
#include<netinet/in.h>
#include<netdb.h>
#include<string.h>
#include<unistd.h>
#define SER_PORT 8013
int main()
{
int a,c;
FILE *f1,*f2;
int sersock,newsock,n;
char str[25],str2[25],host[25];
void *buf,*buf2;
struct sockaddr_in seraddr;
struct sockaddr_in clinfo;
struct hostent *hp;
socklen_t size=sizeof(clinfo);
seraddr.sin_family=AF_INET;
seraddr.sin_port=htons(SER_PORT);
seraddr.sin_addr.s_addr=htonl(INADDR_ANY);
if((sersock=socket(AF_INET,SOCK_STREAM,0))<0)
{
error(" socket\n");
exit(0);
}
 if(bind(sersock,(struct sockaddr*)&seraddr,sizeof(seraddr))<0)
{
error(" bind\n");
exit(0);
}
if(listen(sersock,1)<0)
{
error(" listen\n");
exit(0);
```

```
}
if((newsock=accept(sersock,(struct sockaddr*)&clinfo,&size))<0)
{
 error(" accept \n");
 exit(0);
}
else
printf("connected to m%s \n",inet_ntoa(clinfo.sin_addr));
read(newsock,host,sizeof(host));
printf("%s",host);
hp=gethostbyname(host);
inet_ntop(AF_INET,hp->h_addr,str2,sizeof(str2));
printf("%s\n",str2);
write(newsock,str2,strlen(str2)+1);
close(newsock);
close(sersock);
return 0;
}
```

(Or)

b) Explain the following functions with an example

i) gethostbyname() function ii) getservbyname() function (10+6)

i) gethostbyname function (10)

```
#include <netdb.h>
struct hostent *gethostbyname (const char *hostname);
```

- Returns: non-null pointer if OK,NULL on error

- The most basic function that looks up a hostname is gethostbyname
- It returns a pointer to a hostent structure that contains all the IPv4 addresses for the host.
- It can only return IPv4 addresses
- IPv6 addresses are very long

ii) getservbyname function (6)

```
#include <netdb.h>
struct servent *getservbyname (const char *servname, const char *protoname);
```

- For a given name, this function looks up a service.
- It returns a pointer to the following structure

```
struct servent
{
char *s_name;        /* official service name */
char **s_aliases;    /* alias list */
int s-port;          /* port number, network-byte order */
 char *s_proto;      /* protocol  */
 };
```

15. a) Explain in detail about IPV4 and IPV6 interoperability

- IPv6 server on dual-stack host serving IPv4 and IPv6 clients.
- Processing of received IPv4 or IPv6 datagrams, depending on type of receiving socket.
- Processing of client requests, depending on address type and socket type.
- Summary of interoperability between IPv4 and IPv6 clients and servers

(Or)

b) What is ping command? Write a readloop () function in the ping program and explain it.

The operation of ping is extremely simple:

- An ICMP echo request is sent to some IP address and that node responds with an ICMP echo reply.
- These two ICMP messages are supported under both IPv4 and IPv6

readloop function

- Perform protocol-specific initialization
- Set socket receive buffer size
- Send first packet
- Set up msghdr for recvmsg
- Infinite loop reading all ICMP messages

II. SNS COLLEGE OF ENGINEERING

Department of MCA

Model Question Paper with Answer Key Set – 2

SUBJECT: NETWORK PROGRAMMING MAX. MARKS :100

SUB.CODE: MC9241 TIME : 3HRS

Part-A (10 X 2=20)

1. What is address conversion function?

gethostbyname (), getservbyname(),gethostbyaddr

2. Write the operation of popen() and pclose()

The function popen () does a fork and exec to execute the cmdstring, and returns a standard I/O file pointer. If type is "r", the file pointer is connected to the standard output of cmdstring. If type is "w", the file pointer is connected to the standard input of cmdstring,

The pclose () function closes the standard I/O stream, waits for the command to terminate, and returns the termination status of the shell.

3. Give the syntax of gethostbyname() function

gethostbyname (name) -> Translate Domain name to IP address

4. Define "Quad A"

AAAA record, called a "quad A" record, maps a hostname into a 128-bit IPv6 address. The term "quad A" was chosen because a 128-bit address is four times larger than a 32-bit address.

5. Mention the Resource Records of DNS

Entries in the DNS are known as resource records (RRs).

6. What are TCP Echo Client and Server?

- The TCP client reads a line of text from its standard input and writes the line to the server.
- The TCP server reads the line from its network input and echoes the line back to the client.
- The TCP client reads the echoed line and prints it on its standard output.

7. Mention the advantages and disadvantages of Nonblocking I/O

- Adv :- When the I/O request is not completed, the process is not put to sleep. Instead it returns an error EWOULDBLOCK .Hence there is nu blocking stage.

- Disadv :-

  waste of CPU time

8. What are the features of raw socket?

- Raw sockets allow us read and write ICMPv4, IGMPv4, and ICMPv6 packets.
- With a raw socket, a process can read and write IPv4 datagrams
- With a raw socket, a process can build its own IPv4 header using the IP_HDRINCL socket option.

9. How to create raw socket?

The socket function creates a raw socket when the second argument is SOCK_RAW. The third argument (the protocol) is normally nonzero. For example,

```
int sockfd;

sockfd = socket(AF_INET, SOCK_RAW, protocol);
```

where protocol is IPPROTO_xxx, defined by including the <netinet/in.h> header

10. Write the function of thread creation.

```
#include <pthread.h>

int pthread_create(pthread_t *tid, const pthread_attr_t *attr, void *(*func)(void *), *arg);
```

Part-B (5 X16=80)

11. a) Explain the basic concepts of process relationship.

Terminal login & Network login

Relationship between the login shell that is invoked for us when we log in and all the processes that we start from our login shell

How signal make process relationship

Explain process groups

Orphan process

(Or)

b) Write a short note on environment of UNIX process.

Environment List

Environment Variables

Memory Layout

Process relationship

File Systems

12. a) i) Write a program to implement concurrent server. (10)

Outline for typical concurrent server

```
pid_t  pid;
int  sockfd, connfd;
= socket (............);
// fill in sockaddr_in{ }
 (sockfd, ........);
 (sockfd, LISTENQ);
for ( , , ) {
connfd = accept (sockfd, ........);
if (( pid = fork( )) == 0) {
        close (sockfd);
        doit(connfd);
        close(connfd);
        exit(0);        }
        close (connfd); }
```

ii) Compare UDP and TCP sockets (6)

- UDP is connection-less protocol
- It uses SOCK_DGRAM
- TCP is connection oriented protocol
- It uses SOCK_STREAM

(Or)

b) Write a TCP socket program to transfer the data between client and server.

Refer lab program

13.a) Explain the following functions – select, poll function

Select Function

The process instructs the kernel to wait for any event to occur or until the specified time gets elapsed. Any descriptor can be tested using select

include<sys/select.h>

include<sys/time.h>

```
int select ( int maxfd1, fd_set *readset, fd_set  *writeset,  fd_set *exceptset, const struct timeval *timeout);
```

Poll function

```
#include <poll.h>

int poll (struct pollfd *fdarray, unsigned long nfds, int timeout);
```

The first argument is a pointer to an array of structures.

Functionality of poll is similar to select function

The return value from poll is –1 if an error occurred, 0 if no descriptors are ready before the timer expires. Returns the number of ready descriptors.

```
struct pollfd {
      int fd; /* descriptor to check */
      short events; /* events of interest on fd */
      short revents; /* events that occurred on fd */
      };
```

- The conditions to be tested are specified by the events member
- The function returns the status for that descriptor in the corresponding revents member.
- The number of elements in the array of structures is specified by the nfds argument.
- The timeout argument specifies how long the function has to wait before returning.

  INFTIM - wait forever

  0 - return immediately

  >0 - number of milliseconds to wait

(Or)

b) Write a program to implement TCP Echo Client and TCP Echo Server

TCP Echo Client: main Function Steps

- Create socket, fill in Internet socket address structure
- Connect to server

(i) connect establishes the connection with the server.

(ii) The function str-cli handles the rest of the client processing.

TCP Echo Client: str_cli Function Steps

Read a line, write to server

- fgets reads a line of text
- Writen sends the line to the server

Read echoed line from server, write to standard output

- Readline reads the line echoed back from the server
- Fputs writes it to standard output

14. a) Explain the various functions related to hostent and servent structures

- gethostbyaddr
- gethostbyname
- getservbyname
- getservbyport

(Or)

b) Explain Generic socket options and TCP socket options (12 + 4)

- SO_BROADCAST
- SO_DEBUG
- SO_DONTROUTE
- SO_ERROR
- SO_KEEPALIVE
- SO_LINGER
- SO_OOBINLINE
- SO_RCVBUF and SO_SNDBUF
- SO_RCVLOWAT and SO_SNDLOWAT
- SO_REUSEADDR and SO_REUSEPORT
- SO_TYPE

15. a) Write a program to implement TCP echo server using thread

```
#include    "unpthread.h"
static void *doit(void *);     /* each thread executes this function */
 int  main(int argc, char **argv)
{
int    listenfd, connfd;
pthread_t tid;
socklen_t addrlen, len;
struct sockaddr *cliaddr;
if (argc == 2)
listenfd = Tcp_listen(NULL, argv[1], &addrlen);
    else if (argc == 3)
listenfd = Tcp_listen(argv[1], argv[2], &addrlen);
```

```
else
 err_quit("usage: tcpserv01 [ <host> ] <service or port>");
 cliaddr = Malloc(addrlen);
   for (; ; ) {
len = addrlen;
connfd = Accept(listenfd, cliaddr, &len);
Pthread_create(&tid, NULL, &doit, (void *) connfd);
}
}
static void * doit(void *arg)
{
          Pthread_detach(pthread_self());
          str_echo((int) arg);       /* same function as before */
          Close((int) arg);        /* done with connected socket */
          return (NULL);
}
```

(Or)

b) Explain the important functions of Trace route program.

Main function

- Define proto structures
- Set defaults
- Process command-line arguments
- Process hostname or IP address argument and finish initialization

Traceloop function

- Create raw socket
- Set ICMPv6 receive filter
- Create UDP socket and bind source port
- Establish signal handler for SIGALRM
- Main loop; set TTL or hop limit
- Set destination port and send UDP datagram
- Read ICMP message
- Print reply

III. SNS COLLEGE OF ENGINEERING

Department of MCA

Model Question Paper with Answer Key Set – 3

SUBJECT: NETWORK PROGRAMMING MAX. MARKS :100

SUB.CODE: MC9241 TIME : 3HRS

Part-A (10 X 2=20)

1. What is inter-process communication?

- The main mechanism of an IPC package is to create a communication link between both the related and unrelated processes.
- 4 mechanisms as Pipes, semaphore, message queue, shared memory

2. What is message queue?

Message Queues are a linked list of messages stored within the kernel and identified by a message queue identifier.

3. What is perror () function?

This function produces an error message on the standard error, based on the current value of errno, and returns.

```
#include <stdio.h>
Void perror(const char *msg);
```

It outputs the string pointed to by msg, followed by a colon and a space, followed by the error message corresponding to the value of errno, followed by a newline.

4. What is iterative server? Give an example.

Iterative server serves clients one by one not in parallel. (E.g) Daytime server

5. Differentiate synchronous I/O and Asynchronous I/O

A Synchronous I/O operation causes the requesting process to be blocked until that I/O operation completes

An Asynchronous I/O operation does not cause the requesting process to be blocked.

6. Write the syntax of poll () function.

int poll(struct pollfd fdarray[], nfds_t nfds, int timeout);

7. Define Resource Record (RR)

Entries in the DNS are known as resource records (RR). The following are the types of Resource Records.

- A
- AAAA
- PTR
- MX
- CNAME

8. What is the difference between close and shutdown function?

First, close will deallocate the network endpoint only when the last active reference is closed. This means that if we duplicate the socket (with dup, for example), the socket won't be deallocated until we close the last file descriptor referring to it. The shutdown function allows us to deactivate a socket independently of the number of active file descriptors referencing it. Second, it is sometimes convenient to shut a socket down in one direction only. For example, we can shut a socket down for writing if we want the process we are communicating with to be able to determine when we are done transmitting data, while still allowing us to use the socket to receive data sent to us by the process.

9. What is condition variable?

Condition variable are another synchronization mechanism available to threads. It provides a place for threads to rendezvous. When used with mutexes, it allows threads to wait in a race-free way for arbitrary conditions to occur.

10. Write the function used to terminate the thread.

A single thread can exit in three ways, thereby stopping its flow of control, without terminating the entire process.

- The thread can simply return from the start routine. The return value is the thread's exit code.
- The thread can be canceled by another thread in the same process.
- The thread calls pthread_exit.

Part-B (5 X16=80)

11.a) Define signal. Explain the basic concepts of signal in detail

Signals are a technique used to notify a process that some condition has occurred. For example, if a process divides by zero, the signal whose name is SIGFPE (floating-point exception) is sent to the process. The process has three choices for dealing with the signal.

- Ignore the signal. This option isn't recommended for signals that denote a hardware exception, such as dividing by zero or referencing memory outside the address space of the process, as the results are undefined.
- Let the default action occur. For a divide-by-zero condition, the default is to terminate the process.
- Provide a function that is called when the signal occurs (this is called "catching" the signal). By providing a function of our own, we'll know when the signal occurs and we can handle it as we wish.

Numerous conditions can generate a signal.

- The terminal-generated signals occur when users press certain terminal keys. Pressing the DELETE key on the terminal (or Control-C on many systems) normally causes the interrupt signal (SIGINT) to be generated. This is how to stop a runaway program.
- Hardware exceptions generate signals: divide by 0, invalid memory reference, and the like. These conditions are usually detected by the hardware, and the kernel is notified. The kernel then generates the appropriate signal for the process that was running at the time the condition occurred. For example, SIGSEGV is generated for a process that executes an invalid memory reference.
- The kill(2) function allows a process to send any signal to another process or process group. Naturally, there are limitations: we have to be the owner of the process that we're sending the signal to, or we have to be the superuser.
- The kill(1) command allows us to send signals to other processes. This program is just an interface to the kill function. This command is often used to terminate a runaway background process.
- Software conditions can generate signals when something happens about which the process should be notified. These aren't hardware-generated conditions (as is the divide-by-0 condition), but software conditions. Examples are SIGURG (generated when out-of-band data arrives over a network connection), SIGPIPE (generated when a process writes to a pipe after the reader of the pipe has terminated), and SIGALRM (generated when an alarm clock set by the process expires).

We can tell the kernel to do one of three things when a signal occurs. We call this the disposition of the signal, or the action associated with a signal.

1. Ignore the signal. This works for most signals, but two signals can never be ignored: SIGKILL and SIGSTOP. The reason these two signals can't be ignored is to provide the kernel and the superuser with

a surefire way of either killing or stopping any process. Also, if we ignore some of the signals that are generated by a hardware exception (such as illegal memory reference or divide by 0), the behavior of the process is undefined.

2. Catch the signal. To do this, we tell the kernel to call a function of ours whenever the signal occurs. In our function, we can do whatever we want to handle the condition. If we're writing a command interpreter, for example, when the user generates the interrupt signal at the keyboard, we probably want to return to the main loop of the program, terminating whatever command we were executing for the user. If the SIGCHLD signal is caught, it means that a child process has terminated, so the signal-catching function can call waitpid to fetch the child's process ID and termination status. As another example, if the process has created temporary files, we may want to write a signal-catching function for the SIGTERM signal (the termination signal that is the default signal sent by the kill command) to clean up the temporary files. Note that the two signals SIGKILL and SIGSTOP can't be caught.
3. Let the default action apply. Every signal has a default action, Note that the default action for most signals is to terminate the process.

Explain Signal UNIX System call

(Or)

b) i) Explain the following i) Signal Mask ii) SIG_KILL iii) SIG_USR1 iv) sigprocmask() (8)

Ans:

Explain the following function with example

ii)

SIGKILL This signal is one of the two that can't be caught or ignored. It provides the system administrator with a sure way to kill any process.

iii)

SIGUSR1 This is a user-defined signal, for use in application programs.

SIGUSR2 This is another user-defined signal, similar to SIGUSR1, for use in application programs.

iv) Sigprocmask()

```
#include<signal.h>
int sigprocmask(int how, const sigset_t *restrict set,
    sigset_t *restrict oset);
```

ii) Write a short note on role of kernel in the UNIX process. (8)

In a strict sense, an operating system can be defined as the software that controls the hardware resources of the computer and provides an environment under which programs can run. Generally, we call this software the kernel, since it is relatively small and resides at the core of the environment.

Draw Architecture of the UNIX operating system

The interface to the kernel is a layer of software called the system calls libraries of common functions are built on top of the system call interface, but applications are free to use both.The shell is a special application that provides an interface for running other applications.

In a broad sense, an operating system is the kernel and all the other software that makes a computer useful and gives the computer its personality. This other software includes system utilities, applications, shells, libraries of common functions, and so on.

12.a) Explain all the TCP socket functions with an example.

Ans

Explain the following functions:

int socket (int family, int type, int protocol);

int connect(int sockfd, const struct sockaddr *servaddr, socklen_t addrlen);

int bind (int sockfd, const struct sockaddr *myaddr, socklen_t addrlen);

#int listen (int sockfd, int backlog);

int accept (int sockfd, struct sockaddr *cliaddr, socklen_t *addrlen);

int close (int sockfd);

pid_t fork(void);

(Or)

b) Explain about i) Byte ordering function ii) Address conversion function. (8+8)

Ans:

Byte Ordering Function:

```
#include <netinet/in.h>
uint16_t htons(uint16_t host16bitvalue)
uint32_t htonl(uint32_t host32bitvalue)
uint16_t ntohs(uint16_t net16bitvalue)
uint32_t ntohl(uint32_t net32bitvalue)
```

13.a) Explain about how to implement TCP echo client with multiplexing.

Explain about multiplexing and socket creation.

Part of the program TCP Echo client:

```
Void str_cli(FILE *fp, int sockfd)
{
  int   maxfdp1;
  fd_set  rset;
  char   sendline[MAXLINE], recvline[MAXLINE];
  FD_ZERO(&rset);
  for ( ; ; ) {
    FD_SET(fileno(fp), &rset);
    FD_SET(sockfd, &rset);
    maxfdp1 = max(fileno(fp), sockfd) + 1;
    Select(maxfdp1, &rset, NULL, NULL, NULL);
    if (FD_ISSET(sockfd, &rset)) { /* socket is readable */
      if (Readline(sockfd, recvline, MAXLINE) == 0)
        err_quit("str_cli: server terminated prematurely");
      Fputs(recvline, stdout);
    }

    if (FD_ISSET(fileno(fp), &rset)) { /* input is readable */
      if (Fgets(sendline, MAXLINE, fp) == NULL)
        return;       /* all done */
      Writen(sockfd, sendline, strlen(sendline));
    }
  }
}
```

(Or)

b) Explain the following

i) Crashing of Server Host **(10)**

This scenario will test to see what happens when the server host crashes. To simulate this, we must run the client and server on different hosts. We then start the server, start the client, type in a line to the client to verify that the connection is up, disconnect the server host from the network, and type in another line at the client. This also covers the scenario of the server host being unreachable when the client sends data (i.e., some intermediate router goes down after the connection has been established).

The following steps take place:

1. When the server host crashes, nothing is sent out on the existing network connections. That is, we are assuming the host crashes and is not shut down by an operator
2. We type a line of input to the client, it is written by writen and is sent by the client TCP as a data segment. The client then blocks in the call to readline, waiting for the echoed reply.
3. If we watch the network with tcpdump, we will see the client TCP continually retransmitting the data segment, trying to receive an ACK from the server. Section 25.11 of TCPv2 shows a typical pattern for TCP retransmissions: Berkeley-derived implementations retransmit the data segment 12 times, waiting for around 9 minutes before giving up. When the client TCP finally gives up (assuming the server host has not been rebooted during this time, or if the server host has not crashed but was unreachable on the network, assuming the host was still unreachable), an error is returned to the client process. Since the client is blocked in the call to readline, it returns an error. Assuming the server host crashed and there were no responses at all to the client's data segments, the error is ETIMEDOUT. But if some intermediate router determined that the server host was unreachable and responded with an ICMP "destination unreachable' message, the error is either EHOSTUNREACH or ENETUNREACH.

ii) Crashing and Rebooting of Server Host (6)

In this scenario, we will establish a connection between the client and server and then assume the server host crashes and reboots. In the previous section, the server host was still down when we sent it data. Here, we will let the server host reboot before sending it data. The easiest way to simulate this is to establish the connection, disconnect the server from the network, shut down the server host and then reboot it, and then reconnect the server host to the network. We do not want the client to see the server host shut down.

As stated in the previous section, if the client is not actively sending data to the server when the server host crashes, the client is not aware that the server host has crashed. (This assumes we are not using the SO_KEEPALIVE socket option.) The following steps take place:

1. We start the server and then the client. We type a line to verify that the connection is established.
2. The server host crashes and reboots.
3. We type a line of input to the client, which is sent as a TCP data segment to the server host.
4. When the server host reboots after crashing, its TCP loses all information about connections that existed before the crash. Therefore, the server TCP responds to the received data segment from the client with an RST.
5. Our client is blocked in the call to readline when the RST is received, causing readline to return the error ECONNRESET.

14. a) Write a note on multiplexing TCP and UDP sockets.

Ans:

- Explain the following:
- What is multiplexing?
- Multiplexing using select () and poll ()
- Implement these functions in TCP and UDP

(Or)

b) Write a UDP socket program to transfer the content of file between server and client.

Ans: (Refer Lab Program)

15. a) Define Thread. Explain the features and functions of thread.

Ans

Threads of control (or simply threads) to perform multiple tasks within the environment of a single process. All threads within a single process have access to the same process components, such as file descriptors and memory.

Explain the following function

Thread Identification

```
#include <pthread.h>
int pthread_equal(pthread_t tid1, pthread_t tid2);
```

A thread can obtain its own thread ID by calling the **pthread_self** function.

```
#include <pthread.h>
pthread_t pthread_self(void);
```

Thread creation

```
#include <pthread.h>
int pthread_create(pthread_t *restrict tidp, const pthread_attr_t *restrict attr,
        void *(*start_rtn)(void), void *restrict arg);
```

Thread Termination

If any thread within a process calls exit, _Exit, or _exit, then the entire process terminates. Similarly, when the default action is to terminate the process, a signal sent to a thread will terminate the entire process. A single thread can exit in three ways, thereby stopping its flow of control, without terminating the entire process.

1. The thread can simply return from the start routine. The return value is the thread's exit code.
2. The thread can be canceled by another thread in the same process.

3. The thread can call pthread_exit.

```
#include <pthread.h>
void pthread_exit(void *rval_ptr);
```

Thread join

```
#include <pthread.h>
int pthread_join(pthread_t thread, void **rval_ptr);
```

(Or)

b) Explain the features and steps needed to create the raw socket.

Ans:

Raw Socket Creation

The steps involved in creating a raw socket are as follows:

1. The socket function creates a raw socket when the second argument is SOCK_RAW. The third argument (the protocol) is normally nonzero. For example, to create an IPv4 raw socket we would write

   ```
   int sockfd;
   sockfd = socket(AF_INET, SOCK_RAW, protocol);
   ```

   where protocol is one of the constants, IPPROTO_xxx, defined by including the <netinet/in.h> header, such as IPPROTO_ICMP. Only the super user can create a raw socket. This prevents normal users from writing their own IP datagrams to the network.
2. The IP_HDRINCL socket option can be set as follows:

   ```
   const int on = 1;
   if (setsockopt(sockfd, IPPROTO_IP, IP_HDRINCL, &on, sizeof(on)) < 0)
   error
   ```

3. bind can be called on the raw socket, but this is rare. This function sets only the local address: There is no concept of a port number with a raw socket. With regard to output, calling bind sets the source IP address that will be used for data grams sent on the raw socket (but only if the IP_HDRINCL socket option is not set). If bind is not called, the kernel sets the source IP address to the primary IP address of the outgoing interface.
4. connect can be called on the raw socket, but this is rare. This function sets only the foreign address: Again, there is no concept of a port number with a raw socket. With regard to output, calling connect lets us call write or send instead of sendto, since the destination IP address is already specified

IV. SNS COLLEGE OF ENGINEERING

Department of MCA

Model Question Paper With Answer Key Set – 4

SUBJECT: NETWORK PROGRAMMING MAX. MARKS :100

SUB.CODE: MC9241 TIME : 3HRS

Part-A (10 X 2=20)

1. List the functions used for memory allocation

Three functions for memory allocation:

1. malloc(), which allocates a specified number of bytes of memory the initial value of the memory is indeterminate.
2. calloc(), which allocates space for a specified number of objects of a specified size. The space is initialized to all 0 bits.
3. realloc(), which increases or decreases the size of a previously allocated area. When the size increases, it may involve moving the previously allocated area somewhere else, to provide the additional room at the end. Also, when the size increases, the initial value of the space between the old contents and the end of the new area is indeterminate.

2. Mention the signals that cannot be caught or ignored

SIGKILL and SIGSTOP

3. Give the syntax of gethostbyname( ) function

gethostbyname (name) -> Translate Domain name to IP address

4. What is the basic concept in shared memory?

Shared memory allows two or more processes to share a given region of memory. This is the fastest form of IPC, because the data does not need to be copied between the client and the server. The only trick in using shared memory is synchronizing access to a given region among multiple processes. If the server is placing data into a shared memory region, the client shouldn't try to access the data until the server is done. Often, semaphores are used to synchronize shared memory access.

5. Write the operation of popen( ) and pclose( )

The function popen () does a fork and exec to execute the cmdstring, and returns a standard I/O file pointer. If type is "r", the file pointer is connected to the standard output of cmdstring. If type is "w", the file pointer is connected to the standard input of cmdstring,

The pclose () function closes the standard I/O stream, waits for the command to terminate, and returns the termination status of the shell.

6. What is binding operation?

A socket can be bound to a port

7. Define semaphore

A semaphore isn't a form of IPC similar to the others that we've described (pipes, FIFOs, and message queues). A semaphore is a counter used to provide access to a shared data object for multiple processes.

8. Give the syntax of listen( ) systemcall in UDP

Listen (fd,n)

fd-> socket id

n-> no.of clients in the queue

9. Differentiate wait( ) and waitpid( ).

The differences between these two functions are as follows.

- The wait function can block the caller until a child process terminates, whereas waitpid has an option that prevents it from blocking.
- The waitpid function doesn't wait for the child that terminates first; it has a number of options that control which process it waits for.

10. What is address conversion function?

gethostbyname (), getservbyname(),gethostbyaddr

Part-B (5 X16=80)

11.a) Explain the basic concepts of process relationship.

- Explain the following concepts
- Terminal login & Network login
- Relationship between the login shell that is invoked for us when we log in and all the
- processes that we start from our login shell
- How signal make process relationship
- Explain process groups
- Orphan process

(Or)

b) Write a short note on environment of UNIX process.

In a strict sense, an operating system can be defined as the software that controls the hardware resources of the computer and provides an environment under which programs can run. Generally, we call this software the kernel, since it is relatively small and resides at the core of the environment.

(1) Explain Architecture of the UNIX operating system

The interface to the kernel is a layer of software called the system calls. Libraries of common functions are built on top of the system call interface, but applications are free to use both.The shell is a special application that provides an interface for running other applications.

In a broad sense, an operating system is the kernel and all the other software that makes a computer useful and gives the computer its personality. This other software includes system utilities, applications, shells, libraries of common functions, and so on.

For example, Linux is the kernel used by the GNU operating system. Some people refer to this as the GNU/Linux operating system, but it is more commonly referred to as simply Linux. Although this usage may not be correct in a strict sense, it is understandable, given the dual meaning of the phrase operating system. (It also has the advantage of being more succinct.)

Also explain Process relationship, File system in UNIX

12. a) Define signal. Explain the basic concepts of signal in detail

Ans:

- Definition
- Conditions that generate signals
- What kernel does when signal occurs?
- Signal functions

(Or)

b) i) Explain about actions of signals with example (8)

Ans:

Defn: Signals are software interrupts. Most nontrivial application programs need to deal with signals. Signals provide a way of handling asynchronous events: a user at a terminal typing the interrupt key to stop a program or the next program in a pipeline terminating prematurely.

Explain any 10 signal actions with example

sIGABRT	abnormal termination (abort)
SIGALRM	timer expired (alarm)
SIGBUS	hardware fault
SIGCANCEL	threads library internal use
SIGCHLD	change in status of child
SIGCONT	continue stopped process
SIGEMT	hardware fault
SIGFPE	arithmetic exception
SIGFREEZE	checkpoint freeze
SIGHUP	hangup

ii) Write a short note on role of kernel in the UNIX process. (8)

Ans:

- What is kernel?
- Job of kernel generally?
- Explain the job of kernel when process starts, process and terminate

13.a) Explain the concept of shared memory with an program.

Ans:

Shared memory is a Common chunk of read/write memory among processes

Explain the shared memory functions such as shmget(). shmctl(), shmat() with an example.

Sample program:

```
#include<sys/types.h>
#include<sys/ipc.h>
#include<sys/shm.h>
```

```
        char *ptr;
    main()
    {       int pid, shmid;
       shmid=shmget((key_t)50,10,IPC_CREAT|0666);
     if(shmid<0)  printf("\nError");
       else
            printf("\nShared memory id is:%d\n",shmid);
            ptr=shmat(shmid,0,0);
         pid=fork();
      if(pid==0)
        {  printf("\nChild process\n");
            strcpy(ptr,"Hello friend");
        }
      else
        {  sleep(5);
            printf("\nParent process read %s",ptr);        } }
```

(Or)

b) Explain about elementary TCP and UDP socket options with the suitable example.

Ans

Explain the following function with suitable example.

socket (), connect(), bind(), listen(), read(), send() –TCP socket functions

sendto(), recvfrom() –UDP socket function.

14. a) i) What is socket address structure? Explain general socket address structure (10)

Ans

Explain the following type of socket address structure

- General address structure
- IPV4 socket address structure

A. IPv4 socket address structure

Defined by including the <netinet/in.h> header.

```
struct in_addr {
 in_addr_t s_addr;        /* 32-bit IPv4 address */
};
```

```
struct sockaddr_in {
  uint8_t       sin_len;    /* length of structure */
  sa_family_t   sin_family; /* AF_INET */
  in_port_t     sin_port;   /* 16-bit TCP or UDP port num */
 struct in_addr sin_addr;   /* 32-bit IPv4 address */
 char           sin_zero[8]; /* unused (padding) */
};
```

IPV6 socket address structure

B. IPv6 socket address structure

```
struct in6_addr {
      uint8_t s6addr[16];        /* 128-bit IPv6 address */
};
struct sockaddr_in6 {
      uint8_t        sin6_len;    /* length of structure */
      sa_family_t    sin6_family; /* AF_INET6 */
       in_port_t     sin6_port;   /* port num */
      uint32_t        sin6_flowinfo; /*flow information */
      struct in6_addr  sin6_addr;   /*  IPv6 address */
      uint32_t        sin6_scope_id; /* set of interfaces for a scope */
};
```

C. RAW socket address structure

ii) Explain byte ordering functions with suitable example (6)

Ans:

Consider a 16-bit integer that is made up of 2 bytes. There are two ways to store the two bytes in memory: with the low-order byte at the starting address, known as little-endian byte order, or with the high-order byte at the starting address, known as big-endian byte order.

Little-endian byte order and big-endian byte order for a 16-bit integer.

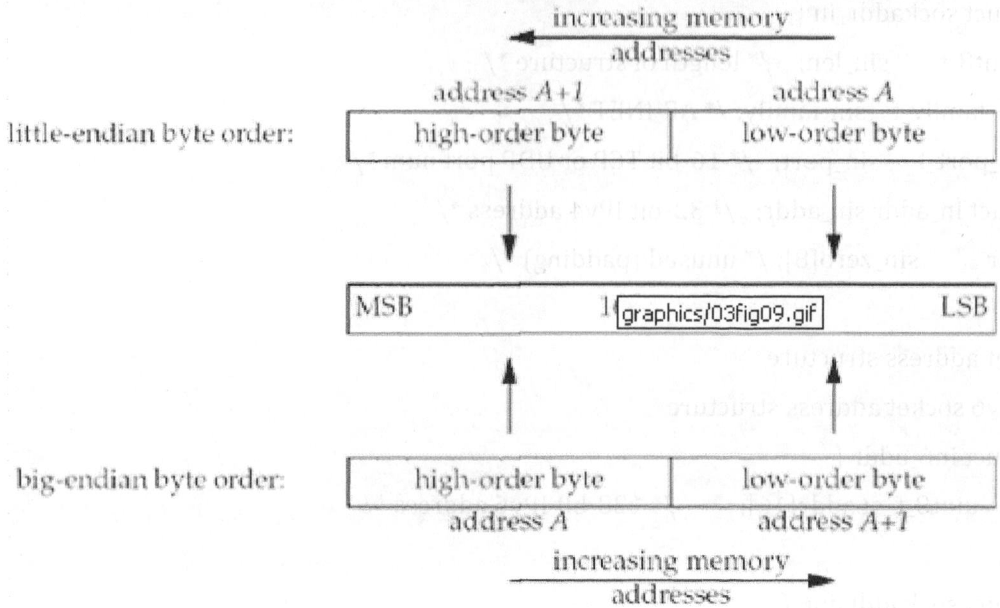

In this figure, we show increasing memory addresses going from right to left in the top, and from left to right in the bottom. We also show the most significant bit (MSB) as the leftmost bit of the 16-bit value and the least significant bit (LSB) as the rightmost bit.

The terms "little-endian" and "big-endian" indicate which end of the multibyte value, the little end or the big end, is stored at the starting address of the value.

- Converts between host byte order and network byte order
  - 'h' = host byte order
  - 'n' = network byte order
  - 'l' = long (4 bytes), converts IP addresses
  - 's' = short (2 bytes), converts port numbers

Explain the following:

#include <netinet/in.h>

unsigned long int htonl(unsigned long int hostlong);

unsigned short int htons(unsigned short int hostshort);

unsigned long int ntohl(unsigned long int netlong);

unsigned short int ntohs(unsigned short int netshort);

(Or)

b) Write a UDP socket program to transfer the content of file between server and client.

Ans: Refer Lab Experiment

15.a) i) Write a program to implement concurrent server. (10)

Ans:

when a client request can take longer to service, we do not want to tie up a single server with one client; we want to handle multiple clients at the same time. The simplest way to write a concurrent server under Unix is to fork a child process to handle each client.

Outline for typical concurrent server.

```
pid_t pid;
int  listenfd,  connfd;
listenfd = Socket( ... );
  /* fill in sockaddr_in{} with server's well-known port */
Bind(listenfd, ... );
Listen(listenfd, LISTENQ);
for ( ; ; ) {
  connfd = Accept (listenfd, ... );   /* probably blocks */
  if( (pid = Fork()) == 0) {
    Close(listenfd);   /* child closes listening socket */
    doit(connfd);      /* process the request */
    Close(connfd);     /* done with this client */
    exit(0);           /* child terminates */
  }
  Close(connfd);       /* parent closes connected socket */
}
```

When a connection is established, accept returns, the server calls fork, and the child process services the client (on connfd, the connected socket) and the parent process waits for another connection (on listenfd, the listening socket). The parent closes the connected socket since the child handles the new client.

ii) Compare UDP and TCP sockets (6)

Ans:

UDP

- Single socket to receive messages
- No guarantee of delivery
- Not necessarily in-order delivery
- Datagram – independent packets
- Must address each packet

Example UDP applications: Multimedia, voice over IP

TCP

- Reliable – guarantee delivery
- Byte stream – in-order delivery
- Connection-oriented – single socket per connection
- Setup connection followed by data transfer

Example TCP applications: Web, Email, and Telnet

(Or)

b) Write a TCP socket program for data transfer.

Ans: Refer Lab Experiment

V. SNS College of Engineering

Department of MCA

Model Question Paper with Answer Key Set - 5

SUBJECT: NETWORK PROGRAMMING MAX. MARKS :100

SUB.CODE: MC9241 TIME : 3HRS

Part-A (10 X 2=20)

1. Differentiate synchronous I/O and Asynchronous I/O

A synchronous I/O operation causes the requesting process to be blocked until that I/O operation completes. An asynchronous I/O operation does not cause the requesting process to be blocked.

2. Define timeval structure

```
struct timeval
{
        long tv_sec;            //seconds
        long tv_usec;   //microseconds
};
```

3. List the fields of pollfd structure

```
struct pollfd {
    int fd; /* descriptor to check */
    short events; /* events of interest on fd */
    short revents; /* events that occurred on fd */
};
```

4. Define select function

The process instructs the kernel to wait for any event to occur or until the specified time gets elapsed . Any descriptor can be tested using select

5. Differentiate SHUT_RD and SHUT_WR

SHUT-RD The read half of the connection is closed. ie, The process can no longer issue any of the read functions on the socket.

SHUT-WR The write half of the connection is closed. ie, The process can no longer issue any of the write functions on the socket.

6. Give the syntax of getsocket function

```
#include <sys/socket.h>

int getsockopt(int sockfd, int level, int optname, void *optval, socklen_t *optlen);
```

7. Define Resource Record

Entries in the DNS are known as resource records (RRs).

8. List the fields of servent structure

```
struct servent
{
    char *s_name;  /* official service name */
    char **s_aliases;         /* alias list */
    int s-port;               /* port number, network-byte order */
     char *s_proto;  /* protocol  */
};
```

9. Give the syntax of gethostbyaddr function

```
#include <netdb.h>
struct hostent *gethostbyaddr (const char *addr, socklen_t len, int family);
```

10. Define DNS

DNS is used to map between hostnames and IP addresses. A hostname can be either a simple name, or a fully qualified.

Part-B (5 X16=80)

11.a) Explain TCP Echo Server

Echo Server Steps are :-

- The client reads a line of text from its standard input and writes the line to the server.
- The server reads the line from its network input and echoes the line back to the client.
- The client reads the echoed line and prints it on its standard output.

TCP Echo Server: main Function

TCP Echo Server: str_echo Function

Steps:-

Read a buffer and echo the buffer

- read reads data from the socket

- The line is echoed back to the client by writen
- If the client closes the connection, read returns 0

(Or)

12. b) Explain the following

i) Termination of Server process (10)

- Start the server and client and type one line to the client to verify that all is okay. That line is echoed normally by the server child.
- Find the process ID of the server child and kill it. All open descriptors in the child are closed. This causes a FIN to be sent to the client, and the client TCP responds with an ACK. This is the first half of the TCP connection termination.
- The SIGCHLD signal is sent to the server parent and handled correctly
- The client TCP receives the FIN from the server TCP and responds with an ACK. The problem is that the client process is blocked in the call to fgets waiting for a line from the terminal.
- Running netstat at this point shows the state of the sockets.
- When the client terminates, all its open descriptors are closed

ii) Shutdown of Server Host (6)

- When a Unix system is shut down, the init process normally sends the SIGTERM signal to all processes , waits some fixed amount of time (often between 5 and 20 seconds), and then sends the SIGKILL signal to any processes still running
- All running processes are given a short amount of time to clean up and terminate.
- If we do not catch SIGTERM , server will be terminated by the SIGKILL signal.
- The process terminates and all open descriptors are closed

13.a) Describe the various I/O Models

Five I/O models are available under Unix :

- blocking I/O
- nonblocking I/O
- I/O multiplexing (select and poll)
- signal driven I/O (SIGIO)
- asynchronous I/O (aio_functions)

(Or)

b) Explain TCP Echo Client with multiplexing.

Implementation of str_cli function using select

i) Call select

ii) Handle readable socket

iii) Handle readable input

13. b) Explain the various system calls in Elementary UDP socket

UDP Client

- socket
- bind (optional) if not specified, connect/sendto/recvfrom will bind
- connect (optional) - allows use send/recv
- sendto/recvfrom (send/recv if connected) retransmit if necessary
- close

UDP Server

- socket
- bind
- sendto/recvfrom
- close

(Or)

b) Explain the various IPv6 socket options

IPV6_CHECKSUM

IPV6_DONTFRAG

IPV6_NEXTHOP

IPV6_PATHMTU

IPV6_RECVDSTOPTS

IPV6_RECVHOPLIMIT

IPV6_RECVHOPOPTS

IPV6_RECVPATHMTU

14. a) Write a DNS program to map hostname with its IP address.

CLIENT

```
#include<stdio.h>
#include<sys/socket.h>
```

```
#include<sys/types.h>
#include<arpa/inet.h>
#include<netinet/in.h>
#include<unistd.h>
#define SER_PORT 8013
int main(int count,char *argv[])
{
int a;
int clisock,x,b,c;
char str[25],host[25];
char str2[25];
struct sockaddr_in cliaddr;
cliaddr.sin_port=htons(SER_PORT);
cliaddr.sin_family=AF_INET;
cliaddr.sin_addr.s_addr=inet_addr(argv[1]);
clisock=socket(AF_INET,SOCK_STREAM,0);
if(clisock<0)
{
perror("\n no socket");
exit(0);
}
if((x=connect(clisock,(struct sockaddr*)&cliaddr,sizeof(cliaddr)))<0)
{
perror("\n no connect");
exit(0);
}
printf("enter domain name");
scanf("%s",host);
write(clisock,host,strlen(host)+1);
read(clisock,str2,sizeof(str2));
printf("%s\n",str2);
close(clisock);
return 0;
}
```

SERVER

```
#include<stdio.h>
#include<sys/socket.h>
#include<sys/types.h>
#include<stdlib.h>
#include<arpa/inet.h>
#include<netinet/in.h>
#include<netdb.h>
#include<string.h>
#include<unistd.h>
#define SER_PORT 8013
int main()
{
int a,c;
FILE *f1,*f2;
int sersock,newsock,n;
char str[25],str2[25],host[25];
void *buf,*buf2;
struct sockaddr_in seraddr;
struct sockaddr_in clinfo;
struct hostent *hp;
socklen_t size=sizeof(clinfo);
seraddr.sin_family=AF_INET;
seraddr.sin_port=htons(SER_PORT);
seraddr.sin_addr.s_addr=htonl(INADDR_ANY);
if((sersock=socket(AF_INET,SOCK_STREAM,0))<0)
{
error(" socket\n");
exit(0);
}
 if(bind(sersock,(struct sockaddr*)&seraddr,sizeof(seraddr))<0)
{
error(" bind\n");
```

```
exit(0);
}
if(listen(sersock,1)<0)
{
error(" listen\n");
exit(0);
}
if((newsock=accept(sersock,(struct sockaddr*)&clinfo,&size))<0)
{
 error(" accept \n");
 exit(0);
}
else
printf("connected to m%s \n",inet_ntoa(clinfo.sin_addr));
read(newsock,host,sizeof(host));
printf("%s",host);
hp=gethostbyname(host);
inet_ntop(AF_INET,hp->h_addr,str2,sizeof(str2));
printf("%s\n",str2);
write(newsock,str2,strlen(str2)+1);
close(newsock);
close(sersock);
return 0;
}
```

(Or)

b) Explain the following functions

i) gethostbyname function **(10)**

```
#include <netdb.h>
struct hostent *gethostbyname (const char *hostname);
```

- Returns: non-null pointer if OK,NULL on error

- The most basic function that looks up a hostname is gethostbyname
- It returns a pointer to a hostent structure that contains all the IPv4 addresses for the host.
- It can only return IPv4 addresses

- IPv6 addresses are very long

ii) getservbyname function **(6)**

```
#include <netdb.h>
struct servent *getservbyname (const char *servname, const char *protoname);
```

- For a given name, this function looks up a service.
- It returns a pointer to the following structure

```
struct servent
{
char *s_name;        /* official service name */
char **s_aliases;    /* alias list */
int s-port;          /* port number, network-byte order */
 char *s_proto;      /* protocol  */
 };
```

15.a) Explain UDP Echo Client

UDP Echo Client: main Function Steps

Fill in socket address structure with server's address

- An IPv4 socket address structure is filled in with the IP address and port number of the server. This structure will be passed to dg_cli, specifying where to send datagrams.
- A UDP socket is created and the function dg_cli is called.

UDP Echo Client: dg_cli Function Steps:-

- Read a line from standard input using fgets
- Send the line to the server using sendto
- Read back the server's echo using recvfrom
- Print the echoed line to standard output using fputs.

(Or)

b) Write a socket program to perform multi-user chat using UDP.

Lab program 1.(c)

VI. SNS College of Engineering

Department of MCA

Model Question Paper with Answer Key Set - 6

SUBJECT: NETWORK PROGRAMMING **MAX. MARKS :100**

SUB.CODE: MC9241 **TIME : 3HRS**

Part-A (10 X 2=20)

1. **Draw a simple Echo Client Server**

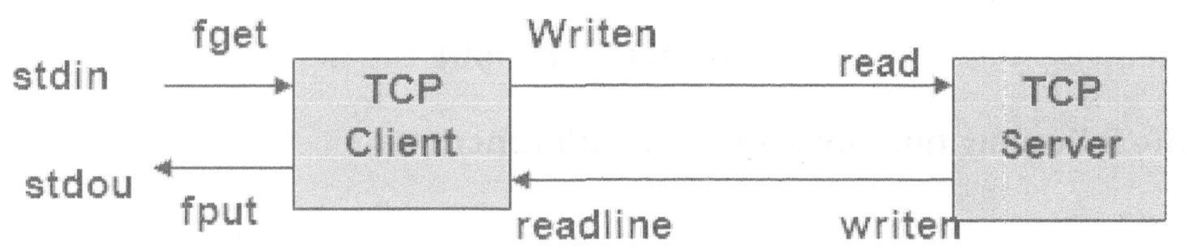

2. **What does an error EWOULDBLOCK represent?**

When the I/O request is not completed in Nonblocking I/O, the process is not put to sleep. Instead it returns an error EWOULDBLOCK

3. **Mention the advantages and disadvantages of Nonblocking I/O**

Adv – The process is not put to sleep

Disadv – waste of CPU time

4. **Define readset**

Specifies the descriptors that we want the kernel to test for reading operation.

5. **What are the types of stream messages?**

(i) high priority
(ii) priority band
(iii) Normal

6. **Give the syntax of setsocket function**

int setsockopt(int sockfd, int level, int optname, const void *optval socklen_t optlen);

7. Define Quad A

AAAA record, called a "quad A" record, maps a hostname into a 128-bit IPv6 address. The term "quad A" was chosen because a 128-bit address is four times larger than a 32-bit address.

8. List the ICMP Socket option

ICMP6_FILTER

9. Mention the Resource Records of DNS

A, AAAA, MX, PTR, CNAME

10. What is the difference between close and shutdown function?

close terminates both directions of data transfer, reading and writing. Shutdown closes either read half ,write half or both based on the option.

Part-B (5 X16=80)

11. a) Explain the following functions – select, poll function

Select Function

The process instructs the kernel to wait for any event to occur or until the specified time gets elapsed. Any descriptor can be tested using select

```
# include<sys/select.h>
# include<sys/time.h>
int select ( int maxfd1, fd_set *readset, fd_set  *writeset,  fd_set *exceptset, const struct timeval *timeout);
```

- Returns positive count of ready descriptors

Poll function

```
#include <poll.h>
int poll (struct pollfd *fdarray, unsigned long nfds, int timeout);
```

- The first argument is a pointer to an array of structures.
- Functionality of poll is similar to select function

The return value from poll is –1 if an error occurred, 0 if no descriptors are ready before the timer expires. Returns the number of ready descriptors.

```
struct pollfd {
int fd; /* descriptor to check */
short events; /* events of interest on fd */
short revents; /* events that occurred on fd */
```

};

- The conditions to be tested are specified by the events member
- The function returns the status for that descriptor in the corresponding revents member.
- The number of elements in the array of structures is specified by the nfds argument.
- The timeout argument specifies how long the function has to wait before returning.

INFTIM - wait forever

0 - return immediately

>0 - number of milliseconds to wait

(Or)

b) Explain TCP Echo Client

TCP Echo Client: main Function Steps

- Create socket, fill in Internet socket address structure
- Connect to server
  1. connect establishes the connection with the server.
  2. The function str-cli handles the rest of the client processing.

TCP Echo Client: str_cli Function Steps

- Read a line, write to server
  * fgets reads a line of text
  * Writen sends the line to the server
- Read echoed line from server, write to standard output
  * Readline reads the line echoed back from the server
  * Fputs writes it to standard output
- Return to main

12.a) Explain the concept of I/O Multiplexing

Five I/O models are available under Unix :

1. blocking I/O
2. nonblocking I/O
3. I/O multiplexing (select and poll)
4. signal driven I/O (SIGIO)
5. asynchronous I/O (aio_functions)

(Or)

b) Explain the following

i) Crashing of Server Host (10)

- When the server host crashes, nothing is sent out on the existing network connections. That is, we are assuming the host crashes and is not shut down by an operator .
- We type a line of input to the client, it is written by writen, and is sent by the client TCP as a data segment. The client then blocks in the call to readline, waiting for the echoed reply.
- If we watch the network with tcpdump, we will see the client TCP continually retransmitting the data segment, trying to receive an ACK from the server.

ii) Crashing and Rebooting of Server Host (6)

- Start the server and then the client. Type a line to verify that the connection is established.
- The server host crashes and reboots.
- Type a line of input to the client, which is sent as a TCP data segment to the server host.
- When the server host reboots after crashing, TCP loses all information about the connection before the crash. Therefore, the server TCP responds with an RST.
- Client is blocked in the call to readline when the RST is received, causing readline to return the error ECONNRESET.

13.a) Write a socket program to perform data transfer using UDP.

Lab program 1(b)

(Or)

b) Explain Generic socket options

- SO_BROADCAST
- SO_DEBUG
- SO_DONTROUTE
- SO_ERROR
- SO_KEEPALIVE
- SO_LINGER
- SO_OOBINLINE
- SO_RCVBUF and SO_SNDBUF
- SO_RCVLOWAT and SO_SNDLOWAT
- SO_REUSEADDR and SO_REUSEPORT
- SO_TYPE

14. a) Explain the following

i) Domain Name System (10)

- DNS is used to map between hostnames and IP addresses
- A hostname can be either a simple name, or a fully qualified domain name (FQDN)
- Example - solaris , freebsd, solaris.unpbook.com
- Resource Records - A, AAAA, MX, PTR, CNAME Explanation
- Example

(ii) Shutdown function (6)

```
#include <sys/socket.h>
int shutdown(int sockfd, int howto);
```

Returns: 0 if OK, –1 on error

howto argument can be :-

SHUT-RD The read half of the connection is closed. ie, The process can no longer issue any of the read functions on the socket.

SHUT-WR The write half of the connection is closed. ie, The process can no longer issue any of the write functions on the socket.

SHUT_RDWR The read half and the write half of the connection are both closed— This is equivalent to calling shutdown twice: first with SHUT_RD and then with SHUT_WR.

(Or)

b) Explain the various functions related to hostent and servent structures

- gethostbyaddr
- gethostbyname
- getservbyname
- getservbyport

15. a) Explain UDP Echo Server

Echo Server :main Function Steps

- Create UDP socket, bind server's well-known port
- The function dg_echo is called to perform server processing.

UDP Echo Server: dg_echo Function Steps

Read datagram , Echo back to sender

- This function is a simple loop that reads the next datagram arriving at the server's port using recvfrom and sends it back using sendto.
- This function provides an iterative server, not a concurrent server. There is no call to fork, so a single server process handles all clients. In general, most TCP servers are concurrent and most UDP servers are iterative.

(Or)

b) Explain about TCP and UDP sockets with multiplexing

Explain the TCP and UDP sockets with multiplexing concepts such as select(), poll()